THE ETHIOPIANS

AN INTRODUCTION TO COUNTRY
AND PEOPLE

EDWARD ULLENDORFF

THIRD EDITION

OXFORD UNIVERSITY PRESS
LONDON   OXFORD   NEW YORK
1973

Oxford University Press

OXFORD LONDON NEW YORK
GLASGOW TORONTO MELBOURNE WELLINGTON
CAPE TOWN IBADAN NAIROBI DAR ES SALAAM LUSAKA ADDIS ABABA
DELHI BOMBAY CALCUTTA MADRAS KARACHI LAHORE DACCA
KUALA LUMPUR SINGAPORE HONG KONG TOKYO

ISBN 0 19 285061 X

© Oxford University Press 1960, 1965, 1973

First Edition 1960
Second Edition 1965
Third Edition 1973

First published as an Oxford University Press paperback 1973

PRINTED IN GREAT BRITAIN BY
THE CAMELOT PRESS LTD, LONDON AND SOUTHAMPTON

ለዓርማዊ፡ ቀዳማዊ፡ ኀይለ፡ ሥላሴ፡
ንጉሠ፡ ነገሥት፡ ዘኢትዮጵያ፡
ይህን፡ መጽሐፍ፡ በታላቅ፡
አድንቆት፡ አበረክታለሁ ፨

" እሱ፡ ራሱ፡ የፍርድን፡ ሥራ፡ እንዲያካሄድና፡
የመንግሥቱንም፡ የአስተዳደር፡ ክፍሎች፡
በቀጥታ፡ እንዲ ቆጣጠር፡ "

'that he might administer justice in his own person and
see all the parts of government with his own eyes . . .'
'Rasselas Prince of Abyssinia'
chapter 49

PREFACE

THE object of this little book is to present a balanced picture of Ethiopia to the general reader, on one hand sufficiently full and rounded to cover many of the principal aspects of country and people, and, on the other, general enough to be intelligible to the non-specialist. Many *éthiopisants* have long deplored—as has the present writer—the absence of a suitable work of introduction which might, between two covers, summarize the present state of our knowledge of historical and modern Ethiopia. This lacuna is particularly serious in English, for in Italian and German we possess two very brief accounts written by such masters of the subject as the late Carlo Conti Rossini and Enno Littmann. But both were written many years ago and have long been out of print.

With this general object in mind, I have been careful to deal almost exclusively with assured results and with positions generally, or at least widely, accepted rather than with some recent and hitherto unproven hypotheses.

Of course, there is no dearth of books on Ethiopia: a few were written by some of the finest scholars in this branch of studies, while others were compiled by people who spent a few days or weeks in the country and returned as 'experts'. There appears to exist little half-way between these two extremes. And while the present writer cannot claim expert knowledge or independent research in every one of the fields covered in the present work, he has at all events given twenty years to the study of Ethiopian languages and civilization—of which five were spent in the country itself. And, thanks to the generosity of the Carnegie Trust for the Universities of Scotland, he was able to refresh his knowledge by a three months' visit to Ethiopia in 1958.

This book is principally concerned with historic Abyssinia and the cultural manifestations of its Semitized inhabitants—not with all the peoples and regions now within the political boundaries of the Ethiopian Empire.[1]

The question of transcribing Ethiopian names has caused me considerable difficulty. Only a scientifically rigorous transcription[2] can do justice to the linguistic data, but such a rendering was clearly out of place in the present context. I have avoided all diacritical marks and have aimed at a version which would appear readily understandable to English readers. Thus I have retained forms such as Magdala on account of their familiarity, yet have altered other spellings which had little resemblance to linguistic reality. That my performance has fallen short of my aims and that I have been guilty of many inconsistencies I recognize not without sadness. I sympathize with any reviewer who is going to take me to task sternly over these shortcomings, and I offer my apologies to those among my colleagues who are purists and perfectionists.

The Select Bibliography is intended as a guide to further reading; its composition is obviously subjective, but I have attempted to be as fair and catholic as possible in the selection.

I wish to record my indebtedness and gratitude to Professors A. F. L. Beeston and A. M. Honeyman for having generously given of their time by reading the typescript and suggesting many improvements. Dr. J. A. Macdonald of the Botany department of St. Andrews University has rescued me from a pitfall in his field of study.

Professors G. R. Driver and D. Winton Thomas have at all times offered me encouragement and advice. My debt of gratitude to them is heavy. And the example of the great masters of Ethiopian studies, Marcel Cohen, Enrico Cerulli, and of my teacher H. J. Polotsky, has constantly been before my eyes—always worthy of emulation, yet ever out of reach. A special word of thanks is due to Sir Malcolm Knox, Principal and Vice-Chancellor of St. Andrews University, who has on all occasions been ready, and indeed anxious, to assist and to further the academic plans and projects of his junior colleagues.

[1] For a more detailed statement of this distinction, see the present writer's *Semitic Languages of Ethiopia*, p. 4.
[2] Cf. op. cit., pp. xiii, xiv.

The officers of the Oxford University Press have made the usually burdensome technicalities of publication a pleasure rather than a disagreeable chore. I am grateful to Professor H. H. Rowley, who has lent such great distinction to the Manchester department of Semitics, for permission to quote from an article I wrote for his *Journal of Semitic Studies* (July 1956).

Her Majesty's Ambassador at Addis Ababa, the senior members of the Embassy, and the Consul-General at Asmara have been of the greatest assistance during my last visit to Ethiopia. Mr. Stephen Wright has become the mentor and guide of all who seek to benefit from his vast experience. The authorities at the Addis Ababa University College and the Theological College, the Mayor and Governor of Addis Ababa, and very many other Ethiopian friends have, by their proverbial hospitality and kindness, contributed to this book more than I can readily acknowledge. And no one living in Ethiopia can fail to be inspired by the high example of His Imperial Majesty to whom this volume is dedicated.

My wife has looked after everything that is unpleasant in writing a book: preparing the typescript, reading the proofs, making the index, and removing some of my worst solecisms.

E. U.

May 1959

PREFACE TO THE SECOND EDITION

I AM much obliged to many helpful reviewers and also to colleagues who have sent personal communications and suggestions for improvements. This gratitude is particularly heavy towards Professor Moreno, Professor Tubiana, Mr. Stephen Wright, and Sir Malcolm Knox. Mrs. Ann Kelly, my secretary, was at all times incomparable in both knowledge and efficiency. The last chapter, 'Ethiopia Today', now reflects the situation in March 1964.

E. U.

March 1964

PREFACE TO THE THIRD EDITION

SINCE this book was first written, in the summer of 1958, a great deal of work has been done in nearly all branches of Ethiopian studies. Scholars like A. J. Drewes, A. K. Irvine, Robert Hetzron, Abraham Demoz, G. Goldenberg, Donald Crummey, Olga Kapeliuk, Asmarom Leggesse, F. C. Gamst, Merid Walda Aragay, Hailu Fullas, Taddasa Tamrat, Mesfin Walda Maryam, W. A. Shack—to name at random but a few of the finest young *éthiopisants*—have come forward and left their imprint on the Ethiopian scene.

With the increase in scholarly output, many of the results seem less assured today than they appeared to be in 1958. Of course, there has, inevitably, also been a good deal of ephemeral work now that Ethiopian studies have become popular. There is greater fluidity as many cherished, and perhaps inadequately proven, assumptions are being challenged. This is all to the good—provided it is not done merely for the sake of novelty.

An American scholar has taken *The Ethiopians* to task for 'worshipping at the shrine of dead Ethiopicists . . . and ignoring the contributions of younger scholars to this expanding field of studies'. To the first charge I plead unashamedly guilty, for men like Ludolf, Dillmann, Praetorius, Guidi, Conti Rossini, Littmann, and others occupy a truly unique position in the world of scholarship. I should be very contrite with regard to the second charge if I were given the names of only two or three of the 'younger scholars' who were writing before 1958 and whose work I culpably ignored. Indeed, it has become a worrying aspect of some recent contributions to Ethiopian studies that there has occurred what Marcel Cohen has termed 'une bien fâcheuse rupture de la chaîne bibliographique'. It is indecorous on the part of these new recruits (none of whom appears among the names listed in the opening lines of this preface) to write in ignorance of Guidi and Cerulli, of Polotsky and Praetorius, of Leslau and Cohen—and yet to cite each other's work with all the trappings of grave import. Someone even felt able to write in 1972 that 'relatively few scholars have published works on Ethiopia. Compared with other countries in Africa, Ethiopia has been neglected.' Could he have seen the 3,000 entries in Fumagalli's 1893 bibliography? Or the 1,635 items in Leslau's linguistic bibliography? Or the many thousands of contributions in various fields and disciplines since Fumagalli wrote?

The select bibliography appended to the present edition has been considerably enlarged. Yet I am only too conscious of the many omissions, of books and articles that ought to have been included and which either escaped my notice altogether or were overlooked when the list was compiled. Others were left out not because I disagreed with their opinions but because they seemed to me (no doubt wrongly on occasion) deficient either in scholarship or in good sense.

Some errors have been corrected in half a dozen reprints and three editions of this book, but I remain profoundly conscious of its many shortcomings which, with the passage of time and despite some attempts at improvement, seem to increase rather than to diminish. On a visit to Ethiopia last month, I was severely upbraided by an Ethiopian student for some cavalier remarks about the Gallas which occur in *The Ethiopians*. He was very largely right, and even my express statement (p. viii) that 'this book is principally concerned with historic Abyssinia and the cultural manifestations of its Semitized inhabitants' cannot wholly atone for these faults.

The Ethiopians was written, after a return visit to Ethiopia in 1958, and completed within a few weeks—almost in one sitting—deliberately without recourse to works of reference. This genesis accounts for many of its blemishes but, perhaps, also for some of its merits. Were I now to re-write it completely, temper some of the more general assertions, qualify many of the hasty judgements, and document as well as argue most of the statements in the light of recent research, a wholly different book would emerge, better no doubt in some respects but no longer the impressionistic picture of the Ethiopians which I had in mind and which has not basically altered since I first saw the country and its people more than thirty years ago.

There is much in recent work on Ethiopian archaeology, history, anthropology, geography, or studies on fauna and flora that I can admire but in which I cannot claim independent judgement. This book remains essentially a general introduction for the non-specialist reader.

E. U.

December 1972

CONTENTS

—————ᴗᴗᴗᴜᴜᴑ⦿ᴖᴜᴜᴖᴖᴖ—————

LIST OF PLATES

———∿∿∿∿◊∿∿∿———

ABBREVIATIONS

BSL	*Bulletin de la Société de Linguistique de Paris.*
BSOAS	*Bulletin of the School of Oriental and African Studies* London University.
CSCO	*Corpus Scriptorum Christianorum Orientalium.*
JA	*Journal Asiatique.*
JAH	*Journal of African History.*
JAOS	*Journal of the American Oriental Society.*
JES	*Journal of Ethiopian Studies.*
JRAS	*Journal of the Royal Asiatic Society.*
JSS	*Journal of Semitic Studies.*
MO	*Monde Oriental.*
OM	*Oriente Moderno.*
RRAL	Rendiconti, Regia Accademia dei Lincei.
RSE	*Rassegna di Studi Etiopici.*
RSO	*Rivista degli Studi Orientali.*
SBWA	*Sitzungsberichte der Wiener Akademie.*
SOAS	School of Oriental and African Studies, London University.
TPS	*Transactions of the Philological Society.*
ZA	*Zeitschrift für Assyriologie.*
ZDMG	*Zeitschrift der Deutschen Morgenländischen Gesellschaft.*
ZfES	*Zeitschrift für Eingeborenen Sprachen.*

I

EXPLORATION AND STUDY

WITH the exception of some scattered information gathered by eye-witnesses of an earlier age, the exploration and study of Ethiopia began as the Middle Ages merged in the modern era. From the fifteenth and sixteenth centuries to the present day, navigators and missionaries, royal ambassadors and traders have made their way to Ethiopia. Many of them have lived to tell the tale of their adventures, and few have been able to resist the beauty and strangeness of country and people which have frequently inspired their pen with a surfeit of colour and a love of the picturesque.

Some of the earlier exceptions deserve a brief mention in this context. We are told in the Old Testament that the River Gihon 'compasseth the whole land of Ethiopia' (Gen. 2:13); or that Moses 'had married an Ethiopian woman' (Num. 7: 1); 'Ebedmelech the Ethiopian' appears in Jer. 38, and in Ps. 68:32 'Ethiopia shall soon stretch out her hands unto God'. But we do not know the precise connotation of the Hebrew 'Cush' which the Septuagint translated into Greek as Αἰθιοπία (Ethiopia), and many of these Scriptural references are of difficult interpretation. Similar considerations apply to the passage (Acts 8:27) about the 'man of Ethiopia, an eunuch of great authority under Candace queen of the Ethiopians'.[1] Classical writers, too, mention Ethiopia not infrequently, but here as well it is hard to assess what measure of actual knowledge and direct acquaintance lies behind their descriptions. Thus Homer speaks (*Odyssey*, i, 22ff.) of 'the distant Ethiopians, the farthest outposts of mankind, half of whom live where the Sun goes down, and half where he rises'. This division into eastern and western Ethiopians probably indicates that the name Αἰθίοπες

[1] Cf. E. Ullendorff, *Ethiopia and the Bible*, pp. 5–15.

('burnt faces') referred to all peoples with dark skins, from the country
south of Egypt, Nubia, to India. Herodotus is at times a good deal
more precise, for he clearly identifies Ethiopia with the Kingdom of
Meroe, Nubia: 'Ethiopians inhabit the country immediately above
Elephantine, and one half of the island; the other half is inhabited by
Egyptians; . . . finally, you will arrive at a large city called Meroe:
this city is said to be the capital of all Ethiopia' (ii, 29). Yet in another
passage (vii, 70) 'Ethiopian' appears to be a generic term for Asians
and Africans of dark skin.

A more clearly defined picture emerges from the *Periplus Maris
Erythraei*, an anonymous second-century account of travel and trade
in the Indian Ocean. Here we hear of the famous harbour of Adulis,
'a fair-sized village',[1] and here we also encounter what is probably
the first reference to 'the city of the people called Auxumites',[1]
i.e. Aksum, the ancient capital of Ethiopia. A far more detailed story
is told by Cosmas Indicopleustes in his *Christian Topography*; Cosmas
had visited the Kingdom of Aksum about the year A.D. 525. He found
Adulis a flourishing port and in close commercial relations with Arabia,
Persia, and India. He visited the antiquities and churches of Aksum
and other places in the Kingdom; and he was present at Adulis when
King Elesbaan (=Ella Asbeha) was preparing his expedition against
the Himyarites.[2]

But from the threshold to the close of the Middle Ages Ethiopia
was generally removed from the view of the outside world and lived in
an isolation which was tumultuous rather than splendid. This long
period of darkness is scarcely illumined by the extraordinary narrative
of the ninth-century Jewish traveller, Eldad had-Dani, who claimed
to be a descendant of the Danites who were to have established a
Jewish kingdom 'beyond the rivers of Abyssinia' (Cush). And an
even more impenetrable maze of fact and fiction has been created in
the legend of the Prester John.[3] We reach firmer ground with the

---

[1] § 4 of Schoff's trans.   [2] Pp. 55–6 of McCrindle's trans.

[3] Cf. C. Conti Rossini, 'Leggende Geogr. Giudaiche', *Bollettino della Regia
Società Geografica Italiana*, 1925; *idem*, 'L'itinerario di Beniamino da Tudela
e l'Etiopia', *Zeitschr. f. Assyr.*, XXVII; S. Krauss, 'New light on geographical
information in Eldad Hadani and Benjamin of Tudela', *TARBIZ*, 1937; Beckingham, *The Achievements of Prester John*.

arrival in Ethiopia, in 1407, of Pietro Rombulo, an Italian who remained
in Ethiopia for thirty-seven years till 1444. Rombulo's own report has
not survived, but copious extracts from it were embodied in Pietro
Ranzano's *Annales omnium temporum*. Unfortunately, Ranzano, who
possessed no scientific bent, thought it necessary to harmonize Rombulo's account with that of classical and other writers; we may thus
surmise that some of the more fictional aspects of the story are attri-
butable to Ranzano rather than to Rombulo.

In 1441 two Ethiopian monks from the Ethiopian community in
Jerusalem attended the Council of Florence, and no doubt they contributed to some extent to the knowledge of Ethiopia in Europe. A
few years later, Fra Mauro produced at Venice his map of Africa,
which contained a prominent section on Ethiopia and was based on
data furnished by travellers, merchants, missionaries, and diplomats.
The Republic of Venice had long taken an interest in Ethiopia which
was primarily economic, and Venetian prosperity, derived from the
highly profitable trade in spices, was not impaired till, towards the
close of the fifteenth century, Bartholomeu Diaz discovered the sea
route by way of the Cape of Good Hope. Meanwhile, King John II
of Portugal had, in 1487, despatched Pedro de Covilham and Alphonse
de Payva to find out about the country of the Prester John and to divert
the trade in spices from Venice to Portugal. Both explorers reached
Ethiopia, though by different routes and at different times. Payva
probably died in Ethiopia (although nothing more is known about
him), while Covilham arrived in the interior of the country by way of
Zeila. His reception by the Emperor was cordial, he was offered lands
and honours—but was never allowed to leave the country. He married
an Ethiopian lady and acquired a profound knowledge of the languages
and customs of Abyssinia. This knowledge proved to be a great asset
when, thirty years later, the Portuguese Embassy under Rodrigo de
Lima came to Ethiopia (1520). A good deal of Alvarez's famous narrative of this expedition is, in fact, based on information supplied by
Covilham, who, in the judgement of Alvarez, was 'a man who knows
all the languages that can be spoken, both of Christians, Moors, and
Gentiles, and who knows all the things for which he was sent; moreover, he gives an account of them as if they were present before him'.[1]

[1] *Narrative of the Portuguese Embassy to Abyssinia*, p. 270.

Francisco Alvarez was the first to produce a coherent and reliable work on Ethiopia which excited considerable interest in Europe. Above all, his story was based on first-hand knowledge of the country. The Portuguese Embassy landed at Massawa (where it transformed the mosque into a church), proceeded to the monastery of Bizen, and then went to stay at Debaroa, the headquarters of the Bahr Negash (the Viceroy of the sea province—now Eritrea), before continuing its progress to the court of the Negus. Here their reception was amicable enough—despite the King's dissatisfaction with the presents the Embassy had brought him. Alvarez became involved in many theological disputations, and while one cannot always admire his doctrinal proficiency, his tact and understanding gave him a position of some influence. For a time there was a distinct danger that the Embassy might have to share Covilham's fate in being denied permission to leave the country, but the growing menace of Muslim invasion made it imperative for the King to summon Portuguese assistance from abroad.

Contact between Europe and Ethiopia was thus established, the Portuguese adventure in Ethiopia had begun, and the country had, at least temporarily, abandoned its isolation from the rest of the Christian world.

When the Portuguese mission of Rodrigo de Lima left Ethiopia, in 1526, they took with them an Ethiopian envoy, Saga za-Ab, and left behind Bermudez, a member of their expedition. Bermudez subsequently had a most adventurous career in Ethiopia where he remained some thirty years. It is still not clear whether he was a common impostor or an astute politician who used the predicament in which the Abyssinian Church and State found themselves at the time of the Muslim invasion to further the cause of the Church of Rome. He claims, in the generally valuable account which he published in 1565 after his return to Portugal, to have been nominated Abuna (head of the Ethiopian Church) by the aged Archbishop Mark and by command of King Lebna Dengel, who no doubt hoped by this action (if, in fact, it ever occurred) to induce the Christian powers to come to his aid more readily. Bermudez's story must, however, remain suspect, for no Abuna was empowered to appoint his own successor. The new 'Abuna' was then despatched to Europe to summon assistance against the invaders; and after a long and dangerous journey to Rome he claims to have been confirmed in his episcopal office by Pope Paul III in 1536. Bermudez then went on to Portugal, where he started on a concentrated campaign in favour of Portuguese intervention in Ethiopia. In this he appears to have been supported by the Holy See, and shortly afterwards King John III ordered the Viceroy of India to send an expeditionary force to Abyssinia.

The Muslim assault on Ethiopia—under Ahmad ibn Ibrahim Grañ ('the left-handed')—had been remarkably successful (for details, see the historical chapter below). When the Portuguese, under the command of the young and gallant Christopher da Gama, landed some 400 men at Massawa in 1541, large parts of the country had already been overrun. In a battle with Grañ more than half the Portuguese, including their commander, were killed. But the Ethiopians rallied to the Emperor Claudius—who had succeeded Lebna Dengel—while the remnant of the Portuguese were desperately anxious to avenge their leader. The combined force encountered Grañ near Lake Tana, killed him, and put his army to flight. The Muslim challenge to the Christian Empire had thus been successfully met, but of the Portuguese force no more than a handful saw their own country again.

The intervention of the Portuguese had secured them a position of privilege in Ethiopia. Their political, economic, and religious ascendancy was complete, and conversions to the Church of Rome gained momentum. But undoubtedly the greatest benefit of the Portuguese interlude in Ethiopia is connected with their activity as explorers and scholars. They reached the southern parts of the country, into which Europeans did not again penetrate until the last century. They studied the languages of Ethiopia and its history—laboriously pieced together from fragmentary indigenous chronicles. They investigated the physical, social, and ethnic conditions which had never before been studied or described. There are many valuable observations in the report (published in Lisbon in 1564) of the Portuguese campaign of 1541–3 written by an officer, Castanhoso, in Christopher da Gama's party. Pedro Paez (died 1622), a Spaniard by birth, visited Lake Tana and saw the sources of the Nile. He left a sizeable and most interesting *Historia da Etiopia* and did much work that redounded to the credit of the Jesuit achievement in Ethiopia. He was cautious, tactful, and tolerant, and the success of the Jesuits, culminating in the conversion to Catholicism of the Emperor Susenyos, was largely due to him. Two years after Paez's death there arrived in Ethiopia Manoel de Almeida, whose excellent *Historia de Ethiopia* (for long only known in the abridged version by Balthasar Tellez) represents another important landmark in the history of the exploration of Ethiopia. He was also the first European to reach Lake Zway in the south of the country. Antonio Fernandez, too, had traversed some of the most remote regions in southern Ethiopia in his unsuccessful attempt at reaching the East African coast at Malindi. Manoel Barradas, on the other hand, lived for nine years (1624–33) in the northern province, the Tigrai, and left us a faithful description of this region, the cradle of Ethiopian civilization. A document of particular interest is Jerome Lobo's *Voyage to Abyssinia*, of which we possess an English translation by Dr. Samuel Johnson, made from Le Grand's French version. The Portuguese original was not discovered until 1947 (see Beckingham in *JSS*, 1965, pp. 262–4) and was not published until 1971 (see Bibliography). Lobo gives a vivid account of the incredible hazards and dangers to which his journeys had exposed him; he offers an outline of Ethiopian history, laws, customs, and religion; he describes the sources of the Nile (though it is probable that this account is borrowed from Paez rather than based on his own observation); and finally, he relates in some detail the expulsion of the Jesuits from Ethiopia in 1633. Lobo was well placed to chronicle this story, an essay in futility, for he had been a companion of the last Latin Patriarch in Ethiopia, Alphonse Mendez, a Spanish Jesuit like Paez before him. But Mendez lacked all the qualities of tact and tolerance which Paez had so amply possessed. He treated Ethiopians as infidels rather than Christians: he re-ordained the clergy, re-baptized the people, and forbade circumcision. While the converted King at first acquiesced, the people were only strengthened by these measures in their adherence to their historic faith. When the inevitable explosion occurred, in 1632–3, the departure of the Jesuits from Ethiopia marked the conclusion of a strange chapter in Ethiopian history. The achievement of the Jesuits was immense: they had helped a Christian nation to maintain its identity and independence against Muslim encroachment; they had notably contributed to the education of the people; and, above all, they had explored the country with remarkable diligence and truly

astonishing courage and perseverance; and they have left us the worthy
records of their learning, monuments of scholarship far in advance of
their time. Yet the damage was almost equally great: by religious
intolerance and narrow-mindedness, they rendered nugatory all
attempts at real advance; they implanted in the people a deep-seated
suspicion of Europeans, especially *et dona ferentes*, and threw them back
into an isolation and aloofness which lasted for centuries.

While the Portuguese were working in Ethiopia, proselytizing the
people and exploring the country, the study of Ethiopia had begun in
Europe. The centre was Rome. We have already heard of Ethiopian
delegates to the Council of Florence in 1441; others followed these first
envoys, and the fifteenth and sixteenth centuries saw a steady trickle of
Abyssinian pilgrims to the Holy See. They often settled in Rome and
provided Europe with information about their country. At first most
of these Ethiopian pilgrims came from Jerusalem, where an Abyssinian
community had long been settled, but later we encounter others who
had undertaken the arduous journey from their mountain fastnesses in
Africa. The Pontifical Archives contain documents which authorize the
Vatican Treasurer to disburse certain sums of money for the support of
such pilgrims.[1] The Ethiopians at Rome had been attached to the
Church of St. Stephen, but it was not until 1539 that the Holy See
bought a house for them, situated just behind St. Peter's, as their
permanent home.[2] 'Santo Stefano dei Mori', as it was to be called,
became the cradle of Ethiopian studies in Europe; and, one might
mention in passing, its successor at Rome, the *Collegio Etiopico*, is to this
day the only theological college within the Vatican City.

It was at Santo Stefano that J. Potken of Cologne had heard Mass
celebrated in Ge'ez (classical Ethiopic) and so was impelled to embark
on a study of this language. Fortunately, Potken was also a typographer
and promptly set up a small Ethiopic printing press at Rome which, in
1513, produced the Psalter, Canticles, and some Old and New Testament hymns. The last pages of this book contain the Ethiopic alphabet
or syllabary and a few grammatical notes. A little later, about 1540,
three Ethiopian monks from Debra Libanos in Shoa, Ethiopia's premier

[1] Lefevre, 'Documenti Pontifici', *RSE*, V, Nos. XV–XVII.
[2] *Ibidem*, Nos. XLVIII, XLIX, LXXXIX.

monastic institution, arrived at Rome via Jerusalem. The senior one among them, Tesfa Sion, was a well-educated man and attained, under the name of 'Pietro Indiano' or 'Pietro Etiope', a good deal of local fame. He printed large parts of the Ethiopic New Testament in 1548–9 and succeeded in exciting some interest in Ethiopia and its classical tongue among educated persons at Rome. One of these was Marianus Victorius (1518–72), who studied Ge'ez with Tesfa Sion and, in 1548, published the first grammar of Ethiopic,[1] a pioneering achievement. Tesfa Sion had thus been instrumental in laying the foundations of Ethiopic scholarship in Europe. His manifold plans for the encouragement of Abyssinian studies were cut short when he died suddenly in 1550 and was buried in the Church of Santo Stefano.[2]

Among those who sought information from the monks of Santo Stefano dei Mori were Joseph Scaliger (1540–1609), the famous scholar, who incorporated in his *De emendatione temporum* such knowledge as he had gained about the Ethiopian calendar during his sojourn in Rome; Th. Petraeus and J. G. Nissel, who with their skill in the art of typography were responsible for some fine editions of Ethiopic texts;[3] J. Wemmers of Antwerp, who, with the help of the Ethiopian monks, was able to publish, in 1638, the first Ethiopic dictionary—no mean achievement in the circumstances of the time;[4] and Athanasius Kircher (1601–80), who, in the compilation of his encyclopaedic writings, had often appealed to the Ethiopians of Santo Stefano for advice and instruction.

All these works had received their impetus from the only source then available in Europe, the little convent behind St. Peter's. Some of the basic tools had now been made available to a wider circle, and Ethiopic scholarship could thus be established in other centres as well. Brian Walton (1600–61) in England included in his *Introductio ad lectionem linguarum Orientalium* (London, 1653) a section which dealt with the Ethiopic alphabet, pronunciation of consonants, accent, etc. This is, I

---

[1] *Chaldeae seu Aethiopicae linguae Institutiones*, Rome.

[2] See his epitaph in Conti Rossini's *Storia d'Etiopia*, plate I.

[3] A. Rahlfs, 'Nissel und Petraeus, ihre aethiopischen Textausgaben und Typen', *Nachrichten der Königlichen Gesellschaft der Wissenschaften*, Göttingen, 1917, pp. 268–348.

[4] *Lexicon Aethiopicum*, Rome, 1638.

believe, the first time that Ethiopic characters were printed in Britain. In the preparation of his polyglot Bible, Walton had the assistance of, among others, Edmund Castell (1606–85) who became Professor of Arabic at Cambridge and who is the author of the immense *Lexicon Heptaglotton* (1669), which also includes the Ethiopic language.

But the most illustrious name in Ethiopic scholarship is that of Job Ludolf, who, by his massive contributions to the study of Ge'ez, Amharic, and Abyssinian history, may justly be called the founder of Ethiopian studies in Europe. Ludolf was born at Erfurt in 1624. He first studied medicine and natural science, but his interest soon turned towards languages and music. Apart from Latin and Greek, he was said to possess a good knowledge of French, Italian, Dutch and, later on, of Russian and Swedish as well. Thereafter he was introduced to Hebrew, Arabic, and Syriac, but he soon became conscious of a serious gap in his Semitic equipment: the lack of adequate *instruments de travail* for the study of Ethiopic. At first he was entirely dependent on Potken's Psalter and some fanciful material supplied by his teacher Karnrad. The insufficiency of these aids soon forced Ludolf to compile his own grammar and vocabulary and to move on to Leiden, an important centre of Oriental studies. There he gained access to the manuscripts in the Scaliger Bequest (containing a Psalter and a collection of Ethiopic prayers) and to the Ethiopic dictionary which had been published at Rome in 1638 by J. Wemmers. He convinced himself, however, that Wemmers' work contained little or nothing that he had not already found out on his own. Ludolf was able to travel in many European countries and to gain a practical acquaintance with languages which he had hitherto known from books only. His insistence on a living knowledge of European as well as Oriental languages distinguished Ludolf from many of his contemporaries and successors in Oriental scholarship. He visited France and England and regretted very greatly that the brevity of his stay made it impossible for him to inspect the Oriental treasures of the Bodleian Library at Oxford.

A decisive turn in Ludolf's life came when, in 1649, he was asked by the Swedish Court to search for certain documents at Rome. He failed to find the documents, but he found his true vocation. When he visited Santo Stefano dei Mori he met there one of the four Ethiopians who lived at the Abyssinian hospice at that time, Abba ('Father')

Gregory from Makana Sellasie in the Amhara province. Gregory knew no Latin and, at that period, no Italian, so that conversation had to be carried on through a half-caste interpreter. Ludolf's knowledge of Ethiopic was, however, so excellent that he was soon able to converse with Gregory in classical Ethiopic—at first an unaccustomed task to Gregory as well, for his mother tongue was, of course, Amharic. But the Abyssinian priest was a man of learning and also—as the results of Ludolf's investigations have proved—an informant of truth and reliability. After Ludolf's return home he managed to arouse the interest of Duke Ernest of Gotha, who offered to invite Gregory to his court for further study with Ludolf and to defray all expenses. The Ethiopian readily agreed and, during the year 1652, spent several months at Gotha working with his learned friend, first mainly on Ge'ez and history, but later also on Amharic which Ludolf found an extremely difficult language—as indeed it is. In the following winter Gregory went back to Italy and then, driven by a deep longing to return to his own country, took a ship across the Mediterranean, but perished at sea near the Syrian coast. His services to Ludolf and to Semitic scholarship in general were inestimable.

Ludolf's further career was one of great distinction in diplomacy, politics, and finance, but after the death of his wife, in 1677, he retired to Frankfort and dedicated himself to purely scholarly pursuits. His Ethiopic and Amharic dictionaries and grammars were of an importance far transcending his own time and remained, for well over a century and a half, the indispensable tools for the study of these languages, while his monumental history of Ethiopia (with an extensive commentary) can still be read with profit as well as enjoyment.

From the study of Ethiopia in the seventeenth century we must now return to the exploration of the country. The expulsion of the Jesuits had brought about the withdrawal of the Ethiopians within their inaccessible mountain ranges and had caused a well-nigh complete severance of relations with the outside world. The exceptions are few and slight and are quickly recounted. An Italian, Giacomo Baratti, visited the country towards the close of the Portuguese hegemony (and, perhaps, managed to remain there for a while after the expulsion of the Jesuits). The narrative of his travels has not survived in its original language, but an English translation was published in 1650. Of somewhat greater value is the account left by the French physician Charles Jacques Poncet, who had been called from Cairo to attend to King Iyasu I at Gondar. He travelled by way of Sennar and was accompanied by a learned French Jesuit, Father de Brèvedent, who, to Poncet's great grief, died shortly before reaching Abyssinia. Poncet arrived at Gondar in 1699 and stayed there for nearly a year. He cured the king and seems to have enjoyed considerable popularity. His travels did not extend far beyond the Gondar area, and, while he gives an adequate account of what he saw in Ethiopia, his narrative can in no way be likened to the great works of exploration and description produced by the Portuguese before him.

The first half of the eighteenth century is entirely uneventful in the history of Ethiopian exploration, but the second half of that century is illumined by the overpowering and colourful personality of the great Scottish traveller James Bruce, whose achievements in the field of travel and exploration are comparable to those of Ludolf in the sphere of study and patient scholarship. He was the first European, after the expulsion of the Jesuits over a century earlier, to have attained a position of some importance in Ethiopia and to have contributed a great mass of valuable information to our knowledge of country and people.

Bruce was born in 1730 at Kinnaird House, Stirlingshire, and was educated at Harrow and Edinburgh University. He soon abandoned the study of law and acquired instead a knowledge of Italian, Spanish, and Portuguese as well as of drawing and painting. He married in 1752 the daughter of a wealthy wine merchant and, entering his wife's family business, had ample opportunities of travelling in France, Spain, and Portugal. He was, however, much more interested in the customs, society, art, and antiquities of these regions than in their vintages. Journeys through southern Spain and the monuments of its Muslim past stirred in him the wish to study Arabic manuscripts in the Escurial —which marked the beginning of Bruce's career of Oriental scholarship. On his return to London in 1758 he added to the study of Arabic that of classical Ethiopic, which he acquired from the writings of Ludolf. It was doubtless in this context that Bruce first became impressed with the desirability of discovering the sources of the Nile. This was to become the principal aim of his life when, in 1761, he could

afford to resign his share in the wine business and devote himself
entirely to travel and exploration.

In 1762 Bruce was appointed Consul-General at Algiers, and his
commission included the task of exploring the North African littoral.
This he did with characteristic bravado—examining the Roman ruins
in Algeria, Tunis, and Tripoli, exploring the coasts of Barbary and the
Levant, preparing the most careful and, indeed, most beautiful drawings of temples, columns, arches, etc., and, at the same time, continuing
his studies of Arabic and Ethiopic. He reached Egypt in 1768, and then
went on to Luxor and Assuan; later he embarked at Cosseir for Jeddah,
and finally arrived at Massawa, the gate to Abyssinia, in 1769. The
details of his journeys in Ethiopia, including a vast amount of geographical, historical, ethnological, and scientific information, are contained in the massive and splendid volumes of his *Travels*, which,
despite minor shortcomings and exaggerations, bear witness to a career
of adventure, fortitude, perseverance, versatility, and erudition. Bruce
made a great impression in Ethiopia—not least on account of his
extraordinary physique, which was long remembered in both Africa
and Scotland: 'Profound pity was felt all over the countryside for the
steed he rode whose back was strikingly "howed" from the man's
extraordinary weight.'[1]

Bruce visited large parts of northern Ethiopia, including Aksum and
Gondar and the region to the south of Lake Tana, took many recordings with the aid of the scientific instruments which he had brought
along and, together with his Italian secretary, Luigi Balugani, made the
most meticulous entries in his diaries and produced large numbers of
fine drawings of the fauna and flora of Abyssinia. Some of the drawings
have been published; others are kept in two heavy folio volumes
presented by Bruce to King George III and now in the Royal Library,
Windsor Castle. Perhaps the most important result of Bruce's travels
was the collection of Ethiopic manuscripts which he brought with him
from Ethiopia. They opened up entirely new vistas for the study of
Ethiopian languages and history and placed this branch of Oriental
scholarship on a much more secure basis. He presented a fine and
specially prepared copy of the Book of Enoch (of which the full text
has been preserved in the Ethiopic version only) to Louis XV in Paris.

[1] W. Nimmo, *History of Stirlingshire*, 3rd ed., II, 283.

Bruce mentions in his *Travels* that the royal chronicles of Ethiopia, beginning with the restoration of the so-called Solomonic line of kings, which are presented in the second volume of the first edition of his work, are based on an Ethiopic original which has been lodged in the British Museum 'to satisfy the curiosity of the public'. But the bulk of Bruce's precious manuscripts was purchased by the Bodleian Library, which now possesses twenty-five of his volumes, nearly all of them stately tomes in fine Ethiopian bindings and constituting a representative sample of Ethiopic literature. Bruce's contribution to scholarship in this sphere alone, the treasures of his drawings and manuscripts, should securely establish his reputation as one of the great universal savants and men of action of the eighteenth century.

Alas, Bruce's most cherished claim, to be the discoverer of the source of the Nile, is unfounded. Pedro Paez had—as we have seen—been there already in 1618, and his description is so detailed and accurate that its author's veracity cannot be doubted. More recently, C. Conti Rossini established with a fair degree of probability that even earlier, in 1588, Giovanni Gabriel, son of an Italian father and an Abyssinian mother, had visited the sources of the Nile.

Bruce remained in Ethiopia for over two years and then set out on his return journey by way of Nubia, travelling along the Blue Nile down to its confluence with the White Nile. He reached Cairo early in 1773 and went on to France, where he was given an enthusiastic reception by the world of learning. London, too, celebrated the arrival of the traveller whom it had long believed dead; but the incredulity with which Bruce's accounts of his experiences were received gave him deep offence, and he quickly retired to Kinnaird. Except for an audience of the King, Bruce received no official recognition for the singular services he had rendered to Ethiopian and oriental scholarship. The effect of Ludolf's great work had nearly spent itself in Bruce's day. The Laird of Kinnaird re-kindled the flame, and the stimulus he gave to Abyssinian studies became the basis on which so much has been built. With Bruce the 'classical age'[1] of African discovery opens.

Some thirty years passed before further exploration was attempted in Ethiopia. By then the nineteenth century had begun, which saw a

[1] Perham and Simmons, *African Discovery*, 1942, p. 24.

considerable number of geographical and scientific expeditions to the horn of Africa—not infrequently coupled with political and economic aims. At the same time interest was revived in the academic study of Ethiopia, its civilization and its languages, and with the publication of a number of fundamental works in this sphere the basis was created on which these studies could be established as a proper university discipline.

The first mission in Ethiopia after Bruce was also undertaken by a Briton. It was carried out—as indeed was most of the work in the nineteenth century—in the northern regions of the country, the area of the old Aksumite Kingdom. In the year 1804 George Annesley, Viscount Valentia, was in command of a British ship that was lying in the Red Sea for hydrographic studies. Viscount Valentia had been in correspondence with the powerful Ras of the Tigrai, Walda Sellasie, and, following an invitation by the Ras, sent his secretary and draughtsman, Henry Salt (1780–1827), accompanied by three other Englishmen, to explore the country and to negotiate commercial contracts. The party left Massawa in the spring of 1805 and, crossing Eritrea, went to Antalo, then the headquarters of the Ras of the Tigrai. They were well received and were permitted to proceed in a south-westerly direction towards Gondar, but the internal conflicts which then convulsed the country forced them to abandon this plan. Salt therefore decided to return to Massawa by way of Aksum and Adwa, where he inspected the rich field of antiquities and also prepared drawings. Some of these drawings, together with scientific records and observations, were published by Lord Valentia in his *Voyages and Travels* (London, 1809).

In January 1809 Salt was sent to Abyssinia for the second time, but now on an official mission for the British Government, to carry gifts and a letter from King George III to the King of Abyssinia, to make a report on the country, and to explain the importance of trade to the tribes along the coast. At Massawa he was met by Nathaniel Pearce, one of his former companions, who had stayed behind in Ethiopia. But on this occasion as well the internal situation made it impossible for Salt to reach Gondar. He handed his gifts to Ras Walda Sellasie, thus establishing the first official communication between Britain and Ethiopia. Salt then made an extensive tour of the Takkaze region and later stopped again at Aksum for the study of inscriptions. In 1814 he published his *Voyage to Abyssinia*, 'executed under the orders of the British Government'. His contribution to our knowledge of the geography of northern Ethiopia was considerable, and his accurate and reliable descriptions of the country—though much less detailed and voluminous than those by Bruce—were of great value. This applies in particular to his epigraphic studies and his lists of basic vocabulary, including Amharic and Tigrinya as well as the Agaw, Galla, and Somali languages.

In 1830 Samuel Gobat (born in 1799, later Anglican Bishop at Jerusalem) went to Abyssinia and visited Gondar—the first European to do so since the days of Bruce. He published in 1834 a *Journal of Three Years' Residence in Abyssinia*, and a year later he returned to the country accompanied by three Protestant missionaries. One of them, J. L. Krapf, wrote an interesting report on his travels (published in London in 1860) and did some very valuable pioneering work on the Galla language, while another, C. W. Isenberg, compiled an excellent dictionary of Amharic (London, 1841), the most widespread of the Semitic languages of Ethiopia, followed the next year by a competent grammar of Amharic. At first both these missionaries worked in the Adwa area; later they moved south into the Shoa province.

The pace in exploration and study had quickened: while Isenberg was still working on his dictionary, the German scholar Eduard Rüppell (1794–1884) was exploring Ethiopia. He was a man of proven ability and experience gained during his travels in Egypt and Arabia. A scientist and naturalist, he first engaged in astronomical calculations, in the preparation of a more accurate map of the country, and in listing specimens of the fauna and flora. He explored the regions to the north and south of Gondar and was able to furnish a large mass of information about Lake Tana. His meteorological observations established for the first time the general lines of the climatology of Ethiopia.

It was at that time, in the 1830s, that France made her entry into the field of the exploration of Ethiopia, a branch of scholarship in which she has taken a prominent part ever since. The first travellers, Combes and Tamisier, were somewhat unfortunate in that their traversing of Ethiopia from Massawa to the Galla country was overshadowed by the splendid results of Rüppell's work. But Rochet d'Héricourt was able to add to our knowledge of the topography and geology of the southern parts of Ethiopia. He stayed for some time at a small place near Ankober which was the residence of King Sahela Sellasie of Shoa and accompanied the King on two expeditions against the Gallas. In 1840 the French Government organized a scientific mission headed by Ferret and Galinier. They worked at Adwa and Gondar, mainly on problems of geology and meteorology. Another French expedition under official auspices was that led by the naval officer Th. Lefèbvre, which remained in the Ethiopian highlands from 1839 to 1843 and produced six tomes packed with historical, archaeological, and ethnological observations.

But the first name in French exploration of Abyssinia is that of Antoine d'Abbadie (1810–97), who, together with his brother Arnaud, spent many years in Ethiopia and brought back an enormous body of material in different fields of study. With instruments designed by himself he set out from Gondar for a survey of Lake Tana and its surroundings. He visited the ancient city of Lalibala with its famous rock-hewn churches and also carried out astronomical, trigonometric, and cartographic studies in the Gojjam province. D'Abbadie's work of ten years' exploration and research also included languages, history, and human races. He himself catalogued the treasures of his Ethiopic manuscripts which, later on, were subjected once more to the masterly scrutiny of C. Conti Rossini. Unfortunately, large parts of his notes and journals remain, unedited and unpublished, in the vaults of the Bibliothèque Nationale in Paris.

Meanwhile, in 1854, Sir Richard Burton had been the first European to reach the mysterious city of Harar—a journey of terrible hazards and epic courage. A second official communication between Britain and Ethiopia had taken place in 1841, when Major W. C. Harris was sent on an official mission to King Sahela Sellasie, with whom he concluded, in the name of Queen Victoria, a treaty of friendship and commerce, the first treaty to be negotiated between the two countries. The stately Amharic of this document (which is kept in the Public Record Office, London) also shows many interesting features from a linguistic point of view. A member of Harris's embassy was the traveller and scholar C. T. Beke, who remained in the country for some time and greatly enriched our knowledge of the geography of the Blue Nile region and of southern Ethiopia. He also studied the

The Emperor Haile Sellasie I

(b) Job Ludolf

(a) Abba Gregory, Ludolf's teacher

languages and dialects of this region, recognized that Gafat was on the eve of extinction, and produced a linguistic map of Abyssinia.

Mention must be made here of the fascinating story of the Swiss traveller and adventurer Werner Munzinger. He arrived at Massawa in 1854 and was one of the few Europeans to turn his attention to the neglected northern parts of Eritrea. The results of his travels were the very valuable *Ostafrikanische Studien* (1864) as well as a small vocabulary of Tigre, the Semitic tongue of the tribes of eastern, northern, and western Eritrea. His books became a precious guide to the Italians in their first years of colonization in Eritrea. Munzinger was also a successful businessman and later became Governor of Massawa on entering into the service of the Egyptian Government. But he returned to Keren, the lovely town in western Eritrea (in more recent years the scene of the bloodiest battle in the Abyssinian campaigns of 1940-1). In 1875 Munzinger Pasha's army was heavily defeated by the Ethiopians and he himself was killed—the end, at the same time, of an extraordinary career and of Egypt's imperialist ambitions in the horn of Africa.

In the historical chapter below we shall hear something of Lord Napier's expedition in 1867-8, which led to the fall of Magdala and the suicide of King Theodore. The aim of the British Government's military intervention in Abyssinia was the release of a number of British and other European prisoners detained by King Theodore. When this purpose was achieved, speedily and effectively, the British Army withdrew at once. Yet the expedition had an importance far transcending the freeing of a small number of captives. Lord Napier's troops landed at the port of Zula and set out from there on their 'epic march' to Magdala, over 300 miles of difficult terrain in a virtually unknown country, with heavy artillery carried on elephants. The progress of the expedition and its equipment left a lasting impression in all the regions through which it passed, and stories and 'traditions' about it, true as well as apocryphal, may still be heard now—a century later. During World War II one could still meet a few Ethiopians who, in their childhood, had witnessed the majestic march of the elephants—a spectacle never to be forgotten.

From a scientific point of view, the expedition had results of major importance. Apart from a large number of miscellaneous writings by

B

members of the campaign, books and stories by journalists (including a sumptuous volume by the *Illustrated London News*, containing a hundred illustrations), official reports, etc., there were invaluable scientific observations and collections of manuscripts. T. J. Holland and H. M. Hozier produced the three volumes of the official *Record of the Expedition to Abyssinia*, while the geographer C. R. Markham and the geologist W. T. Blanford placed the results of their detailed surveys before the world of scholarship. The haul of some 400 manuscripts from the library of the Church of Madhane Alam ('Saviour of the World') at Magdala was not only the greatest accession to Ethiopic manuscript literature ever made, but placed the study of Ethiopic literary history on an entirely new basis. Apart from this official collection a large number of MSS., probably no fewer than 150–200, were brought to Britain by individual members of the expeditionary forces. Most of these found their way into university libraries, notably the Bodleian and the Cambridge Libraries, but a few remained in private hands and reappear occasionally at auction sales. The British Museum[1] received 373 manuscripts of great value, while six were deposited in the Royal Library at Windsor Castle.[2] The campaign undertaken to release a few captives had thus far-reaching and quite unexpected results.

With the disappearance of King Theodore, the exploration and study of Ethiopia were taken up with renewed fervour. The extension of Ethiopian dominion over the southern parts of the territory led to increased activities in fresh areas of investigation. The 'classical age' of exploration was now at an end, and we enter the era of expeditions that were frequently government-sponsored and well equipped with all manner of instruments and tools. The lonely and heroic explorer now makes room for the carefully organized scientific mission, though there still remain many individual achievements of courage and perseverance. It is not possible in this context to recount the exploits of all the expeditions or even to name their leaders. But mention should be made of the important voyage, under the auspices of the Italian Geographical

[1] W. Wright, *Catalogue of Ethiopic MSS in the British Museum*, London, 1877.
[2] E. Ullendorff, 'The Ethiopic MSS. in the Royal Library, Windsor Castle,' *RSE*, XII, 1953. See now also Rita Pankhurst, 'The Library of Emperor Tewodros II at Magdala', *BSOAS*, XXXVII.

Society, to the equatorial lakes. Though Italy has not, perhaps, produced travellers of the fame of Bruce or d'Abbadie, she has sent out many men who have notably contributed to the general body of knowledge by a great number of studies of detail, such as cartography, climatology, agriculture, ethnology, linguistics, etc. One thinks especially of Antonio Cecchi and Giuseppe Chiarini, who investigated the south-west of the country, or of missionaries like Massaia[1] and Sapeto, or of administrators like Pollera and Martini. No praise can be too high for the scholarly work accomplished by Swedish missionaries in Eritrea, while in the archaeological field the outstanding event was the German Aksum expedition led by Littmann in the early years of this century.

But we must now retrace our steps and meet the men who, in the seclusion of their studies, worked on the raw material supplied by the explorers in the field. There is, first and foremost, the great name of the re-founder of Abyssinian studies, August Dillmann (1823–94), the Ludolf of the nineteenth century. He wrote the three works which are still the indispensable tools to the student of classical Ethiopic: a detailed grammar (1857) which has been translated into English by Crichton, a truly monumental dictionary of Ge'ez (1865), and a chrestomathy (1866) which is based on his vast reading of Ethiopic literature. He prepared the first catalogues of Ethiopic MSS. in the British Museum, at Oxford, and Berlin. To this one must add his historical studies of the Kingdom of Aksum and the reigns of Zar'a Ya'qob and Amda Sion as well as his pioneering biblical editions.

Dillmann's work was taken up in France by Halévy (noted especially for his archaeological expedition to the Yemen and his contributions to Falasha literature), Zotenberg, and Basset, while in Germany men of the rank of Th. Nöldeke (1836–1930) and F. Praetorius (1847–1927) followed in Dillmann's footsteps. Praetorius wrote grammars of Amharic, Tigrinya, and Galla which have remained models of accuracy, exhaustiveness, and sound method.[2] In Italy Ludolf and Dillmann have found some of their most illustrious disciples: first among them

[1] I am grateful to Dr. E. Cerulli who conducted me, during a recent visit to Rome, over the Massaia Museum near Frascati.
[2] Cf. Ullendorff, *Amharic Chrestomathy*, pp. 3–4.

was Ignazio Guidi (1844–1935), a Semitist and *éthiopisant* of unusual distinction. In 1885 he succeeded in including Ethiopian languages, literature, and history within the scope of his teaching at Rome University. He edited and translated the *Fetha Nagast* ('legislation of the kings'), the law code of Ethiopia, as well as numerous other texts. He had a profound knowledge of Amharic (which was deepened by collaboration with Kefla Giyorgis of Santo Stefano dei Mori), and his Amharic dictionary (and later supplement) has remained unsurpassed in accuracy and arrangement, though the rapid development of Amharic urgently requires further lexicographical work.[1]

Guidi's achievements were continued and matched by Carlo Conti Rossini (1872–1949), who contributed with great distinction to virtually every aspect of Ethiopian studies. He was a cautious, accurate, and most reliable scholar. He had begun his career in Eritrea and then devoted his entire life to the critical investigation of a country for which he cared deeply. Of his generously designed *Storia d'Etiopia* unfortunately the first volume only appeared.[2] Everyone concerned with Ethiopian scholarship is profoundly conscious of the debt owed to Conti Rossini.

No student of Ethiopia can afford to neglect the connection between that country and South Arabia. Among those who have recognized this vital link are Eduard Glaser and Eugen Mittwoch, while Leo Reinisch is the undisputed master of the Semitic connection with the Hamitic (Cushitic) languages of Ethiopia. In Britain, Walton, Castell, and Bruce found their successors in William Wright, author of the great catalogue of manuscripts in the British Museum, and Sir E. A. Wallis Budge, a most assiduous editor and translator of Ethiopic texts and author of a two-volume history of Ethiopia. Earlier still Richard Laurence and Thomas Platt had edited religious and biblical texts, while Enoch studies will always remain connected with the name of R. H. Charles. In Russia B. Turaiev and I. Kratchkovsky were outstanding exponents of Ethiopian studies. The latter's posthumous *Introduction to Ethiopic Philology* (1955) is a valuable bibliographical tool.

Of the recently deceased one remembers especially C. H. Armbruster

[1] Now largely accomplished by Gankin's dictionary.
[2] An index to this indispensable work has since been published in *RSE*, xviii, 1962.

(1874–1957) whose Amharic attainments were of a high order, while Enno Littmann (1875–1958) is universally considered one of the most outstanding Semitists of this century. His epigraphic work in the German Aksum expedition, his four volumes of Tigre texts, his posthumous Tigre dictionary, and hundreds of smaller contributions make his departure from the scene of Ethiopian scholarship an irreparable loss. M. M. Moreno (1892–1964) wrote many profound studies on Galla, Somali, and Amharic, as well as on numerous aspects of the contemporary Ethiopian scene.

Among the living, there stand out the names of Marcel Cohen, the great master of linguistic research who for sixty years has been the teacher of all working in this field, and of Enrico Cerulli who has proved his mastery in everything he has touched, from the study of the South Ethiopian languages to his great works on medieval Oriental and Occidental literature and civilization. H. J. Polotsky has shown, in a few well-directed forays, how finality and perfection can be attained by superb method. W. Leslau has made weighty and prolific contributions, especially to the study of the Semitic tongues of southern Ethiopia, and S. Strelcyn has greatly enriched our knowledge of magical texts and early Amharic.

Many other names from past and present could be cited to bear witness to the abiding fascination which Ethiopian studies have exerted on Europeans of many nations and over a long period.[1]

---

[1] In 1959 the Accademia dei Lincei (upon the initiative of E. Cerulli) convened the First International Conference of Ethiopian Studies at Rome (cf. *Atti del Convegno Internazionale di Studi Etiopici*, 1960). The Second International Conference of *éthiopisants* was held in the University of Manchester in 1963 (cf. *JSS*, Spring, 1964), the third at Addis Ababa in 1966, and the fourth again at Rome in 1972.

II

THE COUNTRY[1]

━━━◦◦◦◦◦◦◎◦◦◦◦◦━━━

ETHIOPIA (including the northern province of Eritrea) covers an area of about 400,000 square miles, that is more than four times the size of Great Britain and Northern Ireland. Its most southerly point reaches within 200 miles of the Equator, while its northern extremity lies within the same distance from Mecca. In its long history the country has always formed a bridge between Africa and Asia, and many of its inhabitants were immigrants from South Arabia from which it is separated only by the narrow straits of the Bab-el-Mandeb, a distance of less than twenty miles. With its ancestry astride two continents and its position in the horn of Africa, Ethiopia has always occupied a favoured place at a cross-road of civilizations and a meeting point of many races.

In the north-east it touches the Red Sea for nearly 500 miles along the Eritrean-Dankali coast with the ports of Massawa and Assab; in the east and south-east the Somali territories form a somewhat awkward frontier; in the south its neighbour is Kenya and in the west and north the Sudan. The country is relatively narrow in the north and broadens out progressively towards the south, reaching a maximum width of some 900 miles somewhere near the line of 8° N. Ethiopia is commonly likened to a triangle with its apex to the north.

The physical configuration of the country is marked by a vast mountain massif with a mean height of between 7,000 and 8,000 feet. It rises from the torrid plains abruptly and almost perpendicularly, and this steep escarpment has had a profound influence on the course of

[1] See now Mesfin, *An Introductory Geography of Ethiopia*, Addis Ababa, 1972.

Ethiopian history in its deterrence of the would-be conqueror. It has also for many centuries enabled the people to live in isolation from the outside world and to stem the flood of advancing Islam. The abruptness of the physical contours is reflected in astonishing contrasts of climate within a distance of a few miles and in linguistic barriers of uncompromising incisiveness. This great massif is cleft, in a direction from north-east to south-west, by the rift valley which is marked by the Awash River and the group of large lakes in south-west Ethiopia. To the west of these mountain ranges lies the immense valley of the Nile and its tributaries which is fed, in part, by the romantic Abbay (or Blue Nile), winding its tortuous course from Lake Tana, and by the torrential rains which, from late June to September, gush down the mountains as mighty rivers.

The great rift valley divides the eastern plateau of the Somalis and Gallas from the central plateau of Abyssinia proper—and it is with the latter in particular that this outline is concerned. These fertile and beautiful highlands extend for 700 miles or more from Asmara in the Hamasien province in the north to Addis Ababa and Jimma in the south. They are frequently rent asunder by river beds and narrow valleys, by cracks, fissures, and deep gorges. Then there are the mountains: the great elevation of Semien where Mt. Dashan (Dajan) reaches nearly 14,000 feet and many others exceed 13,000 feet: Abuna Yosef in Lasta, Mt. Birhan in Gojjam, or Mt. Guna to the east of Lake Tana. No less impressive are the beautiful crater lakes of the Abyssinian plateau such as Lake Tana, the largest, or Lake Hayq, one of the smallest, with their islands and ancient monasteries, where time has stood still and the world of the Old Testament is yet alive.

Ethiopia's first river is the Blue Nile, the *Abbay* of the Ethiopians or *Bahr al-azraq* of the Arabs—perhaps the Gihon (called *Giyon* by the inhabitants of the region) of Gen. 2: 13. The secret of its source had roused the passionate curiosity of men, from Alexander the Great and Julius Caesar to James Bruce and, in our day, R. E. Cheesman, the British Consul who made a most able survey of the area and wrote an excellent book about it. From its source at Gish, in the Sakala region, the Small Abbay flows into Lake Tana. The point of its origin had been a place of worship since pagan days; now a church dedicated to St. Michael and Zar'a Buruk is situated there, and many Abyssinians come here in search of cure by the holy waters. The Small Abbay empties its waters into Lake Tana (whose main supply it is) and then emerges, at the overflow point at Chara-Chara Cataract, as the Big Abbay. Thence it proceeds on its slow course of 1,000 miles to meet the White Nile at Khartoum. But before then it encompasses the large province of Gojjam and forms the great falls at Tis-esat ('smoke of fire'), a spectacle of rare beauty.

Next to the Abbay the most prominent river is the Takkaze (*takkazi* or *takkaze* means 'river' in classical Ethiopic). It has its springs in central Ethiopia and, flowing due north, it bisects the northern part of the country before turning west and, under the name of Setit, joining the Atbara. In its upper reaches it has perennial waters, but in the parched areas of the western lowlands it dries up once it has shed the flow of the big rains into the Atbara. The Atbara itself, under the name of Gandua, rises near Lake Tana, but it soon leaves Ethiopia and runs most of its 500-mile course in the Sudan. The Mareb is the Eritrean river *par excellence* and traverses a large part of the country, south of Asmara, from east to west. In its lower reaches it is called Gash, and not far from Kassala loses itself in the hot sand of the Sudan.

Abbay, Takkaze, Atbara, and Mareb are all part of the great hydrographic system of the Abyssinian highlands. They flow west towards the Nile and, ultimately, empty their waters into the Mediterranean. For many centuries it had been known how vital the rains over the Abyssinian plateau are for the level of the Nile; and the legend that the Negus could ruin Egypt by diverting the waters of the Abbay has never lost its powerful attraction.

The other great water systems of Ethiopia are, in the south-east, the Juba and Webi Shebeli rivers, which descend from the great eastern plateau and flow through Somalia; the Barka in the north, which rises in the Eritrean Highlands near Himberti and, after turning west for a short distance, describes a northerly course until, following its confluence with the Anseba, it reaches the Red Sea not far from Tokar; the Awash in the rift valley depression makes its journey from the Shoan plateau towards Tajura Bay, but fails to reach the coast and is lost in the large saline lacustrine depression of the Dankali littoral; in the south-west the Baro, Akobo, and other rivers rise in the Kaffa mountains and, under the name of Sobat, become a tributary of the

White Nile. The Omo group, likewise in the south-west, constitutes a mighty river basin fed by the region of highest rainfall in the entire country.

Of the lakes of Ethiopia Lake Tana is not only the largest, it is also the one that is most deeply steeped in the history of the country. It lies 6,000 feet above sea-level, is heart-shaped, and has an area of about 1,250 square miles. Cheesman, who knew the lake better than anyone else, failed to get a sounding deeper than 35 feet, though previous travellers had alleged depths exceeding 200 feet. It is a beautiful expanse of water, in places 40 miles wide; the water is blue and the land around it green, with hills and mountains in the background. The largest island is called Dek. Along the eastern escarpment we find smaller lakes, Ashangi, Hayq, and Ardibbo. In the south-western part of the rift valley is a chain of beautiful lakes which form part of the depression leading to the equatorial lakes: Lake Zway in Gurage country, Lakes Langana, Shala, Awasa, Margherita, Stefanie, and finally Lake Rudolph, though only a small corner of the last-named is within Ethiopian territory.

Among the most characteristic sights in Ethiopia are the Ambas, the ubiquitous, flat-topped hills whose sides slope down almost vertically. They show the force of erosion, are often denuded of all vegetation except grass, and are impregnable as fortresses. They have played their part in Ethiopian history. Around and in between these Ambas there are often beautifully green meadows and lush vegetation—another reminder of the contrasts, abrupt and unyielding, which Ethiopia reveals in so many spheres.

Ethiopians themselves divide their country into three main zones according to altitude and the resultant climate with its influence on vegetation and products: *Dega* is the temperate zone of the highlands, 7,000 feet and above; *Woyna Dega* ('highlands of the vine') is the intermediate zone which was once, though scarcely now, the main region for vine cultivation; its altitude ranges from 5,000 to 7,000 feet. *Quolla* is the low-lying and hot area. The division into zones of altitude and vegetation is paralleled by the indigenous scheme of the distribution of seasons: *Keremt* is the rainy season from the middle or end of June till September, while *Hagay* or *Bega* signifies the dry season; *Metsew* is the harvest period following immediately upon the big rains, and *Tsedey* the sowing season from March to June.

Perhaps the most astounding aspect of the climate in Ethiopia is the fact that the highlands have a tropical rainy season (small rains: March–May; big rains: June–September), while the coastal lowlands, only a few dozen miles away, have a Mediterranean period of rains, though with comparatively slight precipitation, mainly in December and January. Thus while the plateau has its most torrential rains during the summer months, the Red Sea littoral at Massawa, less than ten minutes' flying time away, experiences its hottest and driest season. All this leads to far-reaching social consequences: the winter migration of highland shepherds into the lowlands and their return to the plateau when the sun scorches pastures, animals, and humans alike; the movement of the farmer down the slopes in search of a second harvest.

Ethiopia's proximity to the Equator, in an area from 4 to 18 degrees north, should give it the most tropical and torrid climate; and that indeed is the case along the eastern and western lowlands. But the mitigating effect of the high mountains, where the majority of the population lives, is such that the climate there is among the most temperate, agreeable, and healthy anywhere in the world. It is the mountains which have the most profound influence on the Ethiopian climate in general, for they cause the monsoons of the Indian Ocean to deposit ample rain on the plateau—with certain secondary effects on the coastal area and the slopes. The pressure and wind system affecting Ethiopia is one of great complexity, especially in view of the proximity of the low-pressure area of the Nile Valley.

The highlands show a remarkably even temperature throughout the year. At Asmara in the north and Addis Ababa in the south the fluctuations between the hottest and the coldest months of the year do not exceed 7° F. At Addis Ababa the average temperature of the hottest month (May) is 65°, of the coldest month (December) 58°. The absolute maximum recorded at Asmara is 86°, the absolute minimum 38°. At Massawa, on the other hand, the annual mean temperature is 87°, the highest recorded 115°, the lowest 66°. While the plateau thus has the most agreeably balanced temperatures, Massawa and the Dankali coast (where the thermometer may reach 120°) are among the hottest places anywhere in the world.

The annual rainfall at Massawa is 7 inches, at Asmara 18 inches, at Harar 35 inches, at Addis Ababa 50 inches, at Gore (in south-west Ethiopia) 80 inches (compared with London's 24 inches). There is virtually no rain ever in the Dankali plains.

The flora of Ethiopia is as variegated as one might expect in a country of such contrasts of climate and altitude. In the lowlands vegetation is generally dense and tropical, while in the highlands bushes and trees are found scattered and in small clusters rather than in large forests, though there are thickly wooded hillsides, especially in the medium altitudes. In Eritrea the general aspect of the plateau, though often not devoid of a certain grandeur, is one of considerable bareness, but the further south one proceeds the lusher becomes the vegetation; and in the uplands of the south-west it is very luxuriant.

The two most prominent trees of the highlands are *zegba* and *ted*, both large and evergreen coniferous trees of the juniper type. More recently King Menelik II introduced the eucalyptus tree, which has been a most happy innovation that gives Addis Ababa its wonderfully wooded and green appearance and, incidentally, creates the illusion of mitigating the lack of oxygen at those great heights. The acacia (*grar* in Amharic) is the most important tree in the lower regions of the country; it is used for building and as fuel; it also yields gum. Other trees are sycamores, cedars, date palms, wild olives, and wild bananas, as well as many varieties of plants and shrubs. The *koso*, or *kussa*, is most ubiquitous, and its fruit is widely used by Ethiopians as a cure against the tape-worm. The word 'coffee' is often claimed to be derived from the name of the Kaffa province, where coffee trees grow in profusion. Coffee forests in the south-west may be either wild or may be established in plantations. Coffee is the most important cash crop in Ethiopia and accounts for more than 50 per cent. of the value of all exports.

Tief, or *teff*, is a very common cereal grain with seeds of small size and is extensively grown in areas of the middle and higher altitudes. While *teff* is probably not suitable for the baking of European bread, it is ideal for making *injera*, the indigenous type of flat and porous bread. Even more important is *durra* (*mashella*), a type of sorghum that is commonly grown in India and North Africa. It prospers in the low, hot regions of the country and also in those of medium elevation, especially in many parts of Eritrea and near Harar and Dessie. *Durra* is hardy, of high productivity, and needs little attention; it is therefore a very popular crop. Maize is grown in the high rainfall areas of south-west Ethiopia, while wheat is much less widely cultivated—except near Addis Ababa, Ambo, and Gondar, where demand and sales have increased in recent years. Barley is grown in most parts of the plateau, but the amount of rice cultivation is extremely limited.

Among vegetables, peppers, onions, garlic, cabbage, tomatoes, beans, asparagus, lettuce, and artichokes are very common. Fruit is plentiful and is grown especially in the Harar area and in south-west Ethiopia; bananas, mangoes, lemons, grapefruit, and oranges can be seen in many parts of the country. Papaws (papayas), guavas, pineapples, and peaches are grown in the middle and lower regions, while the fruit of the cactus, the prickly pear, is most popular and plentiful on the plateau.

Ethiopians keep a large number of the usual domestic animals. Cattle are either hump-backed or, less frequently, straight-backed. The raw meat of the cow is still a favourite food. Goats and sheep are extremely numerous; the latter are not usually woolbearing. The mule is by far the most popular animal, for both riding and the carriage of loads. It is exceedingly sturdy and, above all, remarkably sure-footed along the dangerous mountain-slopes. Horses and asses are somewhat less frequently encountered. Chickens abound everywhere and are an important element in the Ethiopian's diet. They are very small and their eggs are tiny. Camels will generally be found in the lower and hotter areas only; they are rare in the highlands.

Elephants and crocodiles can, I believe, be found only in some of the lowlands of western Ethiopia, especially in the Sobat Valley, but some large crocodiles have been seen on the sandbanks of the Abbay. Lions and leopards are by no means common; their habitat is in the south and west of the country, but the surroundings of Harar and Dire Dawa have also been visited by them in recent years. Giraffes and zebras are rare nowadays. Most common is the spotted hyena, which can be seen, or more often heard, on its nocturnal outings; the striped hyenas are smaller, shyer, and less noisy by night. Both kinds fulfil an important sanitary function. Gazelles exist in large numbers in the lower-lying districts. Baboons can be extremely dangerous to crops, animals, and humans alike. They appear in large troops, descending from mountain-tops, and have a most penetrating bark.

Birds are numerous and often of beautiful plumage. Eagles are infrequent, but bustards are quite common, especially in the Dankali plains. Guinea-fowls and partridges can be found in most parts of the country; the same is true of grouse, duck, and goose. Poisonous serpents are not widespread in Ethiopia. Leslie Brown has written, knowledgeably, of tawny eagles and lammergeiers, of Walia ibex and Semien fox, and has published some beautiful photographs (*Ethiopian Episode, passim*).

Gold is found both in Eritrea and in the south, but reports about deposits and their commercial exploitation vary—even though attempts have often been made to locate Ophir and the riches of the Queen of Sheba on the western side of the Red Sea. Other minerals and oil have not so far been traced in any large quantities. An American oil company has been granted a concession; they have undertaken explora-tory drillings, but reports so far give little cause for extravagant hopes.

III

THE PEOPLE

———————•~^~^~^~(O)~^~^~^~•———————

Nobody quite knows how many people there are within the boundaries of the Ethiopian Empire. Since no properly controlled census has ever been undertaken, all population figures are bound to be estimates. In 1936, *L'Africa Orientale*[1] thought that 6–7 millions was a realistic guess, while the figure in the *Guida dell' Africa Orientale* (p. 82) is 7½ million. The 1954 Ethiopian *Guide Book*[2] contains an estimate of just under 17 millions, and the U.S. Army *Area Handbook* of 1960 considers a total of 21 millions 'far beyond all competent estimates' (p. 53). The 1967 *Trade Directory and Guide Book to Ethiopia* mentions a figure of 22 millions (p. 11). The Ethiopian geographer, Ato Mesfin Walda Maryam, in a carefully documented study,[3] has convinced me that previous guesses[4] ranging between 10 and 15 millions were too low and failed to take account of the modern growth-rate which Ato Mesfin assumes to be at least 2 per cent. His own well-documented estimate of 28 millions (1971) is based on sample surveys (*An Introductory Geography of Ethiopia*, p. 169). At any rate, Ethiopia ranks after Nigeria and Egypt as the most populous state in Africa.

American aerial mapping experts in Ethiopia have told the present writer that aerial photography may assist demographic investigations, for the photographs are sufficiently detailed to show every house or hut

[1] *R. Soc. Geogr. Ital.*, pp. 195–7.
[2] Issued by the Ethiopian Chamber of Commerce.
[3] *Ethiopia Observer*, v, 2, pp. 135–42.
[4] Including my own in the first edition of this book.

in the country. By sampling the number of inhabitants per house, it may thus be possible to arrive at an approximate figure for the country as a whole.

Estimates for the numerical distribution of ethnic groups vary widely and are scarcely better than guesses, but the following figures may claim a reasonable basis of probability:

Amharas, Tigreans, Agaw, etc.	40%
Gallas	35%
Sidamas	10%
Somalis	6%
Danakil-Afar	4%
Negroes	5%

The population is mainly concentrated upon the salubrious highlands, while the sweltering lowlands support only a small fraction of the inhabitants of the Empire. The Abyssinians proper, the carriers of the historical civilization of Semitized Ethiopia, live in the central and northern highlands. From the mountains of Eritrea in the north to the Awash Valley in the south we find this clearly distinguishable Abyssinian type who for many centuries has maintained his identity against the influx of the negroid peoples of the Nile Valley, the equatorial lakes, or the Indian Ocean littoral. The steep escarpment has been the bulwark against which successive waves of would-be invaders have battled and failed, while others have ascended the mountain plateau only to be assimilated and to be merged in the dominant Abyssinian element.

There are three great ethnic groups within the political boundaries of the Ethiopian Empire: (1) Peoples of Cushitic (i.e. Hamitic Ethiopian) stock who have, over a long period, received Semitic admixtures originating from the Arabian shores of the Red Sea and who themselves speak Semitic languages; (2) Cushitic groups of the Beja, Sidama, etc., type who have remained comparatively free from the influx of such outside elements; (3) peoples of Nilotic origin.

Of course, this seemingly simple picture of ethnic grouping is somewhat misleading, for Ethiopia is a country which embraces a complex variety of ethnic elements representing a veritable mosaic of races, tribes, and linguistic groups: 'l'Abissinia è un museo di popoli', in the words of Conti Rossini.[1] Neither the Semitized peoples nor the Cushitic groups are in any way racially pure; indeed, they have absorbed so much alien blood, partly from each other, partly from negroid groups, and from sources difficult to identify that the term 'race' (vague and all-too-often abused) has little meaning in this connection.

In this outline of racial grouping we shall constantly have to invoke the criterion of linguistic affinity as a guide to ethnic distribution. That this is by no means a completely satisfactory criterion need hardly be stressed, for some groups have changed their language (and more often their religion) in the past—recent or remote. But in the absence of any safer means of identification we shall have to use language as a rough-and-ready indication of ethnic origins.

Generally speaking, the predominant Ethiopian type reveals fairly close anthropometric affinities to that commonly found among the Arabs of South Arabia, i.e. medium stature, long face, and a fairly straight and thin nose—all characteristics not encountered among the neighbouring African peoples. The hair is curly or frizzy, lips are thinner and very much less protruding than is otherwise the case in Africa. The colour of the skin varies a good deal, but is generally rather light, somewhere between olive and light brown.

(1) If we disregard recent Semitic immigrants, mostly Arabs settled along the Red Sea coast in towns like Massawa, Assab, etc., the most noticeably Semitized part of the country is the north, the area of the old Aksumite Kingdom. Here, proceeding from north to south, we first encounter the Tigre-speaking tribes. They inhabit the northern hills of Eritrea as well as the eastern and western plains. The Beni Amer are the largest tribe and occupy a considerable portion of western Eritrea. They number about 60,000, with an additional 30,000 tribesmen in the Sudan. The Beni Amer are, strictly speaking, a federation of tribes who owe allegiance to a paramount chief, the Diglal. Not all of them speak Tigre; smaller sections are Beja-speaking, while some are bilingual. This linguistic position accurately reflects the heterogeneous origin of the Beni Amer. They are Muslims, and most of them acknowledge the religious leadership of the Mirghani family in the eastern Sudan. A

[1] *L'Abissinia*, p. 20.

small minority of the tribe engage in agriculture, while the great majority are nomadic herdsmen with some wealth in camels, cattle, sheep, and goats. During the rainy season a section of the tribe settles temporarily along the Barka River.

In the northern hills of Eritrea we must first mention the tribal federation of Bet Asgede, which consists of three component sub-tribes: the Habab, the Ad Tekles, and the Ad Temariam. They claim to be descended from a common ancestor, but for all practical purposes they now represent autonomous tribal units with separate habitat and their own chiefs. Like most of the tribes in the Keren division, whether Tigre- or Bilen-speaking, the Bet Asgede have the characteristic social distinction between the ruling class (*shumagalle*), generally of foreign origin, and the serfs or vassals (*Tigre*). The original linguistic difference which this nomenclature reflects has long been blurred, for the alien overlords (in the case of the Bet Asgede of Abyssinian (plateau) origin) have, in the course of time, adopted the language of their serfs. Thus the Asgede rulers have not only given up their language, Tigrinya, and taken over Tigre, they also abandoned monophysite Christianity in favour of Islam, the religion of the tribes they had conquered.

The Ad Sheikh tribe have their encampments between the Habab in the north and the Ad Tekles in the south. They claim descent from a *Sherif* in Mecca, but most of these tribal memories are incapable of proof. They are certainly fervent Muslims, and their hereditary chief is styled *Nazir*. To the east of the Ad Sheikh are three smaller tribes, Ad Tsaura, Ad Muallim, and Bet Mala, who are, of course, Muslims and very largely nomadic. In the north of Eritrea, along the Red Sea coast, we find the Rashaida, recent immigrants from Arabia, who keep themselves separate from the neighbouring Tigre tribes. Their language and culture are Arabic, and they have not so far undergone any measure of assimilation, either physically or linguistically.

In the Keren region itself there are two large tribes, the Marya in the north-west and the Mensa in the east. The Marya, in their turn, have split into two branches, the Red and the Black Marya. They were originally monophysites, but are said to have been converted to Islam early in the nineteenth century. The Mensa, who border on the Hamasien division, have among their number a small contingent of

Tigrinya speakers who are monophysite Christians, but the great majority of the tribe are Muslims and speak Tigre. More than 1,000 of the Mensa have become Protestants under the strong influence of the Swedish Mission in that region.

The eastern plains, along the Red Sea coast, extend from the frontiers of the Sudan in the north to the border of French Somaliland in the south—with the towns and ports of Massawa and Assab. The northern part is very sparsely populated and has, in part, already been discussed. The southern area, the large plains of the Danakil, will be subjected to closer scrutiny when we reach the tribes of Cushitic speech. At present we are concerned with the central area of the long Red Sea littoral, the Tigre-speaking Massawa region and the foothills leading up to the plateau, with Ginda at their centre. Ginda is a small town amidst luxuriant vegetation halfway between Asmara and Massawa and also halfway between the ethnic regions of the mountain plateau and the coastal plains. It is the pivot of many migrations, of the nomadic groups who move into the hills for grazing or cultivation and of the mountain tribes who go down to the foothills and the plains. Here is the abrupt boundary of language, religion, economic habit, etc., all provoked by the sudden and striking geographical contrast of plateau and plain, of temperate climate and sweltering heat, of rainfall and barrenness. There is constant seasonal movement of smaller and larger tribal units between the area of the foothills and the Samhar plain. The villages here, Ailet, Zula, Otumlo, Monkullo, etc., are small and largely composed of primitive grass huts, but at and near Massawa the urban style of building is prominent. The population of Massawa (12,000) and Arkiko (6,000) is very cosmopolitan and includes tribesmen from the hills, Danakil, Sudanese, Arabs, Indians, West Africans, and groups of Turkish descent. But the unifying factors are predominant: the religion is Islam, and the languages are Tigre and Arabic.

Tigre is also the principal language of the people of the Dahlak islands off the Massawa coast. This archipelago is made up of over 100 islands of incredible barrenness and desolation, though some of them are not devoid of a rugged kind of beauty. The people, no more than 2,000 to 3,000, are mostly fishermen; some own a few camels or goats. The Dahlak islanders were amongst the first in East Africa to be converted to Islam, and many tombstones in Kufic characters bear witness to this early Islamic connection.

Turning to the great Tigrinya-speaking block of the Eritrean and north Ethiopian highlands, we enter the area of the old Aksumite Kingdom whose dominion was, in later centuries, carried southwards by the people of Amharic speech. Here is historic Abyssinia *par excellence*, the Semitized people of the plateau with their Semitic language and Old Testament way of life.

As the following chapters on history, religion, language, social structure, etc., will be primarily concerned with this population of the northern and central highlands, we can here be brief. Tigrinya—as the name implies—is the language of the Tigrai province. It is spoken throughout the Eritrean plateau and extends as far south as Lake Ashangi and the Wojerat district; it then crosses the Takkaze westwards to the Tsellemti and Wolkayt regions. And the people who speak this language are the authentic carriers of the historical and cultural traditions of ancient Abyssinia. In Eritrea the three highland provinces of Hamasien, Serae, and Akkele Guzay comprise rather more than half the population of that territory. Although there are some differences of tradition and customary law between these provinces, their ethnic homogeneity is complete: it is expressed not only in physical and linguistic identity but also in long historical and political association as well as in their allegiance to monophysite Christianity. The same system of social structure and land tenure as well as cultural affinity extends beyond the artificial administrative border into the Tigrai. Eritrea was always an artificial creation, for the people on both sides of the frontier are one in race and civilization. In the Tigrai, there is the old cultural capital of Ethiopia, Aksum, now a small market-town, with the administrative centre of Adwa, the city of battle fame, in close proximity. The governmental headquarters of the Tigrai is nowadays at Makalle in the eastern part of the province. The Tigrinya pocket in Wolkayt and Kafta in the extreme west is outside the traditional boundaries of the Tigrai. After the Italo-Ethiopian War the entire Tigrinya block were united in a Greater Eritrea, but this arrangement came to an end shortly after the liberation of Ethiopia.

In the historical survey below we shall see how, with the decline of

Tigrean predominance, political power passed to the Amharic-speaking people who inhabit the great mountain massif to the south of the Tigrai province. The kingdoms of Lasta, Amhara, Gojjam, and Shoa symbolized this southward shift, yet they accepted the Semitized civilization of the north and became its principal militant exponents. While a greater measure of non-Semitic ingredients in the Amharic language may accurately reflect a lesser degree of ethnic Semitization among the Amharas than is the case with the Tigreans, both groups nevertheless form a largely homogeneous entity which is expressed in a common historical consciousness, in their adherence to the mono-physite doctrine, and in a similar social organization—all of which have scarcely been disturbed by linguistic diversity. The political conflicts of the past have never been able to upset the essential unity that has always existed among the Semitized peoples of the Abyssinian highlands, with their keen awareness of cultural and religious identity.

To the east and south of the Tigrinya-Amharic block are two Semitic islands in an otherwise completely Cushitic environment, Harar and Gurage. Both are possibly the result of amalgamation between the original inhabitants of these areas and north Abyssinian military colonies stationed there during the Middle Ages. Harar had also for long been the centre of an Ethiopian Muslim state, and even today, over seventy years after its absorption within the Christian Ethiopian Empire, it still remains the principal exponent of Islamic civilization in Ethiopia. At the same time, the population of the old city-state has retained its special character and has shown astonishing buoyancy in the face of both its massive Cushitic surroundings and the strong impact of the Arabs.[1] The country of the Gurage lies to the south-west of Addis Ababa, is bordered in the north by the River Awash, in the west by the River Omo, and in the east by Lake Zway. The basic Gurage stock appears to be of Sidama origin upon which various layers of military expeditions from the north may have been imposed, resulting in that curious mixture of Semitic and Cushitic traits, in appearance as well as language, which we know also in the case of the Hararis. In many instances we are able to observe similar Tigrean features that can be recognized in both Gurage and Harari and

[1] Cf. *Encyclopaedia of Islam*, new ed., III, 176.

which corroborate indigenous traditions, generally not considered trustworthy in the past, regarding an earlier wave of migration from the northern parts of Ethiopia.[1] In relation to the size of the population, the Gurage exhibit an astonishing fragmentation in terms of religious, linguistic, and tribal conditions. There are among them pagans, Muslims, monophysites, and Roman Catholics; among the numerous tribes the Chaha are the most important—just as Chaha appears to be the most prominent of the large cluster of Gurage dialects.

(2) The peoples of Cushitic speech in Ethiopia occupy not only the vast areas of the eastern, southern, and western plains and mountain slopes, but they also constitute the substrata upon which the Semitic-speaking immigrants have been laid. The substrate population *par excellence* are the Agaw, who inhabit the northern and central Abyssinian plateau. Generally, they are now quite indistinguishable from Ethiopians who speak a Semitic language, and they exhibit the same physical features and social organization. The Agaw are mostly bilingual—reserving their own tongue for use in the family circle; yet the possession of such a 'private' language inevitably fosters the feeling and consciousness of some separate identity and loyalty.

The most northerly Agaw group is represented by the Bilen in the Keren area of Eritrea. The Bilen—also known as Bogos—consist of two large tribes, the Bet Tarke (who probably came here from the Lasta province) and the Bet Takwe, each about 12,000 strong. Many of them are also able to speak Tigre, which they use for all contacts with their neighbours. It appears that the Bilen language is slowly losing ground. Their religion, until the Egyptian invasion of the Keren region in the second half of the nineteenth century, was monophysite Christianity, but since then Islam has claimed the allegiance of the majority of the Bilen, though monophysite pockets survive, together with a sizeable minority of Mission-converted Catholics. The Bilen are sedentary and engage in agriculture. The men are generally of strong build and have well-proportioned features, while their womenfolk are widely renowned for their graceful bearing and beauty.

Another Agaw group comprises the Kemant and Kwara as well as the Falashas, all of whom live in the area west of the Takkaze and north

[1] Cf. Hetzron, *Ethiopian Semitic, passim.*

of Lake Tana. The maintenance of their identity has been favoured by religious factors (see under religions, below) and strict social organization. There may be between 30,000 and 50,000 members of this sector of the Agaw. Further Agaw groups wedged in the massive Amharic body live to the south of Lake Tana in Agawmeder and Damot. Their language, Awiya,[1] appears to be less influenced by Semitized elements and may well exhibit a more purely preserved form of Agaw. The last group of Agaw-speakers, those of Khamir and Khamta, is thrust between the southern Tigrai and the Amharic-speaking Lasta. Bilingualism in this region thus affects Amharic as well as Tigrinya, the latter in the Avergalle district, but Tigrinya seems to be gaining ground at the expense of Khamta.

The most northerly sector of the Cushitic race is composed of Beja tribes. As far as Eritrea-Ethiopia is concerned, the Beja are represented by sections of the Hadendoa and the Beni Amer; a large number of both tribes live in the Sudan. They are, as far as we can judge, the people with the closest affinity to the ancient Egyptians; they are the Blemmyes of Greek and Roman writers from Herodotus to Olympiodorus. The Beja of today can, in the judgement of one authority,[2] best be described as 'a Hamito-Semitic people who are divided into two main groups—a southern one of purer Hamitic strain, but speaking a Semitic language (Tigre), who has only very recently emerged from an agelong serfdom, and a northern one, less pure in blood, but speaking a Hamitic language (Beja) and displaying typical Hamitic characteristics.'

The Saho tribes live in the coastal depression between Massawa in the north, the Gulf of Zula in the east, and the escarpment of the Akkele Guzay in the west. The majority are herdsmen, and their seasonal migrations take them regularly up to the plateau, with the result that a minority section of the tribe have settled on the eastern slopes and adopted Tigrinya as their language. The indigenous language of the two large Saho tribes, the Assaorta and Minifere, is a Cushitic tongue which is akin to Dankali. They are Muslims—with the exception only of those who have settled among the Christian highlanders.

The southern extension of the Saho tribes is represented by the large

[1] The suitability of this nomenclature has been questioned by Robert Hetzron in his fine book on the *Verbal System of Southern Agaw.*

[2] A. Paul, *History of the Beja Tribes,* p. 25.

tribal confederacy of the Danakil who inhabit the vast arid depression behind the Red Sea coast from the Gulf of Zula to the Gulf of Tajura, with the Abyssinian highlands to the west—one of the hottest and most barren regions in the world. The Danakil refer to themselves as Afar, while in some regions the Abyssinian name for them is Teltal. They are basically of Hamitic stock, but considerable admixtures of other racial elements have been added. Their unity has been maintained by a common religion, Islam, and a common language, Afar (or Dankali). Socially, they are divided into two castes: the 'red men' (nobles) and 'white men' (serfs), but the latter have, by dint of numerical preponderance, weakened the hold of the ruling caste and have gained a measure of political autonomy. The Danakil are nomadic herdsmen owning camels, cattle, and goats. There are a few semi-permanent villages of recent creation which also serve as administrative centres, police posts, and markets. Living as they do in a country of desert, salt depressions, and lava streams, their temperament and way of life somehow reflect the cruelty and mercilessness which this appalling environment seems to engender. Their reputation for massacring expeditions and caravans has survived to this day, and it is likely that it was from their ancestors that most of Ahmad Grañ's armies were drawn. Yet their appearance is pleasant with good regular features and thin noses and lips. The total number of Danakil in Eritrea, Ethiopia, and French Somaliland approaches 100,000. They owe allegiance to the Sultan of Aussa, but it is difficult to say what measure of reality this connection retains.

The Galla (or Oromo) are the largest of the Cushitic peoples in Ethiopia, and their language is, despite low prestige value and official discouragement, almost as widely used as Amharic. They occupy an enormous area which extends from the southern tip of the Tigrai to Harar in the east, thence as far south as the Tana River in Kenya and as far west as the tributaries of the Nile. The Ethiopian Gallas are divided into some 200 tribes. In appearance they are somewhat darker than the 'classical' Abyssinian type, but they are brown rather than black. They are strongly built, of tall stature; their lips are not very thick, nor their noses flat or broad. Their original habitat was probably in the corner of the horn of Africa, but continued Somali pressure drove them west and south-west. It was only in the fifteenth and sixteenth centuries that they began to penetrate into the Abyssinian highlands, and once they had ascended the fertile plateau they abandoned their way of life as nomadic herdsmen and became sedentary cultivators. During the reign of Menelik, at the end of the nineteenth century, the Gallas were finally brought under the effective authority of the Ethiopian Empire.

Estimates of the Galla population vary very greatly, and their merging in and intermingling with the Abyssinian inhabitants as a whole make any guesses very hazardous, but a proportion of some 35 per cent of the total population seems to have been generally accepted as reasonable. Islam is the religion of the majority of the Galla tribes, but many of the plateau people have long accepted Christianity, and it is likely that the movement towards the official faith of the country continues to gain momentum. There also remain quite a few pagan pockets.

The Somalis who once displaced the Gallas from the eastern part of the horn of Africa now occupy the vast expanse of country from the Gulf of Tajura along the Gulf of Aden up to Cape Guardafui, thence southwards along the Indian Ocean to the River Tana in Northern Kenya. In the west their territory borders on the foothills of the eastern Ethiopian massif. Politically, the Somalis come under the sovereignty of—

(1) French Somaliland (about 40,000);
(2) Somalia (about $2\frac{1}{4}$ million);
(3) Ethiopian Somaliland, the Ogaden;
(4) Kenya, in the eastern region of the Northern Frontier district.

We possess no population figures for the last two areas, but the Somali population of both together is estimated at close on a million, so that the total number of Somalis approaches the $3\frac{1}{2}$ million mark.[1] They thus constitute a compact ethnic block of what is regarded as a fairly purely preserved branch of the Cushitic race.

The Somalis are divided into three large groups: the Edji, Hawiya, and Sab; their language, a Cushitic tongue which has not been subjected to strong foreign influences, is equally grouped into dialects according to the three major ethnic divisions. Apart from these ethnic and linguistic distinctions, the Somalis readily fall into two categories determined by their way of life as either nomadic herdsmen in the

[1] Cf. I. M. Lewis, *Modern History of Somaliland*, p. 1.

great steppe regions or as cultivators and townsmen in settlements that have been established along the big river systems of their country. It was, of course, in the coastal towns, which had for millennia been in close contact with the people and civilization of Arabia, that Islam gained its first foothold in this part of East Africa. But the Islamization of the tribes of the interior was a hard and very slow process which was opposed, not only by the vigorous paganism of the Somalis, but especially by a deep-rooted system of customary law to which the precepts of the *shari'a* were profoundly alien. Today the religious life of the Somalis is characterized by the pronouncedly Islamic civilization of the coastal region, by the existence of religious brotherhoods (Kadiriyya, Ahmadiyya, Salihiyya), and by the survival in the interior of an ancient paganism.

The Sidama peoples live in the south-west of Ethiopia, in the area of Lake Margherita and the valley of the Omo River and its tributaries. Their territory is among the richest in Ethiopia with its large coffee and cotton plantations. Originally, the area inhabited by them was considerably larger, but the Galla invasions coupled with the Ethiopian expansion southwards have forced them into the region in which they now dwell. The ethnic, linguistic, and religious situation in Sidama country is one of great complexity, and for a more detailed description the reader must be referred to the relevant works in the Bibliography. Here it will suffice to mention that the Sidama retained their independence until the close of the last century, when Menelik's far-reaching campaigns in the southern parts of Ethiopia brought them under the control of the central government. While the majority of the Sidama have adhered to their paganism throughout the vicissitudes of their history over the past 400 or 500 years, an upper layer of the Hadya and Bali tribes did, at one time, accept a veneer of Islam, and not a few have been converted to Christianity in the wake of Menelik's conquests. Nowadays Islam is probably strongest in the market and trading centres of the Sidama country. The total population of the Sidama peoples is estimated to be in excess of one million.

Ethnically and linguistically four main groups have to be distinguished:

(*a*) *Gimira-Maji*, who consist of a number of sub-divisions among whom the Shakko, Benesho, Nao, and Maji are the most important.

Their territory is south of the Kaffa region, but little is known about tribal distribution and administrative districts. Their languages belong to the Cushitic dialect cluster of the Gimira-Maji group. They are all pagans.

(b) *Ometo* (or West Sidama), who live in the valley of the Omo River and whose chief tribal divisions are the Walamo, Gofa, Zala, Basketo, Chara, Kullo, Konta, etc. They are cultivators of *teff*, barley, cotton, and coffee, but they also engage in cattle-breeding and bee-keeping. There are among them many nominal adherents of Islam and monophysite Christianity, but pagan rites continue to have a consider-able hold on the people. Their languages belong to the dialect clusters of Walamo, Chara, and Koyra.

(c) *Sidamo-Kambatta*, whose territory lies between as well as east of Lakes Margherita and Shala. Their tribal components are the Sidamo, Hadya, Darasa, and Kambatta. The principal crops cultivated by the majority of the population are barley, maize, coffee, and tobacco, while the Sidamo engage mainly in the raising of livestock: cattle, horses, and sheep. Their religion consists of a thin layer of Islam among some of the tribes, but Muslim practices have to contend with vigorous and wide-spread pagan cults. The chief languages are Sidamo, Kambatta, and Hadya.

(d) The *Janjero* in the region of the upper Omo and all those in south-western Ethiopia who speak languages of the Kaffa group (Kaffa, Shinasha, Mao).

In conclusion, attention should be drawn to the artificial, but gener-ally observed, distinction between Sidam*o*, the people who live to the east of Lake Margherita, and Sidam*a*, the name which European scholars, probably under the influence of Galla nomenclature, have assigned to the group of peoples, of a closely defined Cushitic linguistic pattern, whose habitat is in the large area of fertile south-west Ethiopia.

(3) The last sector of the population of Ethiopia, the Nilotic (negroid) peoples, can be dealt with summarily, not so much on account of their comparative numerical insignificance, but because they form no integral part of the life and civilization of Ethiopia. These Nilotic races entered the country from the region of the Nile Valley and the Nile tributaries, which lead to the foothills of the Abyssinian highlands, and

settled in the western parts of Ethiopia—generally not far from the Sudan. Their colour is very dark, they are dolichocephalic and prognathous, and their hair is woolly. They appear to be attuned to the severe tropical climate of the western lowlands, from which all true Abyssinians recoil by ascending the cool and salubrious highlands.

In the north, in Eritrea, we find the Kunama and Baria tribes, the former in the Barentu area between the rivers Gash and Setit, the latter north of the Gash. The Kunama language has, as far as we can judge at present, no known connection with any other language. The people are pagans with some relatively recent conversions to Islam and Protestantism. The Baria, on the other hand, are almost completely Islamized.

Among the numerous small Nilotic tribes along the Ethiopia-Sudan border, Mekan, Mao, Gunza, etc., I should mention the Beni Shangul tribes who occupy the area between the Blue Nile and the Sudan frontier. The origin of the name is the Amharic term *shanqella*, which is applied to all Negroes, but was in this case adopted by Arabic-speaking Sudanese to refer to this particular group of tribes. The Beni Shangul were brought within the Islamic fold through the Funj Kingdom of Sennar which penetrated this region and, for a time, exercised a measure of control over these tribes.

To summarize: the Cushitic peoples have been established in the horn of Africa for several millennia; they form the basic ethnic element of the population of Ethiopia. Whether they once came from southern Arabia, whence the Hamito-Semitic race may have sprung, or whether the cradle of the originally united Hamito-Semites was—as some scholars have conjectured—in that part of Africa which is now called Ethiopia, need not concern us here, but the prolonged influx of Semitic elements from south-west Arabia, in pre-Christian centuries and later, has once again brought about a union of the Hamites and the Semites. The stage is the Abyssinian plateau where the result of this renewed fusion has been the emergence of the Hamites as the predominant ethnic factor and of the Semites as the principal linguistic and cultural element.

Physically, the Hamito-Semitic union has produced a handsome race, elegant, subtle, and nervous. It is more difficult to generalize about the Ethiopian national character, for all such pronouncements are of necessity purely impressionistic and subjective. Yet everyone will agree that the Abyssinian is exceptionally intelligent, mentally agile, and extraordinarily eager to learn. His quick absorption of knowledge is at times stupefying, but profundity is not, perhaps, as yet greatly esteemed. Ethiopians are proud people, yet at the same time they display a courtesy and humility towards each other as well as towards strangers that can be deeply moving. Their low bow and their kiss are not an expression of obsequiousness, but an aspect of politeness and considerateness in manner which has all but disappeared in Europe. Most of them are born diplomats, some of them are unduly suspicious, but all are generous and quick to forgive. Many Ethiopians are given to litigiousness, but their sense of honour and justice is satisfied once the matter has been properly argued out; thus they will present a case with great dexterity and a distinct flair for oratory. Of Ethiopian hospitality —generous and uncalculating—one cannot speak too highly; it retains something of a Biblical and patriarchal flavour. Friendship is greatly prized and willingly offered, though often there remains, perhaps, a residue of reserve. Few of those who have come into contact with Ethiopians have been able to resist their compelling charm and the abiding interest of country and people.

IV

THE PAST: AN OUTLINE OF HISTORY

I. SOUTH ARABIA AND AKSUM

AT THE TIME when we get the first glimpses of Ethiopian history the Cushitic peoples of the country appear to be in full occupation. The negroid races had already been pushed back to the western fringes, and if, as seems likely, they once had possession of the entire area, they left little or nothing behind that bears the stamp of this connection. The Egyptians were probably the first outsiders to establish relations with Ethiopia, which, under the name of Cush, was part of Nubia. From here slaves were carried back and gold was washed out of the sandy streams. The Egyptians came to Ethiopia from the west, following the Nile and its tributaries which formed the natural routes of access; but they also travelled by sea to Punt (the Somali coast?)[1] in search of incense, spices, ivory, and gold—all products then to be found in the horn of Africa. One such maritime expedition to the Somali coast is attested for as early a period as the third millennium B.C. during the reign of the Pharaoh Pepi II. The most famous of the Punt voyages was carried out during the reign and by command of Queen Hatshepsut (about the middle of the second millennium B.C.), an achievement that is commemorated in scenes of the great series of Punt reliefs in the Der el-Bahri Temple at Thebes.[2]

[1] Cf. F. Hommel, *Ethnologie und Geographie des Alten Orients* (Munich, 1926), pp. 634–50. See also J. H. Breasted, *History of Egypt*, pp. 127, 142.

[2] See the reproduction in Breasted, op. cit., p. 275.

While relations with Egypt, as a consequence of geographical conditions, have always remained sporadic and fluctuating, the proximity of the horn of Africa to south-west Arabia has been a powerful and steady factor in the history of Ethiopia—at least since the early part of the first millennium B.C. It should at once be noted that, though there have occurred occasional expeditions from Ethiopia into south-west Arabia, the predominant and significant movement was, at nearly every stage, from east to west. This crossing of the Bab el-Mandeb from Arabia to East Africa continues to this day, and thus constitutes a migratory process of great constancy. The Semitic inhabitants of South Arabia, who displayed important differences in development, language, and character as compared with the inhabitants of the central and northern parts of the peninsula, had since very early times evolved a mercantile system and a commercial organization which vied in importance with those established by the Phoenicians in the north. While the latter travelled and settled in the countries and islands of the Mediterranean and beyond, the South Arabians organized their seafaring and trading activities in the countries bordering on the Red Sea and the Indian Ocean. The safety of this traffic and its expansion required dominion over maritime bases and, if possible, the caravan routes leading to these emporia. By the time the South Arabian commercial activities began to flourish, the heyday of the Egyptians had passed and their maritime hegemony in the southern Red Sea had collapsed.

The South Arabians who ventured to travel along the shores of East Africa and the Red Sea islands also succeeded in navigating their craft around and beyond Cape Guardafui and penetrating as far south as Zanzibar, Dar-es-Salaam, and Cape Delgado.[1] But naturally their first attention was given to the shores and the hinterland just across from their own country. On landing at what is now Massawa, or places near it, they could not fail to notice that the western side of the Red Sea littoral exhibited close similarities to the configuration of their own country: a hot, arid, and relatively narrow coastal strip leading up to a mountainous region of some 6,000 feet or more in which the monsoons brought about a well-regulated rainfall with all the attendant benefits of vegetation, agriculture, and the possibility of cultural development.

[1] Cf. also *History and Archaeology in Africa* (SOAS, London, 1955), p. 32.

Thus the South Arabian merchants and seafarers who had established commercial and military posts along the Samhar plain ascended the foothills, the slopes, and finally the steep escarpment itself. Their motive was no doubt to expand their trading activities, to get away from the inclement climate of the coast, and to search still further west for gum, spices, and ivory. The ascent to the plateau must have been made especially attractive by the concurrence, in the summer months, of the most torrid period in the lowlands with the refreshing rains and luxuriant vegetation in the upper regions. Semitic place-names of South Arabian origin in the neighbourhood of Massawa and Assab still testify to the Sabaean progress on African soil.[1]

Once established on the fertile plateau, the traders became immigrants, mingled with the existing Cushitic population, and no doubt reproduced in the highlands of Africa the type of social, political, and cultural organization which they had left behind in Arabia. Above all, they were the carriers of a vastly superior civilization, both material and cultural. Among the former, the camel, incense, and many nutritive plants deserve mention, as well as the manufacture of better arms and the improvement of building. But it is the latter aspect, the cultural advancement, which makes the South Arabian achievement in Africa so notable; and here it is writing and language (to be discussed in Chapter VI) that outshine the importance of everything else.

The early development of south-west Arabia in contrast to the stagnation in the remainder of the peninsula was, of course, due—as has already been suggested—to the terraces, hills, and mountains which attracted the monsoon rains, transformed the countryside, and created a fertile soil and an agreeable climate conducive to agriculture, sedentary pursuits, and the establishment of well-organized urban settlements. The advanced material culture of *Arabia Felix* is attested in large numbers of epigraphic documents from the first millennium B.C. which describe in much detail irrigation systems, property laws, building activities, breeding of cattle and camels—altogether most facets of a progressive agrarian economy and of notable technical and intellectual development.

But the expression 'South Arabia' must not lead us to think of a unified Empire; in fact, there were principally four states, Ma'in,

[1] Cf. Conti Rossini, *Storia d'Etiopia*, pp. 103 et seq.

Qataban, Saba, and Hadramawt, who at times co-existed or succeeded
each other. The great incense road, the most important trading route
towards the north, traversed the territory of all four states, and which-
ever enjoyed political hegemony for the time being also controlled
trade and commerce. For a long period Saba occupied a position of
pre-eminence in south-west Arabia, and finally, in the third century
A.D., a unified Empire replaced the separate existence of the four rival
states. This union was comparatively shortlived, for, in the sixth
century, it lost its independence to the Kingdom of Aksum. Thus the
Aksumites, the Arabian colonists in Africa, re-crossed the Red Sea and
subjected to their rule the very regions from which their ancestors had
emigrated. There followed a brief Persian interlude before South
Arabia was submerged in the flood of Islamic expansion in the seventh
century, but the Abyssinian influence in pre-Islamic Arabia is reflected
in a fair number of Ethiopic loan-words in Arabic.

Having given the briefest, and indeed most superficial, summary of
events in South Arabia, we must now address ourselves to the salient
question of the identity and provenance of the South Arabian settlers in
East Africa. A solution of this problem is, to a considerable extent,
dependent on factors of a linguistic nature and will, therefore, be
discussed in Chapter VI below, but some general considerations must
be rehearsed here. We should certainly not envisage the transplantation
of entire tribes from Asia into Africa; one should much rather think of
the movement of individuals, families, groups, or small colonies. Thus,
if we find the Habashat (hence the name of the country, 'Abyssinia')
on both sides of the Red Sea or if we encounter the Ag'azyan (sing. Ge'ez,
the name of the classical Ethiopic language) in the Akkele Guzay province of what is now Eritrea, there is no warrant to suppose that a
wholesale migration of tribes had taken place. In the first instance, their
organization was not tribal, but territorial; and, secondly, South
Arabian place-names in Africa should be seen in the same light as the
reminiscent and nostalgic onomastics of 'New York' or 'New South
Wales'—the transference by a group of colonizers and settlers of the
name of their original home to their new habitat. Sahartan (Sahart),
Hauzen, Sarw (Sarawe, Serae), etc., are cases in point.[1]

That the colonizers of the west coast of the Red Sea, now Eritrea and

[1] Cf. Conti Rossini, *Storia d'Etiopia*, pp. 103 et seq.

(a) *The great falls of the Blue Nile*

(b) *The snake-like road Asmara-Dessie*

IV

Grain market in Ghimbi (south-western Ethiopia)

northern Ethiopia, hailed from south-western Arabia, the Yemen, has, in my view, been securely established by the researches of Conti Rossini and other scholars.[1] Numerically the South Arabian leaven was not significant, but its superior quality revolutionized life in the Abyssinian highlands and infused into the predominant Cushitic element that peculiarly Semitic ingredient which has throughout the ages given Ethiopian civilization its special character. Obelisks and inscriptions, towns and sanctuaries survive as witnesses of these early achievements on African soil—achievements which were concentrated in two main areas: the eastern Akkele Guzay and the Aksum region. The Ethiopians in the historical sense then represent the amalgam of a relatively thin layer of Semitic settlers from south-west Arabia with the great mass of the existing Cushitic population. While the colonizers from Asia very largely lost their ethnic identity, their political, social, and cultural institutions now became the heritage of the population as a whole.

The period during which at least a trickle of South Arabian settlers crossed the Red Sea westwards was very considerable and may have been as long as a millennium, from as early as the seventh century B.C. to the third or fourth century A.D.—and in a sense this movement has never stopped. It is impossible to be dogmatic about the *terminus a quo*, for the only indications we possess for this dating are South Arabian inscriptions found on African soil. Though their approximate chronology can be established on palaeographical grounds with a fair degree of probability, there must remain an element of uncertainty owing to archaizing tendencies to which these expatriate documents are prone. Some scholars have recently been inclined to shift this dating down to the fifth century B.C.

Before we come to sketch the history of the state which emerged from the fusion of Semites and Hamites on the Abyssinian plateau, reference must be made to the peculiarly Hebraic brand of Semitism that took root in Ethiopia.[2] For the possible infiltration into pre-

---

[1] A somewhat divergent view has been expressed by A. J. Drewes (*Inscriptions de l'Éthiopie antique*) and A. K. Irvine (Habashat in new ed. of *Encyclopaedia of Islam* and *JSS*, Autumn 1965). Their arguments, advanced with great learning and acumen, do not invalidate the belief in the South Arabian origins of Abyssinian civilization but are addressed to the identity of the carriers of those South Arabian elements.   [2] Cf. E. Ullendorff, *Ethiopia and the Bible*.

C

Christian Abyssinia of Jewish migrants from the north, from the
direction of Egypt, we possess very scanty material only. Of course,
there are a few scattered verses in the Old Testament which speak of
Jews who had settled in Egypt (Jer. 44: 1) or of the existence of a
diaspora in Cush (Zeph. 3: 10), but their value is limited, even though
it is known from the Elephantine papyri that Jews had penetrated as far
as Upper Egypt, Nubia, and possibly beyond. The position is different
with regard to Jewish influences that may have entered Abyssinia by
way of South Arabia. Here the source material is somewhat ampler. In
its heyday the Hebrew kingdom included the Sinai peninsula; Solomon and his successors had an outlet to the Red Sea at Elath; we hear of
naval expeditions to Ophir, the gold-producing country (no doubt
somewhere on the coasts of the southern Red Sea); and the reference to
'Arabians that were near the Ethiopians' (II Chron. 21: 16) displays
early knowledge of the proximity and relationship between South
Arabians and Ethiopians. Saba, Ma'in, and Hadramawt are expressly
mentioned in the Old Testament, and there are some references to
Jewish connections with Arabia in Rabbinical literature—such as the
mention of a black (i.e. Ethiopian) 'King of the Arabs' (*Bemidbar Rabba*,
IX): Rabbi Aqiba's journey to Arabia (and probably South Arabia)
would scarcely have been considered worth while unless there had
existed a sizeable Jewish community in that country. So early and widespread a settlement of Jews in the Arabian peninsula (we are well
informed of the later Jewish population at Medinah and of Jewish
tribes in the Khaibar oasis) makes it more than likely that some Jewish
elements were included in the South Arabian colonization and settlement in Abyssinia. It is improbable that they entered the country as a
compact community, a complete tribal *golah*, but they presumably
came in small groups, together with their non-Jewish fellow-merchants
and settlers. Whether they established separate Jewish colonies on
Abyssinian soil or settled together with other immigrants, must remain
within the realm of speculation, though the widespread character of
Hebraic influences and practices in Ethiopia favours the latter alter-
native.

The South Arabian settlers in Africa may have continued for a time
to submit to the authority of the 'home government' and to lead a life
which scarcely differed from that to which they had been accustomed

in Arabia. They built the same houses, constructed reservoirs, and established plantations along the fertile hillsides and mountain slopes. They left us inscriptions engraved on stone which were written in their Sabaean language. But once the ties with the homeland had weakened and the colonizers had fused with the indigenous population and formed a homogeneous element, the independence of the African settlements increased. This appears to have coincided with a period of political debility in Arabia, so that the most prominent of the local chieftains no longer hesitated to assume the title *negusa nagast* which later meant 'King of Kings' (=Emperor) but at this early period probably had no connotation beyond 'commander-in-chief'. We may thus suppose that in the last two pre-Christian centuries the African colonies had successfully asserted their independence without however causing —as far as we know—any rupture of relations with South Arabia. It appears that the settlers in the Aksum area readily won predominance over those in the Akkele Guzay, for the emergence of the Aksumite Kingdom in the first century A.D. is a well-attested historical fact.

The political orientation of this new power was twofold: towards the east, Arabia, where Abyssinian intervention occurred some time between the first and third centuries B.C.,[1] and towards the north-west, the Nile, where the Kingdom of Meroe was languishing. Aksum stepped into this power vacuum and expanded its commerce in ivory, gum, and spices. At the same time trading activities led to a widening of the cultural horizon. Hellenized Egyptians brought commerce as well as the Greek language to the southern Red Sea, and Aksum itself was greatly influenced by these emissaries of Greek civilization. Adulis, the port, opened the road to the Semitic culture of South Arabia and to the Hellenized way of life in the Mediterranean countries. Adulis is, according to the second-century author of the *Periplus of the Erythraean Sea*, 'a port established by law' and 'a fair-sized village' three days' journey from Coloe, 'an inland town and the first market for ivory'. Another five days' journey takes one to 'the city of the people called Auxumites' where 'all the ivory is brought from the country beyond the Nile'. And all these places were governed, so the writer of the *Periplus* tells us, 'by Zoscales who is miserly in his ways

[1] See J. Ryckmans, *Institution Monarchique*, p. 132.

and always striving for more, but otherwise upright and acquainted with Greek literature'.[1] Here, in addition to the South Arabian and Hebraic elements, is another important aspect of the character of Aksumite civilization, the Greek impact which was to endure for several centuries.

Not a great deal is known about the Kingdom of Aksum during the second and third centuries A.D., but towards the close of the latter it intervened decisively in South Arabia and maintained its occupation of the Yemen for a limited period. That was during the reign of the Sabaean King Shamir Yuhar'ish, when the Aksumite ruler, probably called Afilas, assumed the style of 'King of Aksum, Himyar, Saba, Raydan, and Salhen'. Only a little later the Abyssinians reached the Nile and defeated the old Kingdom of Meroe, which was never to rise again. Aksum was now the mistress of the two regions from which it had once drawn its greatest strength.

The fourth century saw the zenith of Abyssinian power and achievement. It was the time of Ezana, their greatest king, who has left us a number of inscriptions, some in the Ethiopic language and characters (either vocalized or just in the consonantal skeleton) or in Ethiopic with South Arabian characters (for details, see Chapter VI), others in the Greek language and script. The attainment by the Aksumites of complete independence and detachment from their Arabian past is also expressed, almost symbolically, in the indigenous development of writing and the incorporation of vowels in the body of the consonants. Ezana did not, it appears, maintain Abyssinian control of the Yemen, but in his monumental inscriptions he relates the story of his wars against the Beja and against other peoples in the region of the Atbara, penetrating very nearly to the confluence of the Blue and the White Niles. He then adds to his royal style (which traditionally retains the South Arabian titles) the countries of Siyamo, Beja, and Kasu.

The greatest event during Ezana's reign was his official conversion—following Constantine's example—to Christianity (see next chapter) which now became the religion of the Aksumite Kingdom. The coins and inscriptions of his early period are still pagan, while the later ones include such Christian invocations as 'By the might of the Lord of Heaven who in Heaven and on Earth has power over all'. Of course,

[1] Schoff's trans., pp. 22–3.

one must not suppose that the introduction of Christianity immediately did away with pagan rites and practices, but when, two centuries later, Cosmas Indicopleustes visited the country he found it thoroughly Christianized.[1] Ezana's claim to fame does not rest only on his military campaigns and on his proclamation of Christianity as the State religion but is also supported by his great building activities; among these the impressive series of obelisks occupies a very special place, the largest of them exceeding 100 feet in height.

None of Ezana's successors could maintain the prestige and prosperity of the country at so high a level, but we lack detailed documentation with regard to the following 100–150 years. The acceptance of Christianity had brought Abyssinia into contact with the Byzantine Empire, which expected a Christian ruler to take on certain obligations for the protection of Christians in areas contiguous to his dominion. In the neighbouring South Arabia both Christianity and Judaism had been spreading rapidly, but rivalry between them developed with equal speed. Dhu Nuwas, the last Himyarite king, had become Judaized and then engaged in a severe persecution of Christians. Justin I, the Byzantine Emperor, is said to have written to the Negus Kaleb, or Ella Asbeha, and to have requested him, as the nearest Christian ruler, to come to the aid of his co-religionists. Ella Asbeha responded to the appeal, if in fact such an invitation was necessary to encourage his intervention, and undertook a military expedition against Zafar in 523. It appears that these operations were temporarily halted and that Dhu Nuwas used this respite to engage in an orgy of hatred which led to the notorious massacre of Christians at Najran, probably in 524.[2] The Negus now prepared a full-scale invasion and a second campaign which, in 525, brought about the death of Dhu Nuwas and with it the end of South Arabian independence.

Aksumite power thus reached a second brief climax in its role as the great empire in the Red Sea area, yet its glory did not last. Ella Asbeha appointed (according to Procopius, the contemporary historian) Esimiphaios (SMYF' of the inscriptions) as governor over his South Arabian possessions, but Abyssinian troops revolted against him and

---

[1] McCrindle's trans., p. 120.

[2] See now also J. Ryckmans, *La Persécution des Chrétiens Himyarites au sixième siècle*, Istanbul, 1956.

placed a certain Abraha on the throne. Abraha refused to submit to the authority of Ella Asbeha, but agreed to pay tribute to the King's successor. We are fortunate in possessing epigraphic sources which throw some light on this episode,[1] especially the long inscription on the Marib dam and one recently discovered at Murayghan which records a defeat inflicted by Abraha on a north Arabian tribe.[2] The remainder of Abraha's career is known to us from Islamic sources only: he built the great Cathedral at San'a, called al-Qulays (= Greek *ekklesia*), and, in the year 570, is said to have led a great expedition against Mecca. This is also the year of Muhammad's birth which is called '*am al-fil* ('year of the elephant') after the elephant(s) which accompanied Abraha on his march.

The Christian rule in South Arabia came to an end with the Persian occupation of the country at the close of the sixth century. The Roman-Persian antagonism found its reflection in the politico-religious events in the Red Sea area. The Persians were anti-Christian in so far as Christianity had become identified with Roman rule, and they encouraged all religious manifestations which might be instrumental in displacing Roman influence. In this way the Jews as well as Christian sects hostile to Rome were favoured, but the Persian hegemony in Arabia soon disintegrated under the dynamic onslaught of nascent Islam.

Aksum itself was now in a state of rapid decline: its supply of fresh Semitic settlers from South Arabia had been cut off, and the end of its Yemenite colonies was a severe setback. Muslim traditions mention friendly relations between Muhammad and the Negus who is said to have offered refuge to some early converts to Islam, but this state of affairs could not last. The Persians had disrupted the sea and trade routes in the Red Sea; the Muslim conquests soon enveloped the whole of Arabia and North Africa; Ethiopia was thus severed, at least temporarily, from its spiritual source, the Patriarchate of Alexandria. In fact, Islam had knocked on the very gates of the Christian kingdom: it had occupied the Dahlak islands. The isolation of Abyssinia, which was to last for many centuries, had now begun. Trade and conquest were a

[1] Cf. especially A. F. L. Beeston, ABRAHA in *Encyclopaedia of Islam*, new edition; *idem*, 'Problems of Sabaean Chronology', *BSOAS*, 1954/1.
[2] G. Ryckmans in *Le Muséon*, Vol. 66, and A. F. L. Beeston in *BSOAS*, 1954/2.

thing of the past, and in the face of the great Islamic expansion there was nothing left to the people but to retire within their impregnable mountain fastnesses.

Only one word has to be added before we close the Aksumite chapter. The beginnings of Abyssinia and its royal house are surrounded by one of the most remarkable and most effective cycles of legends: the Queen of Sheba–Solomon story. We shall deal with this national saga of the Ethiopians in the chapter on literature (VII, below).

2. THE ECLIPSE OF ETHIOPIA

'Encompassed on all sides by the enemies of their religion, the Aethiopians slept near a thousand years, forgetful of the world by whom they were forgotten' (Gibbon, *Decline and Fall*, Chapter XLVII). The rise of Islam, which was so decisive an event for the history of the world as a whole, had a most marked effect on developments in Ethiopia. Of lesser importance was the direct onslaught, the immediate impact of the *jihad*; the indirect results of Islamic expansion, the closure of the traditional sea routes, the severance from South Arabia and Egypt, the extrusion of foreign cultural influences, Greek and Semitic in particular, were much more pregnant in their long-term significance. The cultural atrophy brought about not only a resurgence of pagan practices and the ascendancy of the non-Semitized elements, but it crystallized that peculiarly Ethiopian 'translation of an alien Christianity into indigenous terms'.[1]

Repulsed from South Arabia, from the Red Sea, and the Nile-Atbara region, Abyssinia began to assume much more the physical as well as spiritual contours with which we are familiar. Colonization in the Yemen and the Atbara area gave way to what had become, ever since the seventh century A.D., the traditional direction of Ethiopian policy: the *Drang nach dem Süden*. Semitic speech and Christian religion were carried to the central and southern parts of the highlands; and one cannot but be surprised that this southward move towards what is after all the natural extension of the northern plateau, in which the Aksumites had been entrenched for centuries, should have occurred so late. From now on we may witness a gradual shift of political power away

[1] Trimingham, *Islam in Ethiopia*, p. 44.

from the Akkele Guzay and the Tigrai towards Amhara, Lasta, and, finally, Shoa.

Of these dark centuries we have the scantiest knowledge—only the most general results which are there for all to see, since they were far-reaching, enduring, and full of significance. The Cushitic elements reasserted themselves and influenced the political and juridical structure of the state, as the rapid southward drive was bound to dilute and attenuate the ethnic composition and civilizing *élan* of the erstwhile Aksumites. Yet, as a long-term policy the concentration on the large and homogeneous plateau was sound, for undoubtedly the collapse of the Empire had been facilitated and expedited by the far-flung commitments and geographical decentralization of Aksum. Now, the virtual immurement of the people within its great mountain massif, whatever its consequences in terms of civilization may have been, at least moulded all those diverse elements into a nation which in times of external danger could abandon its centrifugal proclivities and become conscious of its essential unity.

The first onslaught on the weakened Abyssinians came from the north when, in the eighth century, the Beja tribes invaded the Barka Valley and the foothills of the Eritrean plateau. They conquered parts of the Hamasien and the coastal plains at a time when the Aksumite fortunes were at their lowest ebb. Beja tombs have even been found at some of the central points of the Eritrean plateau and testify to the depth of this penetration. At the same period the Beja won control over the Red Sea littoral, and it seems certain that they were established at Massawa as early as A.D. 750.

The Muslim historian al-Ya'qubi describes the situation in the territories overrun by the Beja: it appears that there were several Beja-dominated kingdoms between the Nile Basin and the Red Sea, each one under its own sovereign. Al-Ya'qubi mentions a number of place-names, some of them still identifiable, which prove the extent of the Beja dominion in the north as well as the impotence of the Aksumites in checking this encroachment upon their territory. We also know from a report by al-Mas'udi that the Beja worked the Eritrean gold mines during their occupation of the hinterland of Massawa.

Meanwhile, Islam had been spreading among the population of the coastal region. Arab historians attribute this to the effects of the fall of the Umayyad caliphs and to the refuge which some of their remnants are said to have found among the Beja tribes. Echoes of this opinion are found in certain indigenous traditions in Eritrea, but the general tendency of ancestral ennoblement is such that few of those traditions can withstand critical scrutiny. Some element of truth is, however, reflected in these reports, for the influx of Arabs or Arabicized people into the coastal plains must have been quite considerable at that period. From this substantial foothold they were never dislodged, since life in the hot plains has at no time attracted the true Abyssinian.

While Beja occupation and Islamic penetration persisted in the extreme north, the Abyssinian movement southwards continued, and the valleys of the Awash and Omo were first reached during the ninth and tenth centuries. Again, there is a complete absence of reliable documentation, but linguistic considerations and the stubborn survival of certain traditions, which appear to be worthy of credit, combine to confirm the Semitization of the Harar and Gurage areas through the stationing of sizeable military contingents from the Tigrai. It seems to be a reasonable hypothesis that the peoples and languages of those two regions are the result of notable Semitic admixtures whose origin can be traced, with a fair degree of probability, to the Tigrinya-speaking province in the north. Corroboratory evidence is afforded by the discovery in the south of tombs and obelisks which display a marked resemblance to the Tigrean monuments and monoliths.

By the beginning of the tenth century the decline of Abyssinia had been arrested. Arab historians and geographers convey the impression of a reasonably prosperous and powerful state. Parts at least of the coastal strip were again in the hands of the Negus, who had re-established relations with the Yemen and reconquered the Dahlak islands. Both al-Ya'qubi and al-Mas'udi refer to the great kingdom and the extensive territories of the *Najashi* (Negus), and their accounts are no doubt based on the eye-witness reports of merchants and travellers in the Red Sea area. How this reversal of fortunes was achieved we do not know, nor is there adequate material to trace the origin and cause of the sudden eruption, towards the close of the tenth century, which brought about great destruction and upheaval and is linked with the name of the perhaps legendary Queen Judith.

The *History of the Patriarchs of Alexandria* records a letter which had been written by the King of Abyssinia to the King of Nubia. In this missive the King outlines the misery and dejection of his country and people against whom a woman had risen up, a Queen of the Bani Hamuyah. She had destroyed the churches, persecuted the Christians, and devastated the country. The object of the King's letter was to enlist the Nubian monarch's good offices in persuading the Coptic Patriarch to despatch a new Abuna to Ethiopia without delay—the King's last hope of arresting the total extermination of Christianity in his country. Unfortunately, no people or country by the name of Hamuyah are known. Conti Rossini has suggested that Hamuyah might be a corruption, occasioned by the intermediacy of the Arabic script, of Damot. This might appear a little far-fetched, but it seems clear at any rate that the end of the tenth century saw a most dangerous, and quite unforeseen, revolt of the Agaw peoples intent on overthrowing Christianity and on re-establishing the old Hebraic-pagan cult. It is this latter element which has palpably given rise to the tradition that Jewish tribes, perhaps the Falashas, under a Queen named Judith (in the Tigrai) or Esat (in Amhara), created a Judaized state in Abyssinia.

It is, however, rather more likely that this great upheaval which threatened the very existence of the Abyssinian Kingdom was brought about by recently subdued peoples of the southern regions, probably the Sidama, among whom the matriarchal system had for long been maintained. This would tally well with the story of Queen Judith, who, one might surmise, would have encountered little difficulty in enlisting rebellious Agaw tribes in support of her campaign of loot and destruction. The presence of the Agaw may have lent a Hebraic veneer to a revolt which was principally directed against the southward expansion of the Christian Abyssinian Empire. An interesting concomitant of these developments was the flight of the Bilen from the Lasta province to their present habitat in Eritrea. This marked a return of Abyssinian and Christian tribes to the northern highlands which they had forsaken, some centuries earlier, under the pressure of the Beja invasion.

The great crisis was finally resolved—so we are led to believe—by a strong, almost missionary and messianic, revival of Christianity which had received fresh vigour by the arrival of the new Abuna, Dan'el. He had been sent by the Coptic Patriarch in response to the Negus' urgent appeal and soon became the focus of an intensive campaign of moral and physical rehabilitation. The stability of the Kingdom was clearly dependent on the integration of the Agaw peoples who were now brought within the effective orbit of monophysite Christianity. But the conversion of the Agaw changed as much the character of Abyssinian Christianity as it contributed to the pacification of the country, for it brought about a further instalment in the 'indigenization' of monophysitism which, charged more and more with the residue of Judaic and pagan practices and beliefs, assumed a truly national and peculiarly Abyssinian form. The transformation of Christianity, its moulding in the image of the religious and cultural syncretism of the country, probably received its most notable accession at this period.

While the upheaval in the heart of Ethiopia was at its height, Islamic encroachment along the fringes of the Kingdom became bolder and more dangerous. The internal troubles were eventually checked, and lost ground, both territorially and in the propagation of Christianity, was regained, but the effects of the disturbances on the periphery could not be mitigated in the same manner. Here the losses along the coastal plains proved irremediable; the Islamization[1] of the lowlands continued at an accelerated pace, and foreign Muslim powers succeeded each other in establishing their sovereignty, with varying degrees of effectiveness, over the African Red Sea littoral. But Islam threatened not only the coastal areas, from which the Abyssinian Kingdom had been cut off; it spread its militant faith also among the nomadic groups who lived and moved between the sea and the eastern slopes of the escarpment until, finally, it began to encroach even upon eastern Shoa and the Sidama country. The period from the tenth to the twelfth centuries, the time of greatest internal weakness, saw the systematic penetration of Islam on a wide front: in the Dahlak archipelago, the Dankali and Somali coasts, among the Beja in the north and the Sidama in the south, in the Ifat sultanate of eastern Shoa, at Harar in the east and near Lake Zway in the west, where Arabic inscriptions and Islamic tombs bear witness to the radius of Muslim expansion.

The erstwhile importance of the Dahlak archipelago, as the gateway to Ethiopia and a meeting-place of seafarers and merchants in the Red

[1] For Islam in Ethiopia, see Trimingham's masterly work which deals with the history and special characteristics of Islam in the horn of Africa with remarkably sure touch and excellent documentation.

Sea, can scarcely be appreciated today in view of its desolation and present state of poverty and dejection. Yet, in the Middle Ages, it had won independence of both the Yemen and Abyssinia; its head assumed the title of Sultan instead of the old Aksumite style of *Seyuma Bahr* ('Prefect of the Sea'). It is even probable that the sovereignty of the Dahlak islands extended over Massawa as well, since at some stages the Na'ib of Arkiko acknowledged his dependence upon the Prefect of the Sea. The relative prosperity of the islands at that period must have been accompanied by a high level of cultural development. The most vivid and tangible proof of such civilization is offered by the exceptionally beautiful and elaborate Arabic inscriptions in the stylized Kufic *ductus* (already referred to above) which have been found on Dahlak burial-grounds. Muslim writers, such as Ibn Hawqal and al-Mas'udi, refer to the flourishing slave-trade, of which the archipelago as well as some towns on the East African coast were notorious centres.

The slave-trade proved to be a powerful agent in the Islamization of the coastal plains, for it maintained the link with the Arab world and established or supported such centres as Zeila or Mogadishu with their Dankali and Somali hinterland. Moreover, the slave-raids undoubtedly accelerated the diffusion of Islam among the pagan peoples of East Africa, as conversion was the easiest way of escaping this iniquitous recruitment. The organization of this lucrative trade was enormous: it set up bridge-heads deep in the interior of the country, and what had begun as a raiding expedition developed into permanent control of entire areas and the establishment of a series of petty states and sultanates. Setting out from the Dankali and Somali regions and the coastal towns, the slave-traders enveloped the Harar area, Arussi, and the lake district in the south-west.

It is impossible to say with any degree of certainty whether the origin of the Muslim state in eastern Shoa was due to slavery expeditions. Its beginnings are shrouded in impenetrable darkness, but it must have existed for a considerable period and have been under the rule of the Makhzumi sultans, probably since the late ninth century. The overthrow of this Shoan sultanate, in 1285, and its absorption within that of Ifat, the predominant Muslim state in Ethiopia, is described in a document published by Enrico Cerulli.[1] The sultanate of Ifat under the

[1] *RSE*, 1941, pp. 5-42.

Walasma dynasty had become the focus of Islamic expansion in Ethiopia and of all those southern nuclei of resistance to Abyssinian and Christian encroachment who saw in the spread of Islam the lesser evil. Ifat was firmly established on the south-eastern fringes of the Shoan plateau and has, as we shall see later on, impinged on many points and at several stages in the subsequent course of Ethiopian history.

Returning to the centre of the Abyssinian scene, we find the Zagwe dynasty on the throne of Ethiopia, usurpers according to orthodox tradition (because of their Agaw origin), but some of them able rulers. Their homeland was in Lasta and their capital at Roha. They ruled from 1137 to 1270, and with their advent to power the darkness of the Ethiopian Middle Ages begins to lift. By this time the Agaw appear to have been thoroughly Christianized, for—despite early resistance by the clergy—the Zagwe kings proved to be defenders of the faith, built churches and monasteries, and engaged in missionary activity among tribes not yet converted.

Abyssinian tradition objects to them on the grounds that they were not Israelites, i.e. did not belong to the Semitized layer of the Abyssinian population. Their usurpation of the throne is regarded as a sinister interregnum between the last Solomonic king Delna'od and the re-establishment of the Solomonic dynasty in 1270. The historical fiction of an uninterrupted line of kings descended from Menelik I, the son of King Solomon and the Queen of Sheba, has very deep roots in Ethiopia and must be one of the most powerful and influential national sagas anywhere in the world. King John of Ethiopia, in the second half of the nineteenth century, petitioned the British Government to return to him a copy of the *Kebra Nagast*, which embodies the final proof of the descent of the Abyssinian Royal House from the union of King Solomon and the Queen of Sheba, 'for in my country my people will not obey my orders without it'.[1] The historical kernel of this legend no doubt derives from the identification of the Ethiopian dynasty with the Hebraic-Jewish elements in the Abyssinian past and their insistence on a Semitic, or at least Semitized, ethnic relationship.

Of the first Zagwe kings we know nothing, but at the end of the

[1] Budge, *Queen of Sheba and her only son Menyelek*, p. xv. It has since been established (*BSOAS*, 1969, pp. 135ff.) that this particular phrase does not occur in the Amharic original of the Emperor's missive.

twelfth century the most notable representative of this dynasty, Lalibala, ascends the throne. It is to him that the construction of the famous rock-hewn churches (see Chapter VIII below) at Roha is attributed, a series of astounding monuments of singular impressiveness. Roha itself changes its name and is called after its greatest King and architect, Lalibala. But the Zagwe reign should also be remembered for its contacts with Egypt and Jerusalem, a connection which proved to be fruitful for the development of Ethiopic literature. Above all, it ushered in a new era which was to end the long isolation and eclipse of Ethiopia and marked its re-entry into the world from which it had withdrawn for so long.

In its territorial extent Abyssinia was now more limited, and her sovereignty barely reached beyond the central provinces: Lasta, Tigrai, parts of Begemder and Amhara, and northern Shoa. The Eritrean plateau was still inhabited by the Beja, though the recent northward migration of the Bilen had begun to dislodge them. In the north-west some Agaw groups, notably the Falashas, appear to have clung to their independence with great pertinacity. Of the Muslim encroachments in the coastal plains and in the south-east we have already spoken.

The Zagwe dynasty was overthrown in 1270 by the action of Yekuno Amlak, who had become the focus of discontented and dissident elements. The last Zagwe King was killed in the Church of St. Qirqos, in which he had taken refuge. Yekuno Amlak was proclaimed King, and with him the 'rightful' Solomonic dynasty is claimed to have been 'restored'. But the tradition that the Zagwe dynasty voluntarily abdicated in favour of the Solomonic scion is of much later date and is unlikely to deserve credence. It has been connected with the name of the Saint Tekla Haymanot who is said to have acted as an intermediary and to have received, in recognition of his services, one third of the lands of the state as a perpetual fief of the Church. Tekla Haymanot himself became the founder of Debra Libanos of Shoa, the most important monastery in Ethiopia.

3. THE SOLOMONIC DYNASTY

With the advent of the so-called Solomonic line of kings, which has been reigning in Ethiopia ever since, we enter an era for which a good deal of proper historical documentation is available.[1] The Royal Chronicles provide an uninterrupted sequence of sovereigns together with certain indications about the principal events during their reign. The centre is now Amhara, the true geographical heart of the great plateau, and from here the integration and stabilization of the kingdom were carried out. The aim of the first monarchs after the 'restoration' was clearly to hold on to all the central highland areas without, at first, embarking on fresh ventures in the northern and western regions. The overriding need was to contain and, if possible, to liquidate the Muslim sultanate of Ifat, which had encroached so menacingly upon the Shoa province, one of the great traditional preserves of Christian Ethiopia.

If thus the Solomonic succession is marked by a prolonged series of wars and skirmishes against the Muslim invaders who were holding the fertile country in the south-east, it is also distinguished by a great literary renaissance (about which see Chapter VII, below)—mainly works of an ecclesiastical character and translations from other Oriental languages, it is true, but none the less intense intellectual activity of a kind which gave adequate expression to the Ethiopian national genius. The other great achievement of the Solomonic dynasty was the well-nigh total fusion of Church and State. The number of churches and monasteries founded during this period is truly prodigious, missionary activity was intensified, and national sentiment was concentrated on the monastic tradition and on the powerful institutions connected with it. The influence of Tekla Haymanot in the south and Ewostatewos in the north was both overwhelming and enduring. It was probably during Zar'a Ya'qob's reign that the custom was established that the Prior of Debra Libanos—following the great example of Tekla Haymanot—became Etchege, i.e. the premier monk of the kingdom and the counsellor as well as confessor of the Emperor.[2] Until the Ethiopian Church attained autocephalous status, in the early 1950s, the Etchege was virtually the head of the monophysite Church, for the Egyptian

[1] A major contribution to our understanding of this period has been made by Ato Taddasa Tamrat's fine Ph.D. thesis on Church and State in Ethiopia, 1270–1527, now published by the Clarendon Press.

[2] This honour was probably taken over by the Prior of Debra Libanos from that of the monastery of St. Stephen of Hayq (see Cerulli, Letteratura, pp. 93–5).

Archbishop was frequently ignorant of the language and of Abyssinian traditions—quite apart from the long intervals which often occurred before a new Archbishop took up residence in his diocese.

Conti Rossini has well said[1] that if Yekuno Amlak was the founder of the new dynasty, his grandson Amda Sion (reigned 1314–44) was the founder of its might and power. In fact, Amda Sion must be regarded as the real builder of the Ethiopian state who consolidated the Solomonic kingdom and widened its frontiers through a series of ably conducted campaigns. The history[2] and character of Amda Sion are divided into two distinct periods: that of the flamboyant youth, the great lover according to the indigenous traditions, the seducer of his own father's concubine, and that of the mighty warrior, the suppressor of Islam, and the organizer and administrator. Both phases of his career are depicted in the Ethiopian chronicles, which offer a faithful account of his life and exploits.

After having pushed the boundaries of his kingdom beyond the loop of the Abbay, subjugating Gojjam and Damot and, in the north-west, extending his hold over Begemder, Amda Sion was able to turn his attention southwards to the increasingly dangerous Muslim incursions. The war of attrition between the central Christian highlands and the Muslim sultanates, entrenched all along the eastern and southern fringes of the Abyssinian plateau, is the principal feature of Ethiopian history during the following two centuries. Proceeding from east to west we first encounter the sultanate of Adal (Muslim writers such as Maqrizi[3] refer to it as Zeila, but Adal and Zeila are largely synonymous and their histories closely connected) on the Dankali and Somali coast. At times Adal formed part of the state of Ifat; its ruler was styled *Amir* or *Imam* (*Negus* in the Ethiopian chronicles), and one of them who opposed Amda Sion's march against Zeila, in 1332, was defeated and slain. Harar was, as we have already seen, a Muslim city-state and a great centre of Islamic commerce and cultural propagation. Ifat held the south-eastern part of the Shoan plateau and the slopes of the Awash rift valley; it was the most important of the sultanates. To the west of Ifat, in what is now the Arussi region, the Dawaro kingdom controlled

---

[1] *Etiopia e genti d'Etiopia*, p. 50.
[2] J. Perruchon, 'Histoire des guerres d'Amda Syon', *JA*, 1889.
[3] Maqrizi, *Ilmam*, Rinck's ed., 1790, or Cairo ed., 1895.

large tracts of southern Ethiopia. It bordered upon the Bali sultanate, while the small principalities of Sharkha and Arababni lay between Dawaro and the most westerly Muslim state, Hadya, which comprised the territory of the Sidama and Gurage.

Those were the Muslim sultanates ranged against Amda Sion. They covered a far greater area than that controlled by the Christian Emperor, but the latter had the advantage of a geographically compact state, while the Islamic peoples were spread in a vast semicircle without proper communications or political cohesion. Amda Sion had seized the initiative, attacked Ifat and Hadya, and defeated both. He had thus gained the entire plateau down to the Awash River. And though these Muslim principalities displayed great powers of recovery, for the time being Amda Sion had relieved the pressure of Islamic encroachment. Victory brought mass conversions to Christianity in its wake; many monasteries and churches were founded at that time, and the name of Amda Sion himself was registered among the saints in the *senkessar* (Synaxarium).

Amda Sion's son and successor was Saifa Ar'ad (1344-72), who is principally renowned for his reprisals against Egyptian merchants in Abyssinia to show his disapproval of the persecutions to which Christians in Egypt had been subjected, culminating in the imprison-ment of the Coptic Patriarch. Saifa Ar'ad, in his turn, was succeeded by his son, Newaya Maryam, of whom the Ethiopian chronicles know nothing to relate, but another son, Dawit I, ascended the throne in 1381 and reigned for nearly thirty years. He received an embassy from the Coptic Church in Egypt and later brought about a reconciliation with the Sultan of Egypt, marked by an exchange of gifts. Dawit's eldest son, Theodore, ruled for a brief period only, and after his violent death was succeeded by his brother Isaac (Yeshaq), who defeated Sa'ad ad-Din and occupied the entire sultanate of Ifat. The Walasma dynasty then withdrew to the lowlands out of reach of the Abyssinian armies and adopted the style of Kings of Adal. Isaac's forces also captured Massawa, which at that time was part of the sultanate of Dahlak. His fifteen-year reign was followed by five years of internal strife, when his sons, brothers, and nephews each kept the throne for a few months only.

This inglorious interlude came to an end in 1434, when Zar'a Ya'qob, Dawit's fourth son, became king. He was, perhaps, the greatest ruler

Ethiopia had seen since Ezana, during the heyday of Aksumite power, and few of his successors on the throne can be compared to him. His renown rests not only on his military successes against the Muslims or the extension of the frontiers of the Empire, but is principally based on the notable religious and administrative reforms which are for ever connected with his name. His zeal for the cause of Christianity led to the vigorous suppression of paganism and Hebraic-Jewish nuclei, but it also slid into all the excesses of inquisition and persecution.[1] However, his endeavours on behalf of the Church were overwhelmingly positive: he was responsible for the ecclesiastical reforms which determined the special character of the Ethiopian monophysite Church once and for all; he wrote himself, or caused to be written, some of the basic books of the Abyssinian orthodox faith; he was a patron of literature generally, and some of the oldest Ge'ez manuscripts extant go back to the reign of Zar'a Ya'qob (in fact, there are very few MSS. still preserved which antedate Zar'a Ya'qob's time).

In the Ethiopian struggle against Adal, Zar'a Ya'qob's principal achievement was the defeat of the sultan Badlay ibn Sa'ad ad-Din, who had made deep incursions into the Dawaro province. This victory consolidated the Abyssinian position among the Sidama and at the same time offered a long breathing space before the Muslims were ready to strike again. Zar'a Ya'qob was less successful in his campaigns against the Falashas and other Agaw peoples in the north-west, for the armies which he had despatched to the Semien were forced to withdraw.

His first aim was to strengthen the power and the prestige of the monarchy, which had been greatly undermined by his immediate predecessors during their short reigns. Every attempt at opposition to his plans and reforms was mercilessly suppressed, even if that meant acting against members of his own family: his wife was put to death, and his son was imprisoned for mourning the death of his mother. The reforms which stimulated the strongest opposition were not apparently his ecclesiastical changes, but his reorganization of the secular administration. He attempted to eliminate the power of the hereditary rulers of the provinces and to assume direction of provincial administration either himself or through officials of his choice. It was clear that any

[1] See Taddasa Tamrat's important paper on the Stephanite heresy in *RSE*, XXII, 1966.

success in this field could not last, for the influence of the great Rases was very considerable, and they were the chief exponents of the traditional centrifugal forces of the Empire. But by associating the Church more closely with the throne, Zar'a Ya'qob greatly enhanced the mystery and ritual with which the monarchy was imbued and which have become a mark and symbol of Ethiopian sacral kingship.

A good deal of fresh light has been thrown on Zar'a Ya'qob's ecclesiastical reforms by the publication of the Conti Rossini-Ricci edition of the *Mashafa Berhan* (in the *CSCO* series), by Cerulli's masterly sketch in his *Letteratura etiopica* (3rd ed., pp. 100 ff.), and by Ato Taddasa Tamrat's work (see p. 63 above and bibliography). The central point of controversy in the *Mashafa Berhan* is the question of Sabbath observance in Ethiopia (see p. 101 below; *Ethiopia and the Bible*, pp. 109-13; Hammerschmidt, *Stellung und Bedeutung des Sabbats*) which at one time threatened the unity of the realm. The Council of Debra Mitmaq (1450) resolved many, though by no means all, of the theological problems that beset the Emperor and his country.

With the death of Zar'a Ya'qob the period of the greatest expansion attained during the Middle Ages comes to an end. A large empire had been created, Church and State had been brought into a harmonious union, and the administration had been rationalized. The Muslim sultanates had been conquered and most of their territories were brought under Ethiopian authority. But Zar'a Ya'qob's young son, Ba'da Maryam (1468-78), was unable to maintain so far-flung an empire: some of the outlying provinces recently conquered began to grow restive; the feudal lords whom Zar'a Ya'qob had only ephemerally brought under central control reasserted their regional authority; and the senior clergy relapsed into some of the old-established ways of conduct and ecclesiastical organization. Almost the only success of Ba'da Maryam's reign was his expedition against the Falashas which was made possible by a truce concluded with the Sultan of Adal.

Ba'da Maryam's son Eskender (Alexander) reigned from 1478 to 1494; his energies were again mainly devoted to repelling continued harassing by the Adalites. He was still a young man when he fell during a raid in the lowlands. His son, the child-king Amda Sion II, had only a few months' nominal reign when Eskender's brother, Na'od (1494-1508), became King. He pursued wise policies—advised by the experienced and sagacious Empress Helena—and was the last monarch before the cataclysm of Muslim conquest brought about far-reaching changes in the political, ecclesiastical, and social fabric of Ethiopia.

4. THE MUSLIM CONQUESTS AND THE PORTUGUESE INTERLUDE[1]

The reign of Lebna Dengel (1508–40), Na'od's son, began under the regency of the Empress Helena, who continued her cautious and generally successful policy. At the same time, she was shrewd enough to realize that the tense but 'peaceful co-existence' with the Muslim strongholds on the Red Sea coast could not last for ever. She therefore acted upon a suggestion, first advanced by Pedro de Covilham, to enlist the aid of Portuguese naval forces in the dislodgement of Muslims from the Red Sea littoral. The arrival of a Portuguese exploratory mission was, however, much delayed, and it did not, in fact, reach the country till 1520 by which time the general situation had undergone profound changes.

Lebna Dengel had meanwhile assumed the reins of government and found himself opposed to the prudent course steered by the Empress Helena. The period of Lebna Dengel's rule is marked by two events of transcendent importance to the history of Ethiopia: the climax of the Muslim struggle with the Christian Empire, culminating in the virtual occupation of the Abyssinian highlands, and Ethiopia's entry into relations with Europe in general and Portugal in particular. A broad picture of the Portuguese venture in Abyssinia has already been sketched in the first chapter, and it will be necessary to add here only such aspects of this episode as impinge directly upon the course of Ethiopian history.

While the Portuguese were still considering Helena's request for help, the Adalite incursions had become more audacious under the leadership of the Emir Mahfuz, the Governor of Zeila. But Lebna Dengel was ready when, in 1516, the Muslim armies moved against the foothills and highlands. He stationed his troops on both sides of the mountain gorge through which the enemy had to pass, and when he

---

[1] Ato Merid Walda Aragay has written an exceptionally valuable study of the Portuguese period which, it is hoped, will shortly be published.

struck, the Christian success was complete: the Adalites were killed or routed and Mahfuz himself was slain. Lebna Dengel exploited his victory to the full; he invaded Adal, burning villages and fields and destroying the Sultan's castle at Zankar, a place not yet properly identified. Meanwhile a Portuguese fleet under Lope Soarez had reached Zeila at a time when its garrison was away fighting under Mahfuz. Zeila was occupied and burnt by the Portuguese crew.

Abyssinia was overjoyed, and the young King had a hero's welcome on his return. The Ethiopian chronicles vividly describe the elimination of the Muslim menace and the confident expectation—not unreasonable at the time—that Islam in Abyssinia was *hors de combat* for ever: 'tranquillity and peace now reigned in all the dominions of the Negus'. It was in these circumstances of recent military success and renewed prosperity that the Portuguese Embassy under Rodrigo de Lima (of which we possess Alvarez's most valuable account) arrived in Ethiopia in 1520. When finally the members of the Embassy were admitted into the Imperial presence, they offered precious gifts of silk and velvet instead of the expected firearms. The King was half-hidden behind curtains like a deity; earlier requests for a Portuguese alliance were now disclaimed, and the policies once pursued by the Empress Helena were merely a dim recollection of a remote past. Six years were spent in desultory negotiations (punctuated by disagreements among members of the Mission) about a possible Portuguese occupation of the principal Red Sea ports, thus shielding Abyssinia from a threatened Turkish assault. But no agreement had been reached when the Portuguese left in 1526.

Meanwhile, the sultanate of Adal was convulsed by internal struggles. The recent defeat had done grave harm to the prestige of the Walasma dynasty, whose authority was now constantly challenged by the Emirs and military commanders. The Sultan Abu Bakr had transferred the capital to Harar, possibly to extricate himself from the persistent pressure exerted by the generals who drew their principal support from the Dankali and Somali peoples. Chief among those forceful military commanders was Ahmad ibn Ibrahim (nicknamed Grañ, 'the left-handed') who soon became the effective master of the Muslim possessions in Ethiopia and assumed the title of Imam. We are fortunate in possessing a detailed eye-witness account of the Muslim conquests of the sixteenth century, with the Imam Ahmad as the central figure, written by Shihab ad-Din (*Futuh al-Habasha*, ed. by R. Basset).

Grañ had first made sure of the strength of his position in Adal and had then welded the Danakil and Somalis into a formidable striking force, inspired by the old ideal of the *jihad* and lust of conquest and plunder. He initially concentrated on limited objectives, raids and incursions into the plains and foothills, before venturing upon the distant and difficult highlands. But in 1529, three years after the departure of the abortive Portuguese Mission, he struck and inflicted a major defeat on Lebna Dengel. He was, however, unable to drive home this advantage, as his armies disintegrated, drunk with victory and booty. It was only two years later that he was finally ready to begin the great conquest and invasion which inundated nearly the entire territory of traditional Abyssinia, burning churches and monasteries and forcibly converting large numbers of Christians. Dawaro and the Shoa province were conquered in 1531, and Amhara and Lasta followed two years later. At the same time Bali and Hadya as well as the Gurage and Sidama regions fell into Grañ's hands.

The holocaust enveloped most parts of Ethiopia and brought in its train misery and murder, ruin and devastation. Much of the literary and intellectual heritage of Abyssinia was irretrievably lost, and the barbarism and brutality had an effect far transcending that age. To Ethiopians a good deal of their hard-won civilization was destroyed, while to the historian and *éthiopisant* precious documentation and irreplaceable evidence perished for ever.

When, in 1534, Grañ and his hordes reached the Tigrai, they received at least some temporary checks and setbacks, for the Tigreans were proud, courageous, and combative, and their country mountainous and inaccessible. Yet the Muslim impetus had not yet spent itself. Meanwhile, Lebna Dengel sought refuge in the unoccupied parts of the Tigrai; from there he went to Begemder and Gojjam. But both provinces were overrun by the Muslim armies and shared the common fate of spoliation and pillage. Lebna Dengel then recognized the wisdom of the policies initiated by the Empress Helena and that, having dallied for six years with the Portuguese Embassy, it might now be too late to establish his good faith with the Portuguese.

The expedient which then occurred to him was little short of ingenious, for—if our sources serve us well—he now attempted to bring the monophysite Church, without changing its character or doctrine, under the supreme jurisdiction of the Church of Rome. By this move he hoped to enlist the sympathy and active support of Portugal and other Christian powers. The tool he used for this purpose was João Bermudez (whose career has already been sketched in Chapter I), a detained member of the Portuguese Embassy, whom the King had apparently had consecrated as Abuna and then, in 1535, despatched to Europe to summon help. But before such assistance came Lebna Dengel died in 1540, exhausted, harried, and convinced of the doom of his country.

The accession to the then tottering throne of his son Claudius[1] (Galawdewos) could not have occurred at a more inauspicious moment in the history of Ethiopia—yet within less than two years the situation had radically changed, and the final *dénouement* came so unexpectedly and with such speed that every true Ethiopian could not but see in this the outstretched arm of the God of the Old Testament, who had come to deliver his chosen people. And the deliverance came from the sea. The 400 men under Christopher da Gama had disembarked at Massawa in 1541 and, aided by the valiant Bahr Negash Yeshaq, who had held out at Debaroa, set out on their epic march into the interior. When the Portuguese contingent met the Imam Ahmad, they were successful in two encounters, but could not press their victory home. Meanwhile, Grañ asked for and obtained reinforcements from the Turkish Pasha, with which he prevailed over the Portuguese and their leader, who was put to death. But the remaining 200 Europeans had not been demoralized; they managed to join forces with the remnants of Claudius' armies and, near Lake Tana, fought what was probably—at least until recent days—the most decisive battle in the long and chequered history of Ethiopia. They smote the Muslim troops and slew Grañ himself.

Though there still followed some skirmishes, with the death of Grañ the serious Muslim menace to Ethiopia had been removed for ever. Assisted by the soldiers of a Christian country from Europe, the Ethiopians had finally saved their ancient Christian Kingdom and heritage. But the salvation had come at a very late hour: Ethiopia lay prostrate and exhausted; many of its churches and monasteries existed

[1] Cf. Conzelman, *Chronique de Galawdewos*.

no longer; its clergy was weakened, and its people were either Islam-ized—however superficially—or terrorized and in urgent need of moral and material succour.

Adal, though greatly enfeebled, continued with harassing operations against the Ethiopians. A nephew of Ahmad Grañ moved against the plateau, but he was beaten by Claudius who subsequently advanced on Adal and wrought much devastation. Harar was now the main Muslim stronghold in Ethiopia, and it was from there that another attack was launched which, in 1559, led to the death of the Emperor Claudius.

But despite such isolated successes the Muslims no longer constituted a serious danger to the Abyssinian Empire. By the middle of the six-teenth century the prospect of an Islamized Ethiopia had become very remote. A new threat now arose which was, at least in part, unleashed by the upheavals of recent years and which was equally damaging to Christians and Muslims, i.e. the great Galla migrations which were to become the dominant feature during the next three centuries. The Gallas had been pushed towards the centre of the country by persist-ently exerted pressures from Somalis and, to a lesser extent, Danakil. The vacuum created by the long-drawn wars between Muslims and Christians and the consequent weakening of both enabled the Gallas to scale the mountain chains in the east and south of the great plateau. Some isolated Abyssinian victories scarcely stemmed or even affected the gathering momentum of this tidal wave which, by sheer force of numbers, was utterly irresistible. Abyssinians fled once again from their homes or were swallowed up in this vast immigration. Ethiopian territory became increasingly constricted, and the ethnic composition of the population underwent notable changes. The Gallas swamped most parts of the Shoa province, reached Amhara and extended to the southern and eastern regions of Lasta. They settled all along the outer fringes of the plateau in an immense semicircle, leaving untouched only the northern highlands, the area of the old Aksumite Kingdom.

The Muslims fared no better. The Gallas invaded the Harar region and settled everywhere—except in the city itself. The Imam transferred his seat to Aussa and continued to exercise a measure of authority over Harar till the middle of the seventeenth century. The independent Emirate of Harar then survived till Menelik's conquests at the end of the last century.

The Gallas had little to contribute to the Semitized civilization of Ethiopia; they possessed no significant material or intellectual culture, and their social organization differed considerably from that of the population among whom they settled. They were not the only cause of the depressed state into which the country now sank, but they helped to prolong a situation from which even a physically and spiritually exhausted Ethiopia might otherwise have been able to recover far more quickly.

Claudius' successor, Minas, had only a brief reign of four years which marked the nadir of Ethiopian power. But his son, Sarsa Dengel (1563-97), was a great warrior in the old tradition of Amda Sion. Oddly enough, he turned his major attention first to the north-west, Agaw-Falasha country, which had not been effectively subdued. His battles against the Gallas occupied almost his entire reign, but the buoyancy of this great mass of people was such that every success was purely ephemeral and brought no lasting relief to the hard-pressed Ethiopians.

In the north-east the Turkish occupation of Massawa had not been a serious embarrassment until the Turks sent a military force into the Eritrean highlands and took possession of Debaroa, the headquarters of the Bahr Negash. When the Bahr Negash Yeshaq, who had previously stood so firm in the struggle against Grañ, deserted and joined the Turks, Sarsa Dengel moved against the Ottomans and defeated them in 1578, killing both the Turkish Pasha and Yeshaq. With that the Turkish venture on the plateau collapsed; they still remained at Arkiko and Massawa in a sort of token occupation undertaken on their behalf by a local notable styled *na'ib* ('deputy').

Sarsa Dengel's forceful rule, which had brought a small measure of recovery, was followed by the short and insignificant reigns of Ya'qob and Za-Dengel. When Susenyos (1607-32) acceded to the throne, he ushered in another era of turbulence—but this time commotion of a rather different nature.

After the victory over Grañ, 100 or 150 Portuguese soldiers, the remnant of da Gama's contingent, had stayed in the country and become an integral part of the Ethiopian population. They had brought back with them João Bermudez who still claimed to be the lawful Archbishop of the Ethiopian Church. He was, however, too uneducated to impose the Roman faith by argument and persuasion. Instead, he relied on his spurious authority, and by constant bullying and gross tactlessness made himself so obnoxious that he had to be exiled. The Society of Jesus then despatched a 'genuine' Latin Bishop, Andrew de Oviedo, together with a small mission. The Emperor Claudius explained to them that he already had a monophysite Abuna and that he had no intention of severing his ties with the See of Alexandria or of abandoning Ethiopia's ancient monophysite faith. More positively, Claudius composed a document which is known under the name of 'Confession of Claudius'.[1] The first part is a formal exposition of the monophysite doctrine, while the second half is a defence of the special character of Abyssinian ecclesiastical customs. In this latter part Claudius is particularly anxious to rebut the Jesuit charge of the Hebraic mould of the Abyssinian Church. The value of the 'Confession' has to be judged in the light of the polemical literature of that time, which was a product of the monophysite-Catholic controversy.

The Spanish Jesuit Pedro Paez, who reached Ethiopia in the first decade of the seventeenth century, was by far the most tactful and successful of Roman Catholic missionaries. He had studied the languages and customs of the country, and by his courtesy and knowledge he attained a position of high prestige. The Emperor Susenyos showed him much favour and became more and more susceptible to the influence of Paez's teaching. He relaxed prohibitions against the Roman Church, permitted proselytizing, and discouraged the observance of the Sabbath. When Paez finally induced him to be received into the Roman faith, the King no longer resisted. At that time Paez was replaced by Alphonse Mendez who, in 1626, accepted the Negus' formal oath of obedience to the Roman Pope. But Mendez forced him to link this personal act of submission with a general abjuration of monophysitism for his whole people. There followed an outcry, especially as Mendez had tied this conversion to an abolition of the entire Ethiopian ritual: baptism, circumcision, fasts and feasts, ordination of deacons and priests, etc. The opposition was not confined to the clergy, but included members of the Imperial family and, above all, the ordinary Abyssinian who had no interest in, or knowledge of,

[1] Cf. Ludolf, *Commentarius*, pp. 237 et seq. See also Conzelman, *Galawdewos*, chapters 54-5.

doctrinal matters, yet whose life, in every phase, was deeply anchored in the national ethos of the monophysite Church and the expression it gave to the special character of people and country.

The popular commotion had been so spontaneous and the upheaval so serious that, in 1632, Susenyos was forced to revoke the Roman adherence and to proclaim the return to the old faith of the nation. He himself abdicated in favour of his son Fasiladas who re-established the age-long union of State, Church, and Monarchy, expelled the Jesuits, and thus severed relations with the European power whose interference in the country's religious affairs was construed as an attack upon Ethiopia's independence. We now enter a period of long isolation, of suspicion of Europeans, and the growth of xenophobia.

5. ISOLATION

Although in the outside world the exploration and study of Ethiopia began in earnest between the early seventeenth century and the beginning of the nineteenth, Ethiopia herself remained hidden and concealed, brooding and sullen. The Empire had no firm focus, local chieftains became increasingly independent, the Gallas continued their penetration, and material progress or intellectual development was virtually unknown. There were occasional flickers of light, some able rulers, but the ensuing darkness was only the greater. Not until the advent of King Theodore, in the mid-nineteenth century, does Ethiopia emerge from her isolation. Only then, in her rediscovered unity under the Emperors John, Menelik, and Haile Sellasie, does the country find its soul and genius again, its spirit and its sense of mission.

When Susenyos' son, Fasiladas (1632-67), had banished the Jesuits, he chose Gondar as his capital. This choice had almost symbolical significance, for it reflected the inchoate withdrawal of the monarchy from the centre of the Ethiopian scene. Gondar, situated to the north of Lake Tana, was far removed from the threat of Muslim or other hostile incursions, but it was equally far from the geographical centre of Ethiopia. The foundation of Gondar as the capital thus heralded the steady growth of regionalism, the increasing independence of the great feudal lords, and the progressive reduction of the *negusa nagast*, shorn of all real power, to serve merely as the symbol of the Solomonic connection. In the meantime, the Gallas in the central areas of Ethiopia, remote from their original habitat, began to be assimilated to the social and political organization of traditional Abyssinia. Yet there is little doubt that their continuing influx made its contribution to the decentralization of the Empire and its greatly diminished cohesion.

Another major aspect of this period of isolation and decadence is the resumption of the religious disputation which had been stimulated by the Jesuits and now degenerated—as the chronicles and other writings clearly indicate—into an arid and hair-splitting theological controversy strongly reminiscent of Talmudic dialectics (*pilpul*). In trying to crystallize their opposition to the Chalcedonian Definition, the Ethiopian clergy managed to manoeuvre themselves into ever subtler propositions, be it on the unction of the Holy Spirit or on the Three Births, which in the end led to increasingly serious and disruptive disagreements among themselves.

Fasiladas' reign is mainly distinguished for his attempts to come to terms with the Muslims whom he considered a much lesser evil than the Europeans, for the building of Gondar and its castles (see Chapter VIII, below), and the reconstruction of the Cathedral at Aksum which had been in ruins since the days of Grañ. His son, John I (Yohannes), had a comparatively peaceful reign of fifteen years, during which he continued his father's building activities at Gondar, forced the Franks to join the monophysite Church, and decreed a measure of segregation for Muslims. These laws of *apartheid* coupled with the prohibition to own land had, however, the effect of driving Muslims into commerce, which became increasingly concentrated in their hands, as well as into association with other pariah segments of the population, among whom a slow but steady infiltration of Islam became thus inevitable.

Iyasu I 'the Great' (1682–1706) succeeded his father, John. He was an excellent King and stands head and shoulders above other members of his dynasty during that epoch. He was able to halt, at least temporarily, the decline of state and monarchy and to free himself from the Byzantine intrigues at the Imperial Court. He was a warrior and revived the old Ethiopian pressure southwards. He even introduced tax reforms which were to be applied to the whole Empire and were meant to do away with the iniquities of the tax-collectors. He also visited the traditional colony of exiled princes at Amba Wahni (so vividly depicted in Dr. Johnson's *Rasselas*) and did much to alleviate and to improve their lot.

We are fortunate in possessing a European eye-witness account of the Emperor Iyasu I, written by the French physician C. J. Poncet (see Chapter I, above) who was summoned to the Gondar Court to treat a skin disease from which the Negus was suffering. Poncet tells us that 'the Emperor has great qualities—a quick and piercing wit, a sweet and affable humour, and the stature of a hero. He is the handsomest man I have seen in Ethiopia. . . . He is brave and undaunted in battles . . . has an extraordinary love for justice which he administers to his subjects with great exactness . . . who respect him even to adoration.'[1]

Yet in the end Iyasu was deposed by his son, Tekla Haymanot, and was assassinated in 1706—thus ushering in a long series of royal murders and palace revolts. The only reign of consequence is that of Bakaffa (1721–30) who suppressed, with much success, conspiracies and rebellions and set out to break the power of the constantly scheming nobles. His travels all over the country in disguise have long become part of Ethiopian folklore. He married Walatta Giyorgis (some of her ancestors had been Portuguese) who was a woman of great wisdom and who, as the Empress Mentuab, was to have considerable influence during the following reign. For Bakaffa died in 1730, and the Itege Mentuab exercised the regency during the minority of their son, Iyasu II. James Bruce knew the Dowager Queen in her old age, and he reports that 'she was reputed the handsomest woman of her time . . . the Queen inherited the colour of her European ancestors; indeed, was whiter than most Portuguese. She was very vain of this her descent. . . .'[2]

The effective dominion of Iyasu II (1730–55) scarcely extended beyond Begemder and Gojjam; Shoa and Lasta acknowledged only a token allegiance, while in the Tigrai the long rule of the powerful Ras Mika'el had begun. Iyasu the Little, as he was soon dubbed in contrast to his great predecessor, was defeated in a battle against the Funj Kingdom; the nobles, whom his father had kept in check, reasserted their independence, and the young King lacked the personality and power to impose his authority. He was, however, not without artistic refinements, and the ornamentation and decoration of his palace were greatly admired by Bruce. At his mother's bidding, Iyasu married the

[1] Poncet (Hakluyt, 1949), pp. 130–1. [2] Bruce, *Travels*, 1st ed., II, 611.

daughter of a Galla chief. The old Empress probably thought that her son would thus acquire useful allies, but in fact he alienated the sympathies of the Amhara ruling classes who were now implacably opposed to him. On his death, at an early age, the longeval dowager had his half-Galla son, Iyo'as (1755-69), proclaimed Emperor. This was the first time that the large Galla element in the population had become associated with the government of the country and the Solomonic dynasty itself. The abhorrence of the traditional rulers of Ethiopia was expressed in a further accession of independence and power for Ras Mika'el and a hardening of regional autonomy in general. At the same time, the influential Ras never severed his ties with the nominal Emperor; he even married Woyzaro ('Lady') Esther, the daughter of Mentuab. These three colourful personalities, Mika'el, Mentuab, and Esther, became close friends of James Bruce who has left us a most vivid portrait of their life and character.

When the intrigues at the Court of Gondar had reached such a pitch that Iyo'as was no longer able to deal with them unaided, he called on Ras Mika'el to mediate. But the latter felt doubtful about the King's part in these conspiracies and also of his ability to escape undue Galla influences. Mika'el then cut the Gordian knot by having the Emperor assassinated and by procuring from Amba Wahni an elderly successor, John II. It is this period, from 1769 to the beginning of Theodore's reign in 1855, that is called by Ethiopian tradition the time of the *masafent* ('judges'), for it resembled very closely the era of the Old Testament judges when 'there was no king in Israel: every man did that which was right in his own eyes' (Judges 17:6).

Authority now rested with the great chiefs and military commanders, and in some provinces hereditary kings established themselves who paid no more than lip-service to the paramountcy of a powerless King of Kings at Gondar. Chief among these regional sovereigns was Sahela Sellasie of Shoa, an ancestor of the present Emperor and a ruler of great ability. He negotiated treaties—including one with Queen Victoria[1]—and received foreign ambassadors. Other Rases had attained almost equal power and importance, among them Ras Ali of Begemder, Ras Ubye of Semien, and Ras Hailu of Gojjam. The rivalry between these great chiefs brought about some measure of

---

[1] Cf. *JSS*, 1964, pp. 187-99.

balance, and as none could allow one of their number to assume supreme power, they were content to acquiesce in the continuation of a puppet Solomonian on the throne.

The great unifying agent during that period was the Abyssinian Church which was common to all the provinces and which not only remained the carrier of the ecclesiastical tradition, but functioned as the repository of the national culture and thus embodied a strong sense of historical continuity. There were, in the first half of the nineteenth century, other factors which favoured the awakening of centripetal forces that might under auspicious conditions rekindle the bright light of Imperial cohesion and past glory: the penetration of the Gallas had continued unabated and had, in fact, interposed a solid Galla corridor between Shoa and the remainder of the Abyssinian highlands. Egypt had stirred up fears of Islamic expansion which might eventually envelop the entire Nile and Red Sea area. And, finally, European powers, including widespread missionary activities, had made their appearance in Africa: their motives were suspect, and this new menace could only be met by greater unity.[1] This concatenation of circumstances facilitated the eruption of the great force which the future Emperor Theodore, however illegitimate and un-Solomonic, embodied in the eyes of most Ethiopians.

6. THE EMERGENCE OF MODERN ETHIOPIA

From now on there is an abundant flow of sources, and many of the events are so well known that we need do no more than select the salient features from this *embarras de richesse*.

When Kassa (who later adopted Theodore as his throne-name) was born, in 1818, there was no central authority in Ethiopia. The nominal *negusa nagast*, according to Rüppell who was at Gondar in 1833, barely had the income of an averagely well-to-do Ethiopian, and the great princes of the Tigrai, Shoa, and Amhara were unable to prevent continuous strife and bloodshed. Kassa's homeland was Kwara, in the

[1] Dr. Donald Crummey's Ph.D. thesis (published early 1973) on foreign missions during the nineteenth century is of considerable value to our appreciation of this period. I find it hard, though, to accept his view of the weakness of the Ethiopian Church at that time (pp. 14–15).

west of Ethiopia, Agaw country since time immemorial, and in his
youth he would have known and spoken Kwara as well as Amharic.
His father was Dejatch Haile Maryam, a local prefect, while his mother
was of very humble birth. We are particularly fortunate in possessing
ample information about Kassa's early years—not only reports by
European travellers, but a detailed account (taking us up to 1860)
written by a certain Debtera (=precentor) Zenab who was in close
contact with Kassa during those years.[1] His father died while he was
still a child, and the boy was sent to a monastery to receive the traditional education of a deacon. This early upbringing left a profound
mark upon Kassa's character and found expression in his fervent
attachment to Abyssinian Christianity and in a deep and brooding
mysticism. When the monastery was destroyed during the constant
upheavals of that period, Kassa was one of the few to escape. He then
lived for some time in the house of an uncle, Dejatch Kenfu, before
becoming head of a company of *shifta* ('bandits') who were passionately
devoted to the brave, able, and fiery youth. His stay in the monastery
had given him a taste for, and some knowledge of, Ethiopic literature,
which he could later indulge to the full in the formidable library he
amassed at Magdala (cf. Chapter I, above); and his experience as a *shifta*
laid the foundation of his remarkable talent as a soldier and leader of men.

Kassa's exploits attracted such attention and brought him such fame
and influence that, in 1847, he was able to marry Tewabetch, the
beautiful daughter of Ras Ali of Begemder. By a series of well-executed
strokes, culminating in the capture of the Queen Mother Menen, Ras
Ali's mother, Kassa placed himself in virtual control of the north-west,
including Gondar, and assumed the title of Dejazmatch. Ras Ali now
sought to incite his powerful neighbour, Ras Goshu of Gojjam,
against this tiresome upstart, but Kassa defeated and killed that celebrated old warrior and captured Goshu's son. Ali himself was beaten in a
fierce battle in 1853 and retired for good among the Gallas, thus bring-

[1] The Amharic text was edited by E. Littmann in his *The Chronicle of King
Theodore*, Princeton, 1902, and translated by M. M. Moreno, *RSE*, 1942. A less
detailed, though more complete, version of the King's life was composed by
Aleka Walda-Maryam, and published by C. Mondon-Vidailhet (Paris, 1904). A
third version was recently published by L. Fusella in *Annali dell'Istituto Univ.
Orientale di Napoli*, 1957–9.

ing to a close the period of Galla influence and with it the extinction of the dynasty in whose veins Galla blood had flowed.

At this point there only remained two major regional princes in Ethiopia: Ras Ubye of the Tigrai and Haile Malakot, King of Shoa. Kassa turned his attention first to the northern rival by dissuading the Abuna from crowning Ubye as Emperor (which he had intended to do after the death of Ras Ali) and promising him to expel from the country all Catholics, including the learned Italian de Jacobis.[1] He then defeated Ubye in a battle fought early in 1855 and brought the entire Tigrai under his authority. Kassa was now ready, even before dealing with Haile Malakot (who died shortly afterwards, leaving his young son, Menelik, a vassal of the new master of the country), to take the ultimate step: to be anointed King of Kings by the Abuna Salama. At his Coronation in 1855 Kassa chose, with characteristic adroitness, the name of Theodore which to Ethiopians conjured up the image of a messianic ruler by that name who would restore the Empire to its ancient glory and prevail over all unbelievers.[2]

Within the space of a few years Theodore had thus united a fragmented country, suppressed the foremost feudal lords with their limited territorial aspirations and loyalties, resurrected the Christian character and national concentration which the people needed in the hard times ahead, and prepared the basis for the emergence of modern Ethiopia.

Theodore was of medium height, rather darker than Ethiopians usually are, with a fine nose and strong eyes. All Europeans who met him at this time were greatly impressed by his personal magnetism and regal bearing. His dress was simple, and his habits had barely changed: he still slept in a tent pitched among his soldiers, and went barefoot. He possessed great charm and extraordinary powers of persuasion, but in anger he became immoderate and cruel. The British Consul, W. C. Plowden, and his friend, John Bell, were greatly attached to the Emperor and stayed with him as his intimate counsellors. As long as they and Queen Tewabetch were alive (all three had either died or been killed by 1860), the Negus' excesses could be kept in check.

[1] Cf. Cerulli, *Letteratura*, p. 181.
[2] Cf. now also Rubenson, *Tewodros*, and Jesman in *Ethiopia Observer*, X, 2 (1966).

D

Theodore's first actions in his occupancy of the Imperial throne were the abolition of the slave-trade and of polygamy. In the former aim he had only a measure of success, while in the latter it was clear that a reform of sexual morals was a slow process. The King had a strongly developed sense of justice; he protected the humble against the excesses of soldiers and officials, and each one of his subjects could have personal recourse to the supreme judge in the land. To him Ethiopia and mono-physite Christianity were identical, but his drastic measures of compulsion were bound to miscarry in the long run. Finally, Theodore trans-ferred the capital from Gondar to the fortress of Magdala which was situated more centrally than the city of castles and towers that had been the scene of the progressive dismemberment of the Empire.

It is obvious that the Emperor's reforms were welcomed only by the large masses of the people, while the feudal chiefs continued to give preference to local interests and intrigues. And when Theodore tried to break the influence of such regional nobles by despatching his own men as governors, the latter frequently fell victim to the temptations of power. Insurrections and revolts had to be crushed in many parts of the Empire, but the King went about this suppression with increasing ferocity and tyranny. In his royal loneliness he came to regard himself more and more as the divine instrument in the deliverance of Ethiopia. He lost all sense of proportion, and there was now no one who could reason with him. The streak of cruelty and mercilessness in him gradually submerged the good qualities and finally gave way to passionate megalomania.

A few years after Tewabetch's death the King married Ras Ubye's daughter, Woyzaro Terunesh, who had few of the qualities of his first wife. She treated him as a peasant entirely unworthy of her royal favours. Their son, Alamayahu, was taken to England after the fall of Magdala, but he died there at an early age. The Queen herself had entirely withdrawn from Theodore, and it was only a short while before his death that she returned to him at Magdala. In the meantime, the Emperor took to drink and women, and the corruption of his character brought about ever more severe excesses.

It is in the light of these circumstances that we have to consider briefly the entanglements which led to Theodore's eventual downfall. But it would be wrong to see that end merely as a consequence of the physical intervention by a great European power: the cause of the Emperor's ruin lay in his own character, and the portents were written in large letters long before the British Army arrived on the scene.

In 1862 the British Government appointed Captain Cameron to succeed W. C. Plowden as Consul. When he arrived in Ethiopia, he delivered a letter from Queen Victoria and was received by the Emperor with kindness—even though it was obvious that he did not take to Cameron as he had done to his predecessor. Late in 1862 Theodore sent a letter to Queen Victoria, written in his picturesque style and asking for a reply through Consul Cameron. The letter contained an attack on Muslims in general and in particular on the Turks occupying the Ethiopian coast. Unfortunately, by an oversight in the Foreign Office, no answer was despatched to Theodore's letter. Meanwhile, the King had imprisoned some missionaries, one of whom had included in a book some highly unflattering references to Theodore's mother.

In this general atmosphere of suspicion the Emperor's anger was further aroused when among the despatches Cameron was receiving from England no reply was included to the royal missive. From a variety of indications, wrongly interpreted by a suspicious and highly neurotic King, Theodore concluded that the British were, in fact, supporting Turkish and Egyptian expansionist policies in north-east Africa. He then imprisoned Cameron and his secretary and brought them to Magdala, together with his other European captives, whose number had considerably increased in the meantime. These were soon joined by the Abuna Salama, the Egyptian Archbishop. At this moment of confusion Menelik escaped from Magdala and proclaimed himself King of Shoa.

When the British Government received news of events in Ethiopia, it immediately despatched a reply, signed by the Queen herself, to the King's earlier letter and sent it by the hands of Mr. Rassam and two other emissaries. It took Rassam and his party about eighteen months to be received by Theodore. Their mission appeared at first successful and the prisoners were freed,[1] but shortly before their

[1] Cf. Ullendorff, 'A letter from the Emperor Theodore to Queen Victoria' in *Neue Afrikanistische Studien* (in honour of A. Klingenheben), Hamburg, 1966, pp. 251–5.

departure all of them were bound and arrested once again—including Rassam and his two colleagues. The King now repeated an earlier demand for European artisans, and a letter to this effect was carried to the British Government by Mr. Flad, one of the Magdala prisoners. Engineers and machinery were thereupon sent to Massawa, but when Theodore failed to release the captives, men and equipment returned home.

The Secretary of State now despatched an ultimatum; but when the prisoners were still not freed, a military expedition, under the command of Sir Robert Napier, set out from Bombay. It reached Annesley Bay late in 1867 (see Chapter I). The details of this fascinating campaign may be studied in a number of books written by members of the expedition; the most readable of these is probably C. R. Markham's *History of the Abyssinian Expedition* (London, 1869).

The British march to Magdala was facilitated by the help or neutrality of the chiefs through whose districts the army passed. For by that time Theodore had become anathema to many Ethiopians: his power had faded almost as rapidly as his prestige, and the old centrifugal forces had begun to reappear. The 32,000 men of Napier's army and their equipment left a deep impression wherever they went. There was only one major engagement, at Aroge, not far from Magdala, in which hundreds of brave Ethiopian soldiers met their death. Then followed an exchange of correspondence between the King and Sir Robert concerning the release of the European captives (their number was by that time sixty-seven) and the King's submission to the Queen. Unhappily, these written and oral communications were bedevilled by an incredible sequence of misunderstandings, partly due to faulty translation and interpretation and partly to insufficient knowledge and appreciation of Abyssinian mentality and customs.

The end came quickly: Magdala was stormed and taken on Easter Monday, 1868; Theodore committed suicide by shooting himself through the roof of the mouth. He was buried in the precincts of the Church of Madhane Alam ('Saviour of the World') at Magdala. His end was as violent and impulsive as his life had been. That Theodore was passionately devoted to Ethiopia and her ancient glory and future greatness nobody would deny—nor that the King himself possessed extraordinary valour, high gifts, and more than a spark of genius. But his pride, his distorted sense of honour, his tyranny, and his fearful excesses proved his undoing.

The majority of the manuscripts which Theodore had amassed at Magdala (to form the library of the Madhane Alam Church) found a home in the British Museum (see Chapter I); a chalice given by Iyasu I and Queen Walatta Giyorgis to the Church of Kweskwam is now in the Victoria and Albert Museum, whereas Theodore's crown was returned to the Regent Ras Tafari (later Emperor Haile Sellasie I) by King George V.

The British Army had come and gone: their only purpose, the release of the European captives, had been efficiently and speedily achieved. Yet even those Ethiopian nobles who had been loudest in their denunciation of Theodore and had benefited most from his removal could not entirely forget that their country, invincible Ethiopia, had been defeated and temporarily occupied by a European power—a rankling pain which even the great victory of Adwa was not to dull completely.

Sir Robert Napier's task was to free prisoners and not to decide who was to fill the vacuum created by Theodore's disappearance. There was no dearth of candidates: Menelik, King of Shoa, pressed his claims, even though he had stood somewhat aside from the recent conflict; Kassa, the Ras of the Tigrai, was in a strong position by virtue of the arms he had acquired from the departing British; and the Wagshum Gobazye, ruler of Lasta, was thought the most likely and powerful aspirant to the Imperial throne. Indeed, immediately upon the embarkation of Napier's expedition Gobazye proclaimed himself *negusa nagast* under the name of Tekla Giyorgis II. But when he marched against Adwa, in 1872, to liquidate his Tigrean rival, he was heavily defeated by Kassa, who had himself crowned in the ancient capital of Aksum and assumed the name of John IV (Yohannes). John's accession marked the return of the crown, after a very long interval, to the home of the old Aksumite Kingdom and to the person of a Tigrean prince.

John was, above all, a fanatical Christian, and his reign was characterized by constant wars against the Muslim powers encroaching upon his dominion and by resistance to the incipient European penetration. He was a brave man and as full of zeal and fervour as Theodore—yet without cruelty and intemperance. During his seventeen-year rule he was so harassed by external foes that he had little or no time to devote his energy to internal reforms. He came, however, to terms with Menelik of Shoa, by which, for the sake of Ethiopian unity, the latter recognized John as the King of Kings. Their spheres of influence were carefully assigned, Menelik's in the southern and John's in the northern half of the Empire, and it was agreed that upon John's death Menelik should succeed to the Imperial Crown. Under the same agreement John's son married the Shoan King's daughter, Zawditu.

Egypt, under the Khedive Isma'il, had conceived plans for the conquest of Abyssinia. In these designs she was encouraged by the quick success of the British Expedition in 1868 and by the hope of Ethiopian disunity. In 1875 Egypt directed a three-pronged attack against the Christian Empire; earlier already her agent, the Swiss adventurer Werner Munzinger, had placed himself in charge of the Keren area and also assumed the governorship of Massawa. He now led the assault from Tajura, but was overwhelmed and killed by Dankali forces. The second prong set out from Zeila under the command of Ra'uf Pasha and succeeded in occupying Harar. The Egyptians stayed there until they were dislodged, ten years later, by Menelik's forces. The third and largest column proceeded from Massawa, crossed Eritrea, and during their descent into the Mareb Valley, near Gundet, were attacked by John's Tigrean army and almost totally annihilated.

The shock of this disaster was immense, and the Egyptians at once prepared another expedition, this time of nearly 20,000 men under the command of the Khedive's son. The Emperor now organized a veritable crusade, and the whole country down to Menelik's Shoan hills reverberated with excitement and the call to deal a final blow to the Muslim foe. When the two armies met in 1876 near Gura, the Egyptian *débâcle* was so colossal that it quenched their thirst for Imperial aggrandizement in Ethiopia once and for all.

In 1878 John and Menelik undertook a joint campaign against the Gallas with the aim of bringing as many of them as possible within the orbit of the Christian Church. The Emperor's religious fanaticism and his forcible conversions, both in the service of his beliefs and as an instrument of political unification, had no lasting or beneficial effect. They disturbed the atmosphere of religious toleration which is usually a mark of Ethiopian life and introduced unnecessary strife and dissension. It was, therefore, a wise act on Menelik's part when, shortly after John's death, he allowed a return to religious tolerance and amity.

Meanwhile, the scramble for Africa had brought the Italians to the shores of the Red Sea. Already in 1869 the Rubattino Navigation Company had bought the small port of Assab from the local Sultan, and in 1882 the Italian state took over. Italy had made her modest entry among the colonial powers. But Assab was of no possible use to anyone; the Italians diligently explored the hinterland and made some tentative contacts with Menelik—yet their Abyssinian venture only began in earnest when, in 1885, they landed at Massawa (Britain having previously declared her indifference to action at that part of the Red Sea coast). Two years later they were ready to reconnoitre the Eritrean foothills, but were savagely beaten at Dogali by Ras Alula, the Governor of *Mareb Mellash* (= Eritrea). There was deep resentment in Italy, and General San Marzano was despatched with a strong expeditionary force. The Emperor faced this army for some time without joining battle.[1]

The reason for John's hesitation to attack a well-equipped European force lay in his preoccupation with events on his western flank. The Mahdists in the Sudan were proving dangerous neighbours. In 1887 a large contingent of dervishes had entered western Ethiopia, burnt parts of Gondar, and then retired across the frontier. The Christian Emperor's first duty now was to dispose of this severe threat by the Muslim infidels. He met the dervishes in a great battle at Metemma (1889) and appeared to defeat them, but in the last moments of the engagement the Emperor was mortally wounded, and his army retired when its leader had fallen.

Menelik was now by far the strongest man in Ethiopia, and not even John's death-bed designation of his son Mangasha as successor—in breach of an earlier agreement—could rob him of the Imperial Crown for which he had waited with so much patience and deliberation. The seat of power had now returned from the Tigrai to the southern provinces, and, apart from Ras Alula and Mangasha, the realities of the situation were acknowledged by all Ethiopians.

[1] Cf. Heruy Walda Sellasie's *Ethiopia and Metemma* (a short history of the Emperor Yohannes), Addis Ababa, 1917–18. See also *BSOAS*, 1972, pp. 250–1, and Bibliography under Portal and Zewde.

Menelik was content to leave the Italians a free hand in the Massawa-Asmara-Keren region, where they would relieve him of having to deal with his northern adversaries. The new Emperor had in the past frequently conducted negotiations with the Italians and had received from them considerable supplies of arms; he saw no reason why he should not come to terms with them again now. Under the Treaty of Uccialli, which Menelik and the Italian plenipotentiary, Count Antonelli, signed in 1889, the new Italian territory (to be named 'Eritrea' (from *Mare Erythraeum*) by royal decree of 1 January 1890) was to include Halai, Saganeiti, Asmara, Addi Nefas, and Addi Yohannes. The Italian General had meanwhile reached the Mareb-Belesa line which, however, Menelik refused to accept as the boundary of the new colony.

More serious in its consequences was that clause of the Treaty[1] which stated, in its Amharic version, that the Emperor *might* avail himself of the Italian Government in his relations with foreign states, whereas the Italian text stipulated that he *shall* do so. Italy had thus become, in *her* view, the protecting power of the whole of Ethiopia and had informed other governments accordingly. When Menelik heard of this interpretation of the Treaty—which was certainly far from the spirit in which he had signed it—his relations with Italy became vitiated and tense. The events of the next few years are highly unedifying, and there are few Italians who do not deplore the policy of vacillation and chronic indecision pursued by the Government at home, as well as the manifestations of inexperience, personal disagreements, and intrigues by many of those on the spot. Menelik showed himself patient and willing to compromise, while local Italian officials were backing Mangasha's claim to the Tigrai and, at the same time, acknowledging the Emperor's sovereignty over the whole of the country south of the Mareb-Belesa line. In the end both Menelik and Mangasha became so exasperated and suspicious of the contradictory policies adopted by the Italian authorities that they reached agreement and joined forces. Italy now faced a united and very determined Ethiopia.

At that point the Italian General, Baratieri, moved into the Tigrai province and occupied Adwa. Instructions from his home Government were conflicting: parsimony in the Italian Treasury as well as opposi-

[1] Cf. now also Rubenson, *Wichale XVII*, and Giglio, *Trattato di Uccialli*.

tion to colonial adventures alternated with local recklessness and faulty
judgement. One Italian battalion, under Major Toselli, had advanced
as far as Makalle. Meanwhile, the Emperor had amassed a large and
enthusiastic army and had despatched a forward column under his
cousin, Ras Makonnen (father of the future Emperor Haile Sellasie),
towards Amba Alagi, where Toselli's force was surrounded and annihilated. The northward march of the Ethiopians was now relentless and
increasingly menacing. The final meeting place of the opposing forces
was near Adwa where some 14,000 well-armed, but poorly organized,
Italians faced an enemy six times as numerous, a foe high in morale and
moderately well equipped with Italian arms supplied not long ago in
furtherance of internecine strife. Both sides fought with great bravery
in a battle which settled the fate of Italian ambitions in Ethiopia—at
least for the next forty years. The Emperor did not press his advantage
and still left Eritrea in Italian hands. The Treaty of Addis Ababa (1896)
abrogated the ill-fated Uccialli agreement, recognized the independence of Ethiopia, and, surprisingly, confirmed the Italians in their
possession of the Mareb-Belesa line.

The general aims of Menelik's enlightened policy were threefold:
(1) to contain the European powers on the borders of his country and
to safeguard Ethiopia's independence—which necessitated a series of
elaborate treaties regularizing the frontiers[1] of his far-flung, but land-
locked, Empire; (2) the permanent conquest, followed by the establishment of effective Ethiopian authority, of the neighbouring Muslim and
pagan areas in the south; and (3) internal administrative reforms—
including, first and foremost, the age-long problem of eliminating the
disruptive regional tendencies fostered by the great feudal chiefs and
of introducing, instead, a cadre of qualified governors and administrators.

Already during King John's reign Menelik had started on the systematic conquest of the fertile regions to the west and south of Shoa. This
policy was continued during the first years of his own reign, when the
rich territory in the southern Awash Valley and the Sidama and Janjero
areas were annexed. In 1897 followed the conquest of the Kingdom of

[1] See Ullendorff, 'The 1897 Treaty between Great Britain and Ethiopia' in
RSE, XXII (1966-8); and 'The Anglo-Ethiopian Treaty of 1902' in BSOAS,
1967/3.

Kaffa which had held out for so long. Having dealt with the south, the Emperor turned his attention to the Islamized east. Harar had been under Ethiopian control since 1885, and he now appointed his trusted friend and kinsman, Ras Makonnen, to be Governor of this key province. For from Harar it was possible to control the Galla and Somali tribes in these vast and largely unadministered regions.

With his newly-built capital as far south as Addis Ababa,[1] Menelik had shaped another Empire, different in form and composition from its predecessors. The country had grown out of all recognition in the south, east, and west, but the extreme north, Eritrea, had been abandoned to a European colonial power. There were many Abyssinians in the north who could not forget or forgive this detachment of one of the oldest parts of the ancient Aksumite Kingdom. This bitterness was enhanced by the recent memory of a Tigrean Emperor, John, to whom these lands were the heart, and not the periphery, of his homeland.

Under Menelik's reign the prestige of the country had grown, the foundations of a modern state had been laid, and the Emperor's conduct had been distinguished by wisdom and moderation. He himself had been gravely ill since 1908, but the able and shrewd Empress Taitu stood by his side to aid and to counsel. His paralysis became so severe that the resultant speculation as to the succession began to constitute a serious threat to the unity of the Empire. It was against Taitu's advice that he designated in 1909, by solemn proclamation, his grandson, Lidj Iyasu, as heir to the throne.[2] Once Menelik's competent grip had been relaxed, the grandees began to manœuvre for position, the atmosphere was filled with plots and intrigues, real and imaginary, and foreign powers tried to win influence over the young heir.

When Menelik died in 1913, Lidj Iyasu was a boy of seventeen, not unintelligent, but irresponsible and dissolute. He gave universal offence by disclaiming his Solomonic lineage, by marriage to several Muslim girls, and by having fabricated for himself a genealogy proving his descent from the Prophet Muhammad. When World War I broke out, he did not conceal his sympathy for the Turkish cause. Lidj Iyasu had, however, not only aroused the alarm of the British, French, and Italian representatives at Addis Ababa, he had so deeply offended Ethiopian

[1] See Pankhurst, *Economic History of Ethiopia*, pp. 699ff.
[2] See, *Amharic Chrestomathy*, pp. 24–5.

susceptibilities by speaking of a great Muslim Empire in Ethiopia that his name had become anathema to the Christian majority in his country. Dejazmatch Tafari became the rallying point of the forces of resistance which finally brought about the deposition of Lidj Iyasu in 1916 and the crowning of Zawditu, Menelik's daughter, as Empress, with Ras (as he now became) Tafari as regent and heir to the throne. This arrangement had the blessing of the Archbishop who promptly pronounced excommunication upon Lidj Iyasu.

Ras Tafari[1] is a great-grandson of King Sahela Sellasie of Shoa and a son of Ras Makonnen who was the Emperor Menelik's right-hand man. He was born in 1892 near Harar, where he received his early education from tutors at the French mission, and French has remained his main foreign language. In 1908 he was appointed Governor of the large Sidamo Province, and two years later, upon the death of his father and elder brother, he became Governor of his native province of Harar. In 1911 he married Woyzaro Menen, the future Empress,[2] by whom he had three sons and three daughters.

Ras Tafari was born without any reasonable prospect of ascending the throne. His education was that traditionally given to young Ethiopian noblemen, but his attainments, intellectual powers, and great personal dignity soon became apparent and had already been recognized by the Emperor Menelik. When the decisive hour came, in 1916, he displayed both judgement and courage. It was during the fourteen years of his regency that Ras Tafari prepared the ground for the great work of reform and education which, after 1930, he carried out as Emperor.

The dyarchy of the Empress Zawditu and the young Regent was a difficult and delicate arrangement, but it brought peace and prosperity to Ethiopia. Zawditu, by that time middle-aged, was conservative in her outlook, while Ras Tafari was forward-looking and progressive and soon became the focus for the aspirations of the modernist younger generation. Yet as Regent and Emperor he has shown a remarkable feeling for the pace of reform and progress at which his country could move without disturbance or upheaval. He has always insisted, rightly, that Ethiopia must evolve her own concepts and forms suitable to

[1] See L. Mosley, *Haile Selassie*.
[2] She died in 1962.

conditions prevailing in this ancient realm. Slavish imitation of western ways could only lead to disaster.

Ras Tafari concentrated at first on foreign affairs. In 1923 he had a conspicuous success in the admission of Ethiopia to the League of Nations. In the following year he visited Rome, Paris, and London, and was thus the first Ethiopian ruler ever to go abroad. In 1928, not long after the death of Fitawrari Habte Giyorgis, one of the most powerful men in the Kingdom, he assumed the title of Negus. In the following two years there was considerable manœuvring for position by some of the influential Rases, but when the Empress Zawditu died, in 1930, Tafari prevailed over all his rivals. He was crowned Emperor (*negusa nagast*) in St. George's Cathedral, Addis Ababa, in November and took the name of Haile Sellasie ('Might of the Trinity'). All the great powers attended his Coronation (the Duke of Gloucester representing Britain), and there was a vast array of journalists and special correspondents. The great Rases now bowed in homage before the Imperial throne—Haile Sellasie, the new scion of the Tribe of Judah, had indeed prevailed.[1]

The events of the following years may with advantage be relegated to the last chapter.

[1] An autobiography by the Emperor, entitled *heywatenna ya-Ityopya ermejja* (*My Life and Ethiopia's Progress*—written in Amharic), vol. I, 1892–1937, appeared early in 1973; 264 pp., plates, and genealogical table. It was dictated during the Emperor's exile at Bath.

V

RELIGION AND THE CHURCH

ONOPHYSITE CHRISTIANITY is not only the official
religion of the Ethiopian Empire; it is also the most profound expression of the national existence of the Ethiopians.
In its peculiar indigenized form, impregnated with strong Hebraic and
archaic Semitic elements as well as pagan residua, Abyssinian Christianity had long become the store-house of the cultural, political, and social
life of the people. It is, therefore, to this distinctive conglomerate and
its forms and expressions that the present chapter is devoted. But it will
also be necessary to make brief references to three other religious
manifestations in Ethiopia, Judaism, paganism, and Islam, which are
either genetic ingredients of Abyssinian Christianity or at least elements
of a long historical symbiosis.

According to Ethiopian tradition, in pre-Christian days 'one part of
the people of Abyssinia was under the Mosaic Law, the other was
worshipping the Serpent'.[1] Most scholars accept this tradition as sub-
stantially accurate and confirm that there are adequate historical reasons
to buttress the assumption that, before their conversion to Christianity,
the Abyssinians must have been partly pagans and partly adherents of
some form of Judaized religion.[2]

The religious situation in Abyssinia, before the middle of the fourth
century A.D., must have been very complex. There existed a great deal
of worship of spirits and genii (*zar*), good or evil, who were associated

---

[1] Cf. Béguinot, *La Cronaca abbreviata d'Abissinia* (1901), p. 2; Littmann, *Legend of the Queen of Sheba*, p. 26 et passim.

[2] E.g. Littmann, *Aksum Expedition*, I, p. 51.

with trees or fountains, animate or inanimate objects. The mountain-
tops played a large part in these beliefs as, indeed, did the sky and the
sun. In the *Kebra Nagast* (Chapter 28) the Queen of Sheba declares:
'From this moment I will not worship the sun but the creator of the
sun, the God of Israel.'

The worship of the serpent appears to have been widespread, and
the cult of the *Arwe* (serpent) had its extension in the belief that it was
the first king of Abyssinia. This motif finds expression in traditional
art, where to this day the story of King Solomon and the Queen of
Sheba is depicted as beginning with the reign of the Serpent. The
animistic beliefs of the Cushitic inhabitants, notably the Agaw, have
long continued to exert an influence and have become part of the
Abyssinian type of Christianity. The Semitic immigrants, while
numerically inferior, soon made their influence felt in all spheres of life,
and their superior civilization became—as we have already seen—the
characteristic expression of the Aksumite Kingdom. It is, however,
clear that the immigrants from Arabia brought with them not only a
peculiar type of Judaism, but also many of the other religious forms
that were current in ancient South Arabia. References to members of the
South Arabian pantheon have been found in Abyssinia, and Athtar, the
Venus-star, Almaqah (Sin), the Moon-god, Dhat Himyam (Shams),
the Sun-goddess, were probably equally well known on both sides of
the Red Sea. A specifically Ethiopian development is the appearance of
Meder (Earth), Beher (Sea),[1] and Mahrem (God of War).

Apart from the transplantation to Ethiopia of important aspects of
the South Arabian pantheon, it is clear that South Arabia must also be
considered—as has been shown in Chapter IV—the principal avenue by
which Jewish elements reached the Kingdom of Aksum and gained
admission in a variety of forms.[2] At the same time, it is to be realized
that these elements bore a general Hebraic cast reflecting an early form
of Judaism still fairly free from Talmudic minutiae. That is, of course,
to be expected when one recalls the early date of some Jewish migrations into Arabia, although we should not exclude either customs or

[1] So I prefer to interpret with Guidi (*Enciclopedia Italiana*) and against Conti
Rossini (*Storia d'Etiopia*, p. 142), for *beher* must at that time have possessed a
meaning clearly differing from *meder*.
[2] Cf. *Ethiopia and the Bible*, esp. pp. 15–30.

literary allusions which later on appear in the literature of the Talmud. The period of Talmudic 'gestation' extends over several centuries, and we must therefore expect to find some of its elements among Jewish communities which were severed from the main stream of tradition before its committal to writing.

It must not, of course, be supposed that Judaism was either the only or even the principal monotheistic religion in pre-Islamic Arabia. The great expansion of the monophysite (and, to a lesser extent, the Nestorian) Church beyond the fringes of the desert brought Christianity right into the heart of Arabia. The Syriac story of the Jacobite Bishop Akhudemmeh[1] shows the intense missionary activity of this monophysite zealot among many Arabian tribes. No less important were the religious exertions of the monophysite Kingdom of Ghassan (or of the Nestorians at Hirah) who, by their numerous contacts with the large tribes of the interior of Arabia, contributed so notably to the diffusion of that type of Christianity over wide areas of the Arabian peninsula. The same form of Christianity was, of course, brought into Arabia not only by the Abyssinian conquerors, but also by the vigorous trade in Abyssinian slaves and by commercial relations in general.

It must be appreciated that those forms of Judaism and Christianity which were found at that time in south-west Arabia were not only obviously 'Eastern' in type, but their general Semitic character, the circumstances of their development as well as their entire religious, historical, and emotional atmosphere, rendered them far closer and more akin to each other than is the case with their Westernized counterparts. Monophysite Christianity had a distinctly Hebraic mould, while Judaism in Arabia at that period could not but reflect some of the imprint of the missionary zeal and vigour of early Christianity.

It is possible, of course, to point to certain Jewish influences and manifestations in the emergence of Abyssinian culture, but we possess no explicit information about the identity of the carriers of those influences. For the history of the Jews in Abyssinia we lack nearly all genuine and trustworthy source material. Generalizations of all sorts abound, but there is an almost complete absence of historical detail. The want of proper sources is, however, compensated, at least in part,

[1] Cf. Nau's edition of the *Histoire de Akhoudemmeh* (*Patrologia Orientalis*, III, 1909).

by fairly numerous threads of indirect evidence which, in their cumulative effect, present an impressive picture. Words like Ethiopic *ta'ot* (idol), *gahannam* (hell), *athara* (to purify), *fesh* (Easter), *meswat* (alms), etc., must have been introduced by Jewish merchants or migrants from Arabia at an early date, for they show Hebrew or Jewish-Aramaic forms and a specifically Jewish connotation: *meswat* alone would suffice to demonstrate Jewish religious influence among the Abyssinians.[1] Those terms were imported in pre-Christian times, but survived after the introduction of Christianity with slight shifts in meaning and substance.

Apart from such obvious Hebraic-Old Testament elements as ritual cleanness (particularly in connection with sexual relations), levirate marriage, etc., one has to consider such deeply rooted traditions—many of them reflected in the legend of the Queen of Sheba in all its manifold ramifications—as the Aaronite origin of the Aksumite clergy, the references to Abyssinians as *dakika Esrael* (children of Israel), and the consciousness of having inherited from Israel the legitimate claim to being regarded as the chosen people of God. It is clear that these and other traditions, in particular that of the Ark of the Covenant at Aksum, must have been an integral part of the Abyssinian national heritage long before the introduction of Christianity; for it would be inconceivable that a people recently converted to Christianity should *thereafter* have begun to boast of Jewish descent and to insist on Israelite connections, customs, and institutions—despite the widespread imitation of Israel to which M. Rodinson (*JSS*, 1964) has so rightly invited attention.

The circumstances attendant upon the introduction of Christianity into Ethiopia are sufficiently well known. It occurred about the middle of the fourth century and is attested in the *Historia Ecclesiastica* by Rufinus (345–410) as well as by evidence of a more circumstantial, though scarcely less secure, character. Two brothers from Tyre, Frumentius and Edesius, had worked as missionaries at the Court of Aksum. When they left the country, Frumentius went to Alexandria and was there consecrated Bishop of Aksum by St. Athanasius. Frumentius is called by Ethiopians 'Abba Salama, Revealer of the Light' in recognition of his zealous propagation of the new Faith. He

[1] Nöldeke, *Neue Beiträge*, p. 36; Polotsky, *JSS*, 1964.

was, of course, a Syrian, and this fact assumes—as we shall see presently —considerable significance for the development of Abyssinian Christianity.

These events took place during the reign of Ezana, the Constantine of Ethiopia, the gradual evolution of whose religious policy can be deduced from his coins and inscriptions in their replacement of pagan symbols and phrases by others of Christian connotation. According to Ethiopian tradition, Christianity was introduced at the time of two brothers with the symbolic names of Abreha ('he who has made light') and Asbeha ('he who has brought about dawn'). The motives which led Ezana to adopt Christianity are unlikely to have been entirely religious; the friendship of the Emperor at Constantinople was a factor which no King of Aksum, especially one so traditionally hostile to the Persians, could overlook.

The conversion of Abyssinia to Christianity is bound to have been slow in time and geographically sporadic, at least outside the principal centres. Conditions were thus propitious for both the co-existence as well as intermingling of very diverse strands of religious habits and practices. This may explain, in part, the remarkable syncretism that can be observed in Abyssinian Christianity.

Another factor conducive to the development of this syncretism was, of course, the provenance of the early missionaries in Abyssinia: the Syriac imprint, with which Frumentius and monks following upon him stamped Abyssinian Christianity, is yet a further Semitic element that can be detected not only in a particular doctrinal bias or even the Aramaic loan-words in Ethiopic (*haymanot* 'faith', *orit* 'Thora', etc.), but especially in the peculiarly Semitic religious concepts and semasiological development which those terms represent: *kwerban* (oblation, sacrifice, Eucharist), *salot* (prayer), *makdas* (sanctuary), *som* (fast), etc. The monophysites who rejected the definition of the Council of Chalcedon (A.D. 451) took refuge in Egypt, Arabia, and Abyssinia and thus contributed very notably to the spread of Christianity throughout the Aksumite Empire. At the same time, their infiltration determined once and for all the fanatical adherence of Ethiopia to the monophysite doctrine. Among these fugitives were the famous 'Nine Saints' who came to Ethiopia in the fifth century, founded monasteries and are said to have engaged in the translation of the Bible into Ethiopic. The New

Testament was rendered according to the Lucianic recension current in the Patriarchate of Antioch—yet another aspect of the Syrian monophysite impact.

The canon of the Scriptures of the Abyssinian Church comprises a number of apocryphal or deuterocanonical books such as Enoch, Jubilees, the 'Shepherd' of Hermas, Judith, Tobit, Ecclesiasticus, etc. Equal authority is attributed to the prescriptions of the Old Testament as to those of the New Testament. The Councils of Nicaea (325), Constantinople (381), and Ephesus (431) are recognized, while that of Chalcedon is rejected. In the person of the Incarnate Christ there was but a single, i.e. divine, nature. According to some, the human nature has been absorbed by the divine and thus disappeared, whereas others hold that the human nature has been so perfectly united with the divine that one single nature has resulted from this complete union. The Virgin is the Mother of God, rather than of Christ, and has a very special place in the Ethiopian cult.

Of the seven sacraments two have fallen into disuse: confirmation and extreme unction, although the latter possesses a special Ge'ez ritual (*Mashafa Qandil*). Baptism is practised by threefold immersion; in addition there is an annual commemoration of the baptism in the Jordan. The Eucharist is administered by the priest detaching the form of a cross from the fermented bread; he then dips it into the wine and offers it to the communicant. Confession is not made at regular intervals and usually only during grave illness. Holy Orders are conferred by the Metropolitan, generally upon scant evidence of the candidate's knowledge; but in recent times entrants to the ministry have probably been of somewhat higher attainments. Marriage is celebrated in the presence of a priest; divorce is admissible only in the event of adultery.

Circumcision is generally practised and is held to be a religious duty, even though there exists no specific ecclesiastical injunction. This custom is not confined to Semites alone, but appears in the form of a tribal badge or initiation rite also in other parts of Africa, Australia, and America. The *Fetha Nagast* (Chapter 51) decrees that circumcision is merely a 'custom' and has not the sanction of a 'legal precept'. The doctrinal position of the Abyssinian Church was always unenviable, caught as it was between the deeply rooted Judaic customs of the country and the necessity to maintain its theological prestige as a truly

Christian body. Fortunately, these stresses became acute only in times of foreign pressure or religious controversy; at other times the Abyssinian Church and nation have been at peace with their syncretistic Judaeo-Christian civilization and folklore.

The date of circumcision, i.e. the eighth day, is shared, to my knowledge, by Jews and Ethiopians only. This is the more remarkable because members of the Coptic Church in Egypt are circumcised at an age of between six and eight years, while Gallas, Muslims, and other influences in Ethiopia, with widely varying dates, would all combine to shake the Ethiopian adherence to the eighth day. Yet this date has been steadfastly maintained, no doubt under the impact of the Pentateuchal injunction.

One of the most notable features in Abyssinian Christianity is the survival of magical practices and prayers as well as a whole body of superstitious beliefs. Many of these magical prayers now combine their pagan substratum with a hastily and belatedly superimposed layer of divine invocations or references to the Virgin Mary and the Saints. Widespread is the *lelafa sedeq*, a parchment scroll tied to the body of the deceased and buried with him in order to guide him on the way to heaven. Belief in the *zar* (spirits) or *buda*, a human being possessed of the evil eye which by night is transformed into a mischievous hyena, is still ubiquitous.

It is likely that the majority of superstitious and magical practices are derived from the old Cushitic pagan beliefs; yet a very large body of magical craft, contrivances, and prayers were common to most peoples of the ancient Semitic world. How serious a danger sorcery, witchcraft, and magic constituted to the religion of the Hebrews may be gathered from Lev. 20:6. There is no doubt that many magical practices were so integral a part of the pagan folklore of Canaan that they were taken over into the Hebrew religion and given a fresh and sublimated significance. In this connection, one need only think of the *Urim* and *Thummim*, phylactery, and *mezuza*. The latter two were certainly meant to avert demons and other evil spirits and may be compared to the amulets (*mateb*)[1] worn by Ethiopians for the same purpose. In post-biblical times *Gematria* and *Notarikon* are the vehicles of magical calculations: and from here we get the disposition of letters in magic

---

[1] Cf. Walker, *The Abyssinian at Home*, chapter VI.

squares, the special patterns, the secret charms—all widespread in
Ethiopia. There is little doubt that the shield of David and the seal of
Solomon have a similar origin. Among the countless magical names
and words[1] in use in Ethiopia, *El*, *Elohe*, *Adonay* occur frequently.
Ludolf (*Commentarius*, p. 350) goes so far as to say that 'tota ista detesta-
bilis scientia a Judaeis originem habet' and claims that Kabbalistic doctrines and exercises brought about the abundance of magic and demons
in Ethiopia. If this is, perhaps, a slightly extravagant assertion, Ludolf is
on safe ground when he mentions[2] the extraordinary importance Jews
and Abyssinians alike attach to the effect of *name*. To both, knowledge
of the name means power over the person or the spirit.

Apart from the numerous magical names in Ethiopia which have an
obvious Hebrew origin, there are many others that are undoubtedly
derived from Cushitic lore, but all have been brought into harmony,
at least superficially, with the requirements of Christianity. However
pagan the spirit may be, *Maryam*, *Krestos*, etc., are rarely missing.
Christ himself has become the greatest of magicians, but he is closely
followed by Moses and Solomon.

In considering very briefly the prescriptions governing the consump-
tion of food,[3] it is important to appreciate the discrepancy between the
abstract doctrinal position of the Church and the actual state of affairs.
The *Fetha Nagast* and the *Confessio Claudii* (the purpose of the latter, in
the monophysite versus Jesuit controversy, was to minimize the
prevalence of Judaic elements in Abyssinian Christianity) appear to
deny the existence of special dietary requirements. In reality, however,
the Pentateuchal food laws have been, and are still, observed with some
strictness in Ethiopia. That applies in particular to the division into
clean and unclean animals, but while the prescriptions regarding
mammals and birds are generally scrupulously followed, the same does
not seem to be the case with regard to fish. This is probably due to the
fact that fish does not form part of the Abyssinian's normal diet, though
Conti Rossini has found[4] that fish without scales ranks among forbidden items of food.

[1] Cf. especially Strelcyn's excellent *Prières magiques éthiopiennes*.
[2] *Historia*, lib. III, cap. IV.
[3] Cf. *Ethiopia and the Bible*, pp. 100–3.
[4] *L'Abissinia*, p. 82.

Among the feasts of the Ethiopian Church, it might be well to refer first to the observance of the Sabbath. One of the principal accusations levelled by the Portuguese against the monophysite Ethiopians was the latter's adherence to the Jewish Sabbath in addition to Sunday. The history of Sabbath observance in Abyssinia is fairly chequered, and the sources are often ambiguous or even contradictory, but the retention of the Sabbath drew support from a number of unimpeachable authorities:[1] The Ethiopic *Didascalia* as well as Gregory of Nyssa—whose prestige amongst Ethiopians stands high—enjoin the keeping of both the Sabbath and the Sunday. And most significantly: is not the continued validity of the Decalogue and the Law expressly prescribed in Matt. 5:18 that 'one jot or one tittle shall in no wise pass from the law'?

While the position of the Sabbath has long been firmly established in Ethiopia, there had at one time been acute theological struggle until King Zar'a Ya'qob, in the fifteenth century, intervened to remove successfully the threatening schism between the two great monastic orders in Ethiopia; for the main point at issue in this controversy was the strict observance of the two Sabbaths (Saturday and Sunday) by the northern Eustathian monks (mainly based on Debra Bizen).[2] Zar'a Ya'qob did not introduce a new conception of the equality of the two Sabbaths, but merely gave preference to the long established northern tradition which, in the original home of the Semitized Aksumites, had always preserved Hebraic ingredients more faithfully.

There is a prodigious number of feasts in the Abyssinian Church. Among these one might mention *Keddus Yohannes* or *Addis* (or *hadesh*) *Amat* (New Year), *Maskal* (Feast of the Cross), *Leddat* (Christmas), *Gezrat* (Circumcision of Christ), *Temkat* (Baptism), *Tensa'e* (Easter), *Ergat* (Ascension), and very many others. But the prolificity of feasts in Ethiopia is caused by the very large number of commemorative days—all strictly observed—of angels (that of St. Michael occurs on the 12th of each month) and saints. There are thirty-three days annually in honour of the Virgin Mary!

The New Year and Maskal feasts display distinct Hebraic affinities. The dates, 11 and 27 September respectively, correspond closely to the Hebrew season of the *yamim nora'im*. With the introduction of

---

[1] Cf. Dillmann, *Kirchenordnung*, pp. 45 seq.
[2] Cf. *Ethiopia and the Bible*, pp. 109–13, and p. 67 above.

Christianity it became necessary to transform the celebration of the New Year into a Christian feast—without undue interference with the religious practices then in vogue—and in this way the Christian feast of *Keddus Yohannes*, St. John the Baptist, was superimposed on the ancient Judaic structure. Maskal, the feast of the finding of the True Cross, appears to have received its Christian sanction at the end of the four-teenth century, but the pagan and Hebraic rites associated with it point to a more ancient and more complex origin. The earliest meaning of these feasts—as was also the case in Israel—was no doubt seasonal: the month of Maskaram (= September) marked the end of the rains, the resumption of work, and the reopening of communications.

The days of fasting are even more numerous and are rigorously observed. Wednesday and Friday are regular weekly fasts (comparable to the Monday and Thursday fasts kept by Jews), and the total number of fasting days amounts to about 250 a year of which about 180 are obligatory for all.[1] The longest periods of fasting are those of Lent, Advent, and *Kweskwam* (forty days preceding the feast of the flight to Egypt). Fasts generally imply one meal a day to be taken either in the evening or just after midday, with total abstention from meat, fats, eggs, and dairy products.

It is well known that the liturgy of the Temple and the synagogue has exerted a considerable influence on services of the Christian Church as a whole and on the Eastern Churches in particular. The Ethiopic liturgy strongly reflects this general trend. King Zar'a Ya'qob had decreed in his *Mashafa Berhan* that religious instruction should be part of the divine worship. This tradition of 'learning' as an integral part of the service was undoubtedly inspired by the synagogue: interpretation, discussion, exegesis of the Scriptures go back at least to the days of Ezra and are clearly recognizable in the Hebrew and Ethiopic liturgical and didactic terminology. Zar'a Ya'qob had also reaffirmed that the books of the Old and New Testaments were to be read in their entirety during church services and, in the manner of the Hebrew *parashah* and *haftarah*, he placed special emphasis on the reading from the Law and the Prophets. Antiphonal singing, the importance of the Debtera (pre-centor, cantor), the significance of hymns and psalms in the worship, the liturgical chant accompanied by the sound of sistrum and the

[1] See Pollera, *Chiesa*, p. 299.

rhythmical beat of the prayer-stick are all part of the archaic rites of the Abyssinian Church.

The Ethiopic liturgy, *keddase* (cf. *kedushah* and Trisagion), contains fifteen anaphoras among which one is attributed to the Apostles, one to St. John the Evangelist, others to St. Gregory the Armenian, St. Athanasius, James of Serugh, etc.[1]

Until recently the ties of the Ethiopian Church with the Coptic Church in Egypt had been close, for the Archbishop of Ethiopia, under the authority of the Patriarch at Cairo, had to be an Egyptian Copt. But this arrangement, by which the See of St. Mark appointed an expatriate primate to Abyssinia who wielded supreme ecclesiastical power in an alien country with whose language, culture, and psychology he rarely became acquainted, was never wholeheartedly accepted by Ethiopians. After the return to his country of the present Emperor, in 1941, steps were taken towards having an indigenous bishop appointed as primate. An agreement with the Coptic Church in 1948 provided for the future selection of an Ethiopian monk to this office; and this, in fact, happened when the last Coptic Abuna died in 1950 and Abuna Baselyos was chosen as Archbishop. He was later raised to the dignity of Patriarch. Although the Ethiopian Primate still travels to Egypt for formal consecration, the Abyssinian Church now enjoys autocephalous status. The present Patriarch is Abuna Tewoflos.

As long as the head of the Church was a foreigner, the role of the *Etchege* as the premier indigenous cleric was one of great importance. As has been shown in the preceding chapter, the Etchege is the Prior of Debra Libanos. He has usually been close to the Emperor as counsellor and chaplain, and while the Court was still ambulatory, the Etchege followed it upon its peregrinations. The monks of Ewostatewos do not have a superior monastic office comparable to that of the Etchege, but traditionally seniority is accorded to the Prior of Debra Bizen.

The monastic rules of the Ethiopian Church derive from the founders of Egyptian monasticism, St. Antony and St. Pachomius. Monks make three professions: upon the first they receive the *kenat* 'girdle' or 'belt' (corresponding to the priestly *abnet*—Exod. 28); on the second the

[1] The Ethiopic Anaphoras have been investigated by E. Hammerschmidt in a thesis presented to Oxford University.

kobe (Amharic *kob*) 'skull-cap' (=Hebrew *koba*, and corresponding to
the priestly *misnefet*—*ibidem*); and, finally, the *askema* 'scapular' with its
twelve crosses which no doubt correspond to the twelve stones on the
hoshen (Exod. 28:21), the breast-plate of the High Priest on which the
askema appears to be modelled. The head of a monastery is styled
mamher 'Prior' (lit. 'teacher').

The secular clergy (*kes* (*keshi*) or *kahen*) are not bound by any vows
of celibacy and generally belong to families who exercise the ministry
almost hereditarily. They acquire knowledge by practice[1] and during
their assistantship as deacons. The Debteras are undoubtedly the most
educated class and may be described as lay clerks; they have received
some instruction in the Bible, especially the Psalter, and in the rules of
liturgical chant. They, like the rest of the clergy, cultivate the benefices
(*gult*), often of considerable size, assigned to the Church.

There is a large number of monasteries in Ethiopia, some of which
have played a significant part in the cultural, ecclesiastical, and political
development of the country. Among the most ancient and famous of
these are the northern Debra Libanos and Debra Damo in the Tigrai
and St. Stephen on an island in Lake Hayq. The Shoan Debra Libanos
dates from the thirteenth century and Debra Bizen from the fourteenth.
Churches and monasteries of great antiquity and considerable interest
may also be seen on some of the islands in Lake Tana.

Ethiopia is a country of churches. Their number is immense, and
their size varies from the little round village churches, usually perched
upon a hill, to large rectangular and octagonal buildings or modern
cathedrals constructed at Addis Ababa, Asmara, and some of the other
cities. The rectangular churches are generally older, while the round
ones are considerably more numerous. The most famous rectangular
sanctuary is St. Mary of Zion at Aksum—known already in the sixth
century—whose head is styled *nebura ed* (there exists only one other
dignitary thus styled, the *nebura ed* of St. Mary's Church at Addis
Alem—built by Menelik as the southern Aksum).

All churches have a threefold division which is likely to be modelled
upon that of the Hebrew Temple. That had already been recognized by
Ludolf. The outside ambulatory of the three concentric parts of the
Abyssinian church is called *kene mahlet*, i.e. the place where hymns are

[1] There now exists a well-staffed Theological College at Addis Ababa.

sung and where the Debteras or cantors stand. This outer part corresponds to the *haser* of the Tabernacle or the *ulam* of Solomon's Temple. The next chamber is the *keddest* where communion is administered to the people; and the innermost part is the *makdas* where the *tabot* (see below) rests and to which only priests and the king have access. In some parts of Abyssinia, especially in the north, the *keddest* (the *kodesh* of the Tabernacle or *hekhal* of Solomon's Temple) is called *enda ta'amer* 'place of miracle', and the *makdas* is named *keddusa keddusan* (the *kodesh hakkodashim* of the Tabernacle and the *debir* of the Temple). The form of the Hebrew sanctuary seems thus to have been preferred by Ethiopians to the basilica type that was accepted by early Christians elsewhere. Similarly, churches throughout Ethiopia are usually built upon a small hill overlooking the village or, at any rate, at the most elevated place available. The Tosefta mentions the same requirement for the site of a synagogue which is to be erected at the highest point of the town.

The Ark of the Covenant (Ethiopic *tabot*—according to the *Kebra Nagast*, Chapters 48 seq., it was abducted from Jerusalem) has formed the centre-piece of the Ethiopian Church and its service since time immemorial. In fact, it is the *tabot* and not the church building which is consecrated and gives sanctity to the church in which it is placed. The same is true of the early synagogue in which there was only one essential requirement: the *teba* or *aron* (ark). The veneration accorded to the *tabot* in Abyssinia up to the present day, its carriage in solemn procession accompanied by singing, dancing, beating of staffs or prayer-sticks, rattling of sistra and sounding of other musical instruments remind one most forcefully of the scene in 2 Sam. 6:5, 15, 16, where David and the people dance round the ark. The entire spectacle, its substance and its atmosphere, has caused all who have witnessed it to feel transported into the times of the Old Testament.

We must now consider, very briefly, some of the other religious manifestations in Ethiopia, though all of them are peripheral to our theme. For monophysite Abyssinian Christianity alone represents most truly the essence and substance of Ethiopia and her people.

There are, first, the *Falashas*[1] who live to the north of Lake Tana in Begemder, Semien, and Dembiya, and who are Ethiopians of Agaw

[1] See Leslau's valuable *Falasha Anthology*; also Aescoly's *Recueil de Textes Falachas*.

stock practising a peculiar kind of Judaism. This fact has given rise to the (in my view unsubstantiated) claim among some observers that the Falashas are the Jews of Ethiopia. 'Falasha' is a Semitic word and appears to connote 'emigrant', thus corresponding quite closely to the Hebrew *golah* ('exile'); the Falashas usually refer to themselves as *beta Isra'el* 'House of Israel' or by the Cushitic term *kayla* which is of somewhat uncertain interpretation. Since the fourteenth century they have been established in the Semien and Kwara regions and have been engaged in frequent battles for their independence and faith. Some of the victorious Emperors either dispersed them or ordered their compulsory conversion to Christianity, yet the Falashas have hitherto survived in small nuclei, representing a total number that has been variously estimated at between 15,000 and 60,000.

Their cult embodies a curious mixture of pagan-Judaic-Christian beliefs and ceremonies, but the Falashas are neither the only non-Christian and unconverted tribe nor the only sector of the Ethiopian population that has clung to so strange a religious amalgam. Similar claims have been made for the Gafat, the Kemant, and others. The Falashas do not know of any religious prescriptions outside the Pentateuch; Mishnah and Talmud are unknown to them. They have no knowledge of Hebrew, and the language of their prayers is Ge'ez—as is the case with their Christian compatriots. The feasts mentioned in the Pentateuch are observed by the Falashas in a manner often materially different from that of Jews elsewhere. Post-exilic feasts are not celebrated by them. The Sabbath is observed with considerable strictness, and the prescriptions regarding ritual cleanness are practised with great zeal—both features which exist among most other Ethiopians. In common with their monophysite neighbours the Falashas carry out circumcision on boys and excision (a kind of clitoridectomy) on girls. Monkery plays an important part in their community (and here, surely, is a fundamental distinction from Judaism), and their literature, though it includes some works peculiar to them, is mostly derived from general Ethiopian sources.

A dispassionate appraisal of the ethnic and religious position of the Falashas has generally been vitiated because—as W. Leslau has rightly said[1]—'most of the reports . . . about the Falashas have been incomplete

----

[1] *Falasha Anthology*, p. x.

and characterized by a Christian or Jewish missionary tendency which appreciably diminishes their usefulness and objectivity'.

The present writer feels convinced that all the evidence available points to the conclusion that the Falashas are descendants of those elements in the Aksumite Kingdom who resisted conversion to Christianity. In that case their so-called Judaism is merely the reflection of those Hebraic and Judaic practices and beliefs which were implanted on parts of south-west Arabia in the first post-Christian centuries and subsequently brought into Abyssinia. If this opinion is correct, then the religious pattern of the Falashas—even though it will have undergone some change in the past 1,600 years—may well mirror to a considerable extent the religious syncretism of the pre-Christian Aksumite Kingdom. It is in their living testimony to the strangely Judaized civilization of the South Arabian immigrants and their well-nigh complete cultural ascendancy over the Cushitic and other strata of the original African population of Ethiopia that we must seek the value and great interest of the Falashas today—and not in their rehabilitation as a long lost tribe of Israel (which is historically quite unwarranted). Like their Christian fellow-Ethiopians, the Falashas are stubborn adherents to fossilized Hebraic-Jewish beliefs, practices, and customs which were transplanted from South Arabia into the horn of Africa and which may here be studied in the authentic surroundings and atmosphere of a Semitized country.

Paganism in Ethiopia is now mainly confined to the lowland areas of the west and south. It takes a number of varying forms ranging from the purest animism associated with trees, stones, mountains, etc., to the faith of the Kunama in western Eritrea who believe in a supreme God, Anna, who, after completing the creation of heaven and earth, now rests from his labours and has nothing more to do—save for an occasional beneficent intervention to help his devotees against invaders and other enemies. Belief in spirits, good and evil, the latter mainly connected with illness, is very widespread in Ethiopia, and, as has already been indicated, is by no means limited to pagans. Forms of totemism are also encountered here and there when the eponymous animal is ritually slaughtered by the tribe and then consumed by its members. The Gallas believe in a supreme celestial deity, Wak, whose eye is the sun, but apart from this there are many other minor deities who reside in trees, rivers, and mountains.

Islam can be disposed of very quickly, partly because we have already reviewed the long conflict between Christianity and Islam in the preceding chapter, partly on account of its secondary importance to an understanding of the essential Abyssinia, and also because we possess in J. S. Trimingham's *Islam in Ethiopia* (O.U.P., 1952) an exceptionally competent survey of the subject.

It is interesting to observe that, though today nearly half of the population of the horn of Africa are Muslims, their impact on the character and substance of Ethiopia is as peripheral as is their geographical distribution all around the central highland plateau. The identification of Abyssinian Christianity with the political and cultural life of the country is so complete that no numerical increase in Islam has been able to touch the intrinsic nature of this phenomenon. Yet, any map of the distribution of religions in north-east Africa demonstrates most strikingly the Muslim encirclement of Abyssinia—everywhere except for the predominantly pagan south-west.

To Ethiopia, in this historic conception, the most notable group of Muslims are unquestionably the *Djabart*, for they alone enter into the life of the country. Djabart was originally the name of a region in the territories of Zeila and Ifat,[1] but was later applied to all the Muslim principalities of southern Ethiopia and, ultimately, to all Muslims living in the Ethiopian Empire. The term is sometimes also used by the Christian population of Ethiopia with reference to the Muslims of the Arabian peninsula and thus becomes identical with the term Muslim in general. In modern usage, however, Djabart is almost invariably employed in a narrow sense to describe the Muhammadan nuclei in the Christian plateau provinces of Eritrea, Tigrai, Amhara, Shoa, etc. According to Abyssinian tradition the word is derived from Ethiopic *agbert* 'servants (of God)'; in Amharic a Muslim is called *eslam* or *näggadye* ('trader'—which is a socially indicative, and factually accurate, description).

The Djabart or Djabarti live in families and small groups scattered

---

[1] Cf. Maqrizi, *al-ilmam*, Cairo, 1895, pp. 6 seq. See also DJABART in *Encyclopaedia of Islam*, new ed.

throughout the Christian highlands. Ethnically and linguistically (they speak Amharic, Tigrinya, etc.) they are indistinguishable from their Christian neighbours. Their knowledge of Arabic is generally limited to the minimum necessary for an understanding of the Koran. Some of them claim descent (with little or no justification) from the first Muslim refugees who were sent to the Negus by the Prophet. The majority, however, owe their conversion to the sultanates in south-east Ethiopia and to the invasion of Ahmad Grañ. In general, the relations between Djabart and Christians are friendly, though discrimination against the former was not unknown in the past, particularly in the deprivation of *rest* (the hereditary land-right), which led many of them into commerce and handicrafts.

Estimates of their numbers vary greatly, but it seems safe to say that there are upwards of 20,000 Djabart in the three plateau provinces of Eritrea and not less than 50,000 in Ethiopia. These figures exclude, of course, the fairly substantial number of Muslims, other than Djabart, who live in the Abyssinian highlands. The Djabart maintain a number of mosques and Koran schools; in *madhhab* (rite, especially juridical) they belong to the Malikiyya and Shafi'iyya.[1]

Islam is still making steady progress among the Cushitic and Nilotic peoples in the lowland areas, but none among the highland population of Semitic speech. Perhaps its simple and clear-cut theology makes a special appeal to the less sophisticated peoples in the hot and arid regions, with little or no civilization of their own. The universal call of Islam must have a great attraction in all those quarters where the particularistic and national message of Ethiopian monophysite Christianity can scarcely be expected to penetrate.

The Roman Catholic mission in Ethiopia is, of course, of long standing, but it has never been able to regain the prestige it possessed during the Portuguese Jesuit interlude. Yet, since the nineteenth century the Roman Church has been very active in both proselytizing and educational work. Naturally, the advent of the Italian colonial administration in Eritrea gave a notable fillip to these endeavours which proved to be particularly successful in the Akkele Guzay province. The

[1] For the special characteristics of Islam among the lowland peoples, the Dervish Orders, and juridical rites, see Trimingham, *Islam in Ethiopia*, Part 4. In Eritrea, in particular, the Mirghaniyya (or Khatmiyya) is of great influence and importance.

Catholics have learnt from earlier mistakes and failures, and now the Catholic Church of Ethiopian rite preserves much that is of particular significance or national pride in Abyssinian Christianity. An indigenous bishop is in charge of some 30,000 Roman Catholics in the Empire, and the fine *Collegio Etiopico* in the Vatican City has for long enjoyed the special favour of successive popes.

The most active of the Protestant missions are the Swedish Mission (whose educational work at Asmara, Keren, in the Mensa and Kunama regions as well as at Addis Ababa deserves the highest praise), the Sudan Interior Mission, and the Seventh-Day Adventists.[1]

[1] See now Donald Crummey, *Priests and Politicians: Protestant and Catholic Missions in Orthodox Ethiopia, 1830–1868*, Oxford, 1973.

VI

LANGUAGES

A GLANCE at any linguistic map[1] of Ethiopia will show, almost dramatically, the small, yet compact, Semitic island stretching from northern Eritrea to Addis Ababa in the south—surrounded on all sides by a vast Cushitic sea, with some Nilotic currents in the west and two tiny Semitic islets in the east (Harari) and in the south (Gurage). Numerically, the comparatively densely populated centre is about as strong as the immense, yet disjointed, scattered, and sparsely inhabited, areas of the peoples of non-Semitic speech. There are, perhaps, twelve million Semitic-speaking Ethiopians and nearly as many again who speak languages of the Cushitic and Nilotic groups, though the warning given in Chapter III must be reiterated here: in the absence of properly compiled statistics, all such figures are at best inspired guesses. One thing, however, is certain: the Semitic languages of Ethiopia represent, next to Arabic, the living Semitic tongues spoken by the largest number of people; Amharic is well in the lead, followed by Tigrinya. It is, of course, quite impossible to gauge how many native speakers of Cushitic languages are compelled, by the exigencies of official business or prestige, to use Amharic or, to a lesser extent, Tigrinya.

For the reasons which have already been stated in previous chapters, we shall mainly confine ourselves in this survey to the Semitic languages of Ethiopia, since they express the 'real' Abyssinia as we know it and are the virtually exclusive carriers of Ethiopian civilization, literature,

[1] See especially the maps in Tucker-Bryan, *Non-Bantu Languages of N.E. Africa; L'Africa Orientale*, p. 204; E. Ullendorff, *Semitic Languages of Ethiopia*.

and intellectual prestige. To this must be added the political influence of
Amharic as the official language of the Ethiopian Empire and of
Tigrinya as the principal tongue of the northern provinces. Of course,
the impact of the Cushitic languages on their Semitic superstrata has in
some cases been considerable, especially in the field of syntax, and will to
that extent be touched upon in the following pages. The position has
been well summed up by M. M. Moreno[1] in the form of a general
'law': the socially superior minority imposes its language by virtue of
its prestige, while the majority 'deforms' that language by virtue of its
large numbers.

The racial diversity and variegation of Ethiopia are mirrored in a
linguistic situation of great complexity and unusual interest which will
be a compensation to all those who fail to find in the literature of Ge'ez
the inspiration of Hebrew poetry or the vigour of the Gilgamesh epic.
The special geographical features of the country, the steep escarpment
which causes the most abrupt and sharply drawn linguistic boundaries,
the flux and reflux of population waves breaking against the mighty
mountain massif, have all combined to maintain within small areas the
most diversified conditions and to allow tiny ethnic nuclei to keep their
own linguistic characteristics. While in recent years great progress has
been achieved in the investigation of many little-known languages of
Ethiopia, Semitic as well as Cushitic (one need only think of E. Cerulli's
pioneering work on the Sidama languages (including Kaffa) and Harari
or W. Leslau's endeavours in the field of Gurage and Gafat), the
amount of work that remains to be accomplished, both in detailed
analysis as well as in synthesis and general classification, is truly
prodigious.

On the whole, the most fruitful approach to the Ethiopian languages
is from the *ensemble* of Semitics. True, some of the modern tongues
have been notably, others even very profoundly, influenced by their
Cushitic substrata, but none has yet lost its essentially Semitic character,
its original identity.[2] The Ethiopian languages are an important link in
the chain of the Semitic tongues. They often produce evidence and
corroboration where these have been lost in the other languages. They

[1] *L'azione del Cuscitico*, p. 130.
[2] Cf. on this question E. Ullendorff, 'What is a Semitic Language? (A problem
of linguistic identification)', *Orientalia*, January 1958, especially p. 73.

deserve, therefore, the same study and attention which most of those other tongues have, in fact, received.

In the many classification schemes that have, at one time or another, been proposed for the Semitic languages the position of Ethiopic has, to my knowledge, always been clear: a South Semitic language which is to be grouped with South Arabian. It would be quite possible to show reason why Ethiopic should be classified with, say, Hebrew (on account of many surprising lexical resemblances) or Akkadian (by virtue of similarities in the vocalism of the imperfect) or Syriac (for certain identical syntactical constructions) or Arabic (with like features in the sound pattern and the formation of internal plurals), but the value of all such classification schemes is purely pragmatic and calls for countless qualifications and contingent allowances. For it is comparatively easy to lump together any two languages and show the special affinities they bear. Classification into North, West, East, or South Semitic is unobjectionable if such a grouping is related to present-day habitat, but may obscure rather than illuminate if it is meant to reveal genetic connections and special relationships.

The linguistic significance of the Ethiopian languages lies not only in their geographical position as a bridge between Asia and Africa and in their proximity to the area, i.e. South Arabia, which is frequently considered to have been the original habitat of the Semites, but especially in their close contacts with the Hamitic tongues. In Ethiopia we find the most favourable conditions for observing the interaction of Semitic and Cushitic and thus for revealing the original unity of the Hamito-Semitic languages, a field to which Leo Reinisch and Marcel Cohen have made such massive contributions.

It has long been almost axiomatic that the South Arabian immigrants[1] imported into Africa a Semitic language, perhaps in very

---

[1] The view that the Semitic-speaking peoples of Ethiopia arrived there by way of the Arabian peninsula and by crossing the Red Sea is generally accepted as the most likely, and indeed geographically the only realistic, hypothesis. A. J. Drewes, however, has been at pains to point out (*Bibliotheca Orientalis*, 1956) that we possess no express *written* documents which would provide an indication one way or the other. While there may well be considerable latitude in regard to dating, I find it hard to appreciate Drewes' opinion, advanced with such erudition, that the historical data do not furnish an adequate basis for the hypothesis that Ge'ez 'issued' from South Arabian (*Inscriptions*, p. 92).

slightly varying forms, which in the course of time, by long independent development and through influence of the Cushitic substrata,
evolved into what we now call Ge'ez. The evidence[1] to support this
opinion has generally passed muster, though there have at times been
divergent views as to whether one or several of the South Arabian
dialects were brought westwards across the Red Sea and whether, perhaps, the differences between the various modern Ethiopian languages
have to be explained by derivation from different South Arabian
tongues that came into Africa.

Considering the comparatively small distinctions between the
various dialects of epigraphic South Arabian (at least in the purely consonantal skeleton which alone is known to us), we are, to my mind,
unlikely to find any indications of those rather minute differences in the
fully developed Ge'ez language. Nor does there appear to be any need
to make Amharic claim descent from an unknown 'sister'-tongue of
Ge'ez. It would be beyond the scope of this survey to assemble the
evidence in full, but the evolution of Amharic and the other modern
languages can best be envisaged in this way: classical Ethiopic, in the
course of time, spread over a fairly large area and, when political and
other circumstances were propitious (especially during the period of
disintegration and eclipse in the Middle Ages), eventually became
differentiated to such an extent that the varying speech forms were
mutually unintelligible. Very much the same occurred in the case of the
Romance languages. In both instances the languages of origin, Latin
and Ge'ez, are known to us from literary sources; in both cases the
crucial period between the classical language and the modern tongues,
the stage of splitting and differentiation, is shrouded in darkness; and
the resultant languages show about the same degree of evolution from,
and affinity to, the 'parent'-tongue and one another.

It is obviously quite impossible to be precise about the time when
Ge'ez had ceased to be South Arabian and had become a different
language no longer intelligible to traders from the east coast of the
Red Sea. This process was, of course, slow and gradual, but the distinctive identity of Ge'ez must have been established by the first century
B.C. or even earlier. In any event, it is impossible to pick out the year
or the decade when the African form of South Arabian turned into

[1] See Ullendorff, *Semitic Languages of Ethiopia*, *passim*.

Ge'ez—just as we cannot say at what precise moment Latin, which had spread over a large area, became 'modern Latin', i.e. Italian, or Spanish, or French. These transitions are fluid and progressive.

The most important transformations which Ge'ez has undergone—as compared with South Arabian—are briefly: the elimination of the interdental sounds; the disappearance of *ghayn*; the development of two *p* sounds; the emergence of several labiovelars. In morphology one notices especially the absence of deictic -*n* in the function of a definite article. Unfortunately, in many other important aspects no valid conclusions can be drawn on account of the incomplete state in which epigraphic South Arabian has been transmitted. In particular, we know virtually nothing about its vowels. As the epigraphic texts provide almost exclusively third person forms, we cannot tell whether Ethiopic was the only Semitic language where the suffix of the second person perfect employs -*k*.[1] In many instances the modern South Arabian languages support the evidence supplied by Ge'ez.

Syntactically, Ethiopic shows somewhat greater freedom than most other Semitic languages, an aspect which, under the impact of Cushitic, has been carried much farther in the modern Ethiopian languages where all conceptions of Semitic syntax are in total dissolution. In classical Ethiopic (Ge'ez), however, we can only speak of some greater latitude (attributed by several scholars to the influence of Greek which was quite strong in the heyday of the Aksumite Kingdom), but on the whole the basic ideas of Semitic syntax are intact. Probably through the influence of Syrian Bible translators we find certain resemblances to Syriac in the employment of some syntactical means, notably the proleptic use of the suffix-pronoun and the introduction of the direct object by *l*.

Lexicographically, quite a few words appear to have no Semitic correspondences and are often loans from one or other of the Cushitic substrata. It is, of course, in the sphere of the vocabulary that foreign influences find easiest access, and not infrequently this is the extent of their intrusion. The Ge'ez dictionary shows a marked resemblance to that of South Arabian,[2] but many words have received new and specialized meanings. In other cases it is likely to be purely accidental that the

---

[1] Details in op. cit., p. 10. See also M. Höfner in *ZDMG*, 108/1, 1958, p. 198.
[2] Cf. E. Ullendorff in *Africa*, April 1955, especially pp. 155-7.

limited vocabulary of epigraphic South Arabian (as known to us now
—limited despite the immense number of inscriptions that have been
discovered) does not contain words well attested in Ethiopic. And,
naturally, the vagaries of lexical development and linguistic propagation generally must always be kept in mind. Both South Arabian and
Ge'ez provide some instances of resemblances to North Semitic. Such
parallels between language groups at present widely separated geographically are, of course, well known also elsewhere.[1]

The South Arabian inscriptions in Ethiopia were followed a few
centuries later by Ethiopic epigraphic documents[2] in which Ge'ez
makes its first appearance as a new language—quite distinct from South
Arabian. We possess, unhappily, no Ethiopic literature (see next
chapter) from that period, and, as far as we can judge at present, the
life of Ge'ez as a spoken language seems to have been relatively short.
So, of course, was the full bloom of the Aksumite Kingdom. Its decline
began in the seventh or eighth century and was followed, some 200
years or so later, by the eclipse of Ge'ez as a living tongue, though it
continued to be Ethiopia's literary and ecclesiastical language to almost
the present day. It is, however, interesting to note that the classical
period of Ge'ez literature was between the thirteenth and seventeenth
centuries, i.e. hundreds of years after it had ceased to be a living language used in the day-to-day life of the people.

It is particularly unfortunate that the period from the ninth to the
twelfth centuries is enveloped in such impenetrable darkness owing to
the political upheavals which occurred at that time and which greatly
disturbed the continuity of Ethiopian history. No literary documents
of that period have come to light, and with the 'restoration' of the so-
called Solomonic dynasty in 1270 we find Ge'ez succeeded by a number
of other languages. Thus our knowledge of Ge'ez as a *living language* is
limited to the early epigraphic material (some short and not very
significant Aksum inscriptions reach down to the ninth century A.D.)

---

[1] See C. Rabin, *West Arabian*, pp. 26–8; E. Ullendorff in *Vetus Testamentum*,
April 1956, pp. 190 seq.; W. Leslau, *Ethiopic and South Arabic Contributions to the
Hebrew Lexicon*, 1958.

[2] Cf. Littmann, *Aksum Expedition*, Vol. IV, *passim*; E. Ullendorff, 'The Obelisk
of Matara', *JRAS* 1951; A. Caquot, J. Leclant, and A. J. Drewes in *Annales
d'Éthiopie*, I, 1955; Drewes, *Inscriptions de l'Éthiopie antique*.

and the Bible translations accomplished between the fifth and seventh centuries. If we possessed documents belonging to the tenth to twelfth centuries we might be able to observe more closely the gradual transformation of Ge'ez in the various areas in which it was spoken.

Through the influence of the Church and its wide ramifications (particularly the vast number of priests, village churches, and monasteries) Ge'ez was embalmed and kept in a permanently 'frozen' state throughout the centuries. One is, I submit, fairly safe in assuming that this 'freeze' reflects the stage Ethiopic had reached some time about the seventh or eighth century. From the beginning of the second millennium Ge'ez has occupied a position in Ethiopia which is similar to that of Latin in the European setting up to the seventeenth or eighteenth century. All written work was limited to those, i.e. generally the clergy, who were capable of manipulating the only medium worthy of literary expression. Whether by this ban on all vernaculars for purposes other than oral use much in the way of popular literary creation has been lost —or strangled at birth—must remain a matter for speculation.

Since—as we have seen—the great bulk of our knowledge of Ge'ez is derived from manuscripts which were prepared several centuries after Ethiopic had ceased to be used as a spoken language and which were written by scribes whose vernacular was usually Amharic, the question arises as to how we can know anything at all about the pronunciation of Ge'ez. The answer is that in Ethiopic—as indeed in Hebrew—we are inclined to rely on the traditional pronunciation of the language. But does there, in fact, exist a genuine tradition of Ge'ez pronunciation which embodies elements of the original mode in which Ethiopic was pronounced before its early demise? Or is the so-called traditional pronunciation of Ge'ez merely a reflection of the speech habits current in the various modern Ethiopian vernaculars?

It has often been thought that the 'school' pronunciation of Ge'ez must have been evolved on Amharic territory; yet while the Amharic element is obviously much stronger numerically, there is no reason to suppose that there exists an exclusive 'received' Amharic-influenced tradition of Ge'ez pronunciation. Generally, Ge'ez is pronounced in the Amharic manner in the south and in the Tigrinya manner in the north, i.e. the specific and distinct phonetic habits of these two vernaculars are also imparted to the reading of classical Ethiopic. This is not to say, though, that in a few isolated instances some genuine remnants of Geʿez pronunciation might not have survived. That would be particularly likely in cases where a certain feature diverges sharply from the phonetic practice of the vernacular in question. On the whole, however, it is well to regard all alleged manifestations of this traditional pronunciation with a good deal of scepticism. The process of transformation by which Geʿez merged in its successor tongues must have been so gradual and imperceptible that it is inherently improbable that elements of the *status quo ante* should have been singled out in the consciousness of those involved in this very process and have been handed down for preservation.

It has been shown that the literary exclusiveness of Geʿez had suppressed almost all information regarding the vernaculars. Fortunately, this ban seems to have been applied a trifle more leniently in the south, outside the area of the original Aksumite dominion, where Amharic is spoken.[1] Thus we do possess some old Amharic Imperial songs dating back to the fourteenth century. Later on, a purely temporary fillip was given to Amharic literary activities when, in the sixteenth and seventeenth centuries, the Jesuits employed Amharic for their propaganda against the monophysite dogma and translated into the vernacular such of the writings of their faith as might sway the people.[2] For this purpose they obviously considered Geʿez wholly unsuitable. But with the expulsion of the Jesuits the impetus given to the use of Amharic in writing had been spent and Geʿez regained its literary supremacy— until the middle of the nineteenth century, when Amharic publications began to appear. Of course, there exist earlier Amharic manuscripts and documents of state, even the odd religious treatise, but more often we only find Amharic glosses and admixtures to Geʿez MSS.

Tigrinya is the language which evolved in the area of the original home of the Aksumites, whereas Amharic represents the southern development of Geʿez strongly influenced by Cushitic, notably Agaw, elements. The earliest records of Amharic show that it was not then as far removed from the characteristics of classical Ethiopic as Shoan Amharic is today. In particular, it still preserved then, and possibly up

---

[1] Cf. Strelcyn, 'Matériaux pour l'étude de l'ancien amharique' in *JSS*, Spring 1964.

[2] See Cerulli, *Letteratura*, pp. 206–8.

to the seventeenth century, some of the laryngals, and other sound shifts had also not yet taken place; the vocabulary was somewhat less permeated with foreign elements. Tigrinya, on the other hand, was considerably more resistant to the acceptance of alien admixtures, and, being at the centre of traditional Ethiopian civilization, it was less directly subjected to the impact of so many racially and linguistically diverse substrata. A reconstruction of many Tigrinya and Amharic forms, however, will have to aim less at classical Ge'ez than at the obscure period of late Ge'ez which is so closely parallel to the epoch of vulgar Latin.

We must now have a brief look at the Semitic languages of Ethiopia as they are today:

Amharic has long been called *lesana negus* or *yanegus kwankwa*, 'the language of the king', for, though it has only in recent times become the official language (in the technical sense) of the Ethiopian Empire, it has for centuries been the language of the Court and the great majority of the population of the central tableland. Its indigenous name is Amarinya (or Amharinya) from the province of Amhara (with the gentilitial ending -*inya*, just as Tigrinya is composed of the name of the province of Tigrai + *inya*). Nowadays Amharic is spoken not only in its home province but covers most of the area south of the Tigrai to the edge of the rift valley. Yet even today there is no complete linguistic homogeneity in this region, and one will encounter several Cushitic languages within it of which Galla is the most important. Amharic, as the language of the sedentary population of the central Ethiopian highlands, is spoken predominantly by Christians. For the reasons already indicated, it is very difficult to give a reliable estimate of the number of Amharic speakers; they may range between 8 and 10 millions. There is little doubt that Amharic is slowly gaining ground, and the stationing of Amharic-speaking administrators throughout the country will in time strengthen its status as a *lingua franca* in most parts of the Empire.

There is general agreement that, considering the wide area covered by Amharic, there are remarkably few and insignificant dialectal variants. Such distinctions as do exist occur principally between the speech forms current in the provinces of Shoa, Begemder, and Gojjam. Investigations in this field cannot, however, be considered complete, and there remains wide scope for further detailed examination.

Amharic has undergone profound changes in its phonetic character: the laryngals have been reduced to *h* and the glottal stop—and even the latter is now rare. Palatalization is, perhaps, the most notable feature in the Amharic sound pattern. In verb-formation consistent doubling of the medial radical in the perfect and the use of composite tenses stand out. The far-reaching phonetic changes have resulted in the emergence of many bi-consonantal roots which are reducible to original Geʿez and general Semitic tri-consonantal formations. The use of auxiliaries is a most prominent aspect of the verbal system and of the idiomatic pattern of the language. The construct state has disappeared; the suffix -*n* indicates the direct object. The syntax is extremely involved and totally devoid of all Semitic conceptions: the verb is placed at the end of the sentence, and subordinate clauses are 'encased' and precede the main clause. Foreign students will, therefore, construe an Amharic sentence by beginning at the end. In recent times Amharic stylistic fashion as to long and involved or short and simple sentences has often varied.

The Amharic vocabulary has received many accretions of Cushitic origin, yet the Semitic stock remains appreciable, especially when many severely 'decomposed' roots are restored to their original form. That is, of course, not always possible, and in Amharic and Gurage the etymological game is more than ordinarily hazardous. Amharic is undoubtedly a most expressive language; its lexical resources seem very adequate, and adaptation of new forms or meaning variants can be accomplished with ease. Recent journalese has made rather exaggerated use of European loans which in many instances could have been satisfied from native supplies. The recently established 'Imperial Amharic Academy'[1] will be of great help in eliminating unnecessary foreign ballast and in bringing about a measure of standardization.

Of all Ethiopian languages (with the exception only of Geʿez) Amharic has enjoyed most attention by scholars. The first grammar was written by Ludolf more than 250 years ago; the most prominent of his successors were Isenberg, Praetorius, Guidi, Armbruster, and Cohen who have all written excellent grammars of this difficult, yet most

[1] See *Addis Reporter* of 27 June 1969 and *Negarit Gazeta* of 27 June 1972.

rewarding, language. Amharic literature will be discussed in the follow-ing chapter.

Tigrinya,[1] i.e. the language of the Tigrai province, is spoken in an area largely identical with that of the Old Aksumite Kingdom and may thus lay claim to being—at least geographically—the direct successor of Ge'ez. Its territory covers the eponymous Tigrai province, the three highland regions of Eritrea, Hamasien, Serae, and Akkele Guzay, the fringes of the administrative divisions of Keren and Massawa, and reaches as far south as Tembien and south-west as Wolkayt. The Tigrinya speakers form the compact, densely populated, agricultural block of the Eritrean and northern Abyssinian plateau. They are overwhelmingly monophysite Christians and are proudly conscious of their cultural and linguistic heritage. In 1945 I estimated[2] the number of Tigrinya-speakers at 1,300,000, of whom nearly 500,000 live in Eritrea. The total figure almost certainly requires con-siderable upward revision. There are, in my experience, remarkably few dialectal distinctions in Tigrinya; certain insignificant regional variants can be recognized in the Akkele Guzay and in some of the southern areas.

Tigrinya phonetics do not deviate markedly from the sound struc-ture of Ge'ez: spirantization may occur in some instances under relevant conditions, and two of the laryngals have coalesced in pro-nunciation (which had probably happened already in the later stages in Ge'ez). The morphology displays a few innovations in inflectional affixes and the use of auxiliaries in the determination of tenses, but the syntax is almost as far removed from the Semitic type as is that of Amharic. The vocabulary is a good deal less influenced by Cushitic elements than the Amharic dictionary, but Agaw components are by no means infrequent.

We possess some good Tigrinya grammars compiled by Praetorius,

[1] Correctly *tigriñña*. Often spelt *Tigriña*. Italian and French books mostly write *Tigrigna*. During the British occupation of Eritrea (1941–52) *Tigrinya* was adopted for purely practical reasons. Also referred to as *Tigrai* or *Tigray* and, erroneously, as *Tigre*. Tigrinya speakers themselves call their language *habesha*, i.e. 'Abyssinian' *par excellence*.

[2] *Exploration and Study*, p. 68.

Mauro da Leonessa, Conti Rossini, and Leslau. Francesco da Bassano
has given us a useful dictionary, although meanwhile we require
quite a substantial supplement, a need which even Abba Yohannes
Gebre-Egzi'abher's Tigrinya-Amharic Dictionary has not entirely
satisfied.

Tigrinya literature is still in its beginnings. There is very little
original creation, but among a good deal of translation a recent rendering into Tigrinya of *Robinson Crusoe* might be mentioned. Mission
societies have published the complete Bible in Tigrinya as well as a fair
number of religious books. Several codes of customary law have been
printed in addition to collections of proverbs and songs. The constitution of an autonomous Eritrean government (1952–62) greatly
stimulated the output of works in Tigrinya. It might also be mentioned
that Tigrinya was the first Ethiopian language to possess a regular
daily newspaper (Amharic followed a little later). Yet there have long
existed weekly journals in Amharic, while the first regular publication
in Tigrinya was inaugurated as late as 1942, when the British
Administration founded the *Eritrean Weekly News*.

Tigre (in the Kassala province of the Sudan it is generally referred to
as *al-Khassiya*) might also be called northern or lowlands Tigrinya, for
that is its genesis. But the sharp geographical barrier of the escarpment
and long independent development have brought about a clear differentiation, so that nowadays the two languages are mutually unintelligible. The area of Tigre comprises the eastern lowlands of Eritrea (i.e.
the administrative division of Massawa and the Dahlak islands), the
northern and western plains (the Keren and Agordat divisions), the
Mensa, Marya, Ad Temariam, Ad Tekles, Beni Amer tribes as well as
many smaller tribal units which need not be enumerated here.[1] The
Beni Amer overflow into the Kassala province. Several tribes are
bilingual, e.g. Tigre-Bilen or Tigre-Beja.

The Tigre-speakers constitute the pastoral and nomadic sector of the
Eritrean population. Almost all of them are Muslims. The total number
of Tigre-speakers, in both Eritrea and the Sudan, has been estimated at
some 250,000–300,000.

There appear to exist some dialectal divergences between the eastern

[1] For details see Tucker-Bryan, *Non-Bantu Languages*, pp. 132 seq.

and western lowlands, but owing to the highly unsatisfactory state of
our knowledge of Tigre it is very difficult to express oneself in more
than purely impressionistic terms about the question of dialects in
Tigre.[1] Since the populations of the eastern and western plains have
virtually no contact with each other, the likelihood of divergent
linguistic development is very considerable.

Unlike Tigrinya, Tigre possesses no velar fricatives, and its sound
structure has generally not been subjected to heavy pressure by non-
Semitic substrata. The verbal pattern in the perfect is *qatla* (in contrast
to Ge'ez and Tigrinya *qatala*). The syntax is somewhat less influenced by
Cushitic than is the case with Tigrinya and Amharic, but the existing
documents are generally either translations or songs and proverbs with
little scope for the free flow of prose style. In the sphere of the vocabulary the action of Beja and Bilen can be discerned.

Until recently there existed no proper dictionaries of Tigre, for the
few word-lists that had been published could not be said to have more
than interim value. We now possess Littmann and Höfner's *Tigre
Wörterbuch* whose appearance was a major event for all students of
Tigre. We are poorly placed for grammars. The outline prepared by
the Missione Cattolica is of some practical value but has no scholarly
pretensions; it is also somewhat influenced by the compilers' knowledge
of Tigrinya. Leslau's useful sketch is based on printed texts in the
Ethiopic script rather than on living acquaintance with Tigre. In 1954
a small mimeographed manual of Beni Amer Tigre was issued by two
district officers who had experience of the language during their work
in the Sudan. F. R. Palmer's work on the Tigre noun appeared in 1962.
We are desperately in need of as many well transcribed texts as possible
from all parts of the Tigre-speaking area.

Tigre cannot boast any written literature, but Littmann has taken
down large numbers of songs and dirges which are collected in several
stout volumes of his Princeton texts. The Gospels, the Psalter, religious
books, and some customary law codes have been published by Swedish
missionaries. Tigre-speakers are very largely illiterate, and those who
have pretensions to literacy generally turn to Arabic; as Muslims
and traders they frequently find Arabic a more useful means of

---

[1] Mr. S. Raz is at present concluding a doctoral thesis on Tigre which will, it is
hoped, shed light on many of these problems.

communication. There is no doubt that Tigre is losing ground in favour of Arabic, but it is as yet impossible to express this in terms of figures. The decision of the Eritrean Government, in 1952, declaring Tigrinya and Arabic the official languages of Eritrea (although many Tigre-speakers know little or no Arabic) was significant and augured ill for the future of Tigre.

In order to convey an idea of the relationship of Amharic, Tigrinya, and Tigre towards each other and towards Ge'ez, we might enlist the helpful parallel of the Romance languages. If Ge'ez is compared to Latin, Tigrinya takes the place of Italian (both because it seems most closely akin to the 'parent'-tongue and also on account of its continuance in the original home), Tigre would then be likened to Spanish, and Amharic to French (also because it has been subjected to the most far-reaching changes).

The small Semitic islands to the east and south of the Amharic area vary in size and significance. Some of them have preserved Semitic characteristics which are lost elsewhere, and in a few instances we find curious parallels with the North Ethiopian languages. These parallels are probably due—as has already been mentioned in Chapter III—to the stationing in those regions of military garrisons from the north. Some progress has been made in the disentanglement of traits of North Ethiopian, Amharic, and Cushitic origin, but future tasks are still immense and of great complexity.

Harari (its indigenous name is Adare) is the language spoken in the town of Harar in eastern Ethiopia. It is surrounded on all sides by Galla and Somali which have left their imprint on Harari, but a greater influence, especially in the sphere of the vocabulary, has been exerted by Arabic—owing to the long Muslim conquest and Harar's position as the premier Muslim city in Ethiopia. Since the town came under effective Ethiopian authority, towards the end of the last century, the influence of Amharic has grown, and it seems likely that the latter will slowly displace Harari altogether. The number of those still capable of speaking Harari has been estimated by Cerulli at 35,000.

Harari has generally been written in Arabic, and not Ethiopian, characters. Its literature is limited to some songs and the codification of Muslim customary law. In its scholarly treatment the names of Cerulli, Cohen, Littmann, and Leslau deserve mention.

Gurage has generally been referred to as a 'dialect cluster'. It is spoken in an area to the south-west of Addis Ababa and is circumscribed by the rivers Awash and Omo as well as by Lake Zway. Gurage is surrounded by Galla in the north and east, and by Sidamo in the south and west; from Amharic it is separated by a fairly narrow Galla corridor, and—as Bruce had already mentioned—many Gurage speak Amharic in addition to their own language.

The linguistic situation is one of quite exceptional complexity in an area of such limited extent. According to Leslau, we can distinguish three groups: (1) Eastern Gurage (including Selti, Wolane, and two or three other dialects); (2) Western Gurage (including Chaha, the most important dialect, Ezha, Muher, Ennemor, etc.); and (3) Northern Gurage, represented by Aymallal. Internal classification as well as relationship to other Ethiopian languages are still a matter of debate, and here remains a most promising task for the linguist. As in the case of Harari, northern military colonies have probably been 'grafted' upon a Cushitic stock, in this instance of Sidama origin. The evidence supporting this view is both linguistic and historical.[1] The number of Gurage-speakers is estimated at 350,000.

Gurage is characterized by the extraordinary debility of the liquids and the strange pattern of their interchange which has been clarified in a brilliant study by H. J. Polotsky. It abounds in palatalized and labialized phonemes. The dictionary, apart from having preserved some elements of an old Semitic stock, displays large numbers of Cushitic, mostly Sidamo, words. A study of the 'decay' of Semitic roots in Gurage is a fascinating pursuit. There exists no Gurage literature; a catechism in Chaha has been published, and we are indebted to European scholars for making transcribed texts available.[2] The writings of Cohen, Polotsky, and especially of Leslau, Hetzron, and Goldenberg have considerably

---

[1] Cf. E. Ullendorff in *Africa*, 1950, pp. 336-7.
[2] Of considerable interest is Sahle Sellassie's *Shinega's Village*, a description of Gurage life.

enhanced our knowledge of this language. Their results, at times conflicting, could not be embodied in the present outline.

Gafat was spoken by tribes in the Blue Nile region of the Gojjam
province. All we possess of this language is a seventeenth- or eighteenth-
century manuscript of the Song of Songs in the Bodleian Library, on
the basis of which Leslau has provided a grammatical outline of Gafat.
When he visited the area in 1947 he managed to collect, after considerable endeavours, a total of four people who could still speak the language. In a more recent study Leslau has made the results of this
investigation available, and we may now assume that no further
information on this language is likely to come to light, for already over
a hundred years ago Charles T. Beke had found that Gafat was 'on the
eve of extinction';[1] one may, therefore, expect that it has now virtually
breathed its last.

Argobba is—or rather was—spoken to the north-east of Addis Ababa.
It is disappearing rapidly in favour of Amharic, and only a few hundred
elderly people are still able to speak it. Argobba is closely related to
Amharic. We are indebted to M. Cohen for nearly all the information
we possess about this language.

With a few exceptions, our knowledge of the *Cushitic* languages is
still highly unsatisfactory and grossly deficient. These exceptions are
Galla (thanks mainly to Praetorius and Moreno), Somali (Moreno and
Andrzejewski), the Sidama languages including Kaffa (Cerulli),
Kemant (Conti Rossini), Beja and Bilen (Reinisch and F. R. Palmer).
The best factual survey on the present state of available information
may be found in Tucker-Bryan's *Non-Bantu Languages* (see bibliography); a few general observations on the distribution of the Cushitic
languages have already been made in Chapter III, above.

Here it will suffice to add some remarks on the special importance of
the Agaw languages (now being studied by R. Hetzron), for the Agaw
peoples formed the original population of the northern and central
Ethiopian plateau, and their speech has exerted great influence on that
of the immigrant Semites. Nowadays Agaw is primarily employed for

[1] *Proceedings of the Philological Society*, 1846, p. 92.

'home use', as all official contacts require a knowledge of Amharic, Tigrinya, or Tigre (as the case may be). Virtually all Agaw are, therefore, bilingual, and their own languages appear to be dying out—with the possible exception of Bilen.

In all questions regarding the non-Semitic substrata of Amharic, Tigrinya, and Tigre, Agaw must take first place. Ethiopians themselves refer to all the original inhabitants of their country collectively as Agaw. An Ethiopian historian[1] begins his account of the Agaw: 'The Agaw tribe came [into the country] together with the army of Menelik I'—which has to be understood both as a compliment and an indication of a very early date. In any event, it is the amalgam of the Agaw with immigrant Semitic elements which has given rise to the main Ethiopian type, ethnically as well as linguistically, as it has emerged in historically attested times.

This survey has to be concluded with a few summary remarks on the *Ethiopic script*. As known to us today it represents a quasi-syllabic system of writing in which each character consists of one consonant followed by a vowel (or zero). This syllabary developed in the third and fourth centuries A.D.; we are, however, in possession of some inscriptions in which the early purely consonantal form of the Ethiopic alphabet has survived.

The Ethiopic script, in its unvocalized shape, is derived from the South Arabian alphabet.[2] From a comparison of the two scripts it will be seen that their basic forms are to all intents and purposes identical, and such slight changes as have occurred are due to (a) the tendency towards round forms; (b) the changed direction of writing; (c) the turn

[1] Aleka Tayye in his Amharic *History of the People of Ethiopia*, especially pp. 28 seq.

[2] This hitherto generally accepted view has been challenged by J. Ryckmans. See the exchange of articles between J. Ryckmans and E. Ullendorff in *Bibliotheca Orientalis*, January 1955, and September–November 1955, respectively. Ryckmans' view is, briefly, that the Ethiopic alphabet has its origin not in the South Arabian alphabet, but in a Thamudean form of writing. A. J. Drewes has supported J. Ryckmans' hypothesis (*Annales d'Éthiopie*, I, pp. 121–6), but I agree with W. Leslau's counter-arguments (*AJA*, 1958, p. 112).

For a detailed discussion of the Ethiopic syllabary see E. Ullendorff in *Africa*, 1951, pp. 207–17.

of some characters by ninety degrees. The South Arabian script had often been *boustrophedon* (right- or left-running in alternate lines), whereas the Ethiopic syllabary runs from left to right. This difference is of little moment: it has merely caused certain minor modifications in the shape of some letters and may well be due to the influence of the Greek script (from which the numerals have been borrowed with a subsequent endeavour to adapt them to existing Ethiopic forms). Since there are some distinctions between the South Arabian and Ge'ez sound patterns, Ethiopic has discarded some letters extant in South Arabian and has also fashioned two new characters (both *p* sounds) unknown in South Arabian.

The oldest Ethiopic inscriptions are unvocalized texts of the type well known to us from other Semitic languages. But later Ge'ez pursued the most original course taken by any Semitic script in denoting vowels by a variety of changes in the structure of the consonantal symbol. Vowels have thus become an integral part of Ethiopic writing which now assumed the character of a syllabary—yet without sacrificing the general Semitic conception of the predominance of consonants over vowels. It would seem that the Semitic idea of the consonantal skeleton as the carrier of primary semantic value was so deeply ingrained in the consciousness of the people that no other course appears ever to have been contemplated. It is now widely accepted that the introduction of the vowel denotation came as the result of gradual development rather than as an individual act of reform. Each letter has seven different forms (with the exception of the labio-velars which possess five only) depending on the vowel which it incorporates; in this way the Amharic alphabet (which has a few characters more than Ge'ez) is made up of 33 letters multiplied by seven plus four labio-velars multiplied by five=251.

The seven Ethiopic vowel orders (*ä, u, i, a, e, ə* (or zero), *o*) all express, at least in the present writer's view,[1] qualitative distinctions only, and each one of them can be either long or short. The sequence of these seven vowels is old and well-established, but we know nothing about the underlying reason; it must be purely fortuitous, as there are no apparent graphic or phonetic causes which might explain it.

[1] Expatiated in *Semitic Languages of Ethiopia*, pp. 158 seq.

Of equally difficult explanation is the letter-order of the Ethiopic consonantal signs which differs sharply from that of the Canaanite-Greek alphabet. It has given rise to many theories, some ingenious, others fanciful, but so far a really plausible explanation has eluded us. It is, of course, possible that there is no overriding principle guiding the sequence of the Ethiopic alphabet and that the order is largely accidental. A new element, and one of some promise, was introduced into the consideration of this question when, in 1951, an American expedition to South Arabia, under the archaeological direction of Professor W. F. Albright, discovered at Timna a series of paving stones *in situ*, marked with letters of the Qatabanian alphabet and revealing a sequence resembling that of the Ethiopic alphabet.[1] However, this find has raised some new problems as well, and the question can scarcely be considered resolved.

Another crux connected with the Ethiopic alphabet relates to the names of the letters. It must now be regarded as virtually certain that the 'Abyssinian' letter-names current in Europe and entirely unknown in Ethiopia were invented—as had first been suggested by Aleka Tayye[2]—by Tesfa Sion who had printed the New Testament in 1548. It is in that volume that the names make their first attested appearance, and it is probable that the Ethiopic nomenclature was modelled on the well-known names of the Hebrew-Greek alphabet. The only letters which have names in present-day Ethiopia are those which are no longer distinguished in pronunciation in some of the modern vernaculars and whose specific naming has thus assumed some practical importance.[3]

There are two shortcomings of the Ethiopic script which are very disturbing: (*a*) the absence of a sign showing the doubling of a consonant. This is particularly serious because gemination is not only of phonetic importance, but is frequently indicative of phonemic distinctions as well; and (*b*) the ambivalence of the sixth vowel-order which may either express ə (corresponding to Hebrew *shwa mobile*) or zero, i.e. the naked consonant without vowel (corresponding to Hebrew *shwa quiescens*). Only a knowledge of the languages concerned can

---

[1] See A. M. Honeyman's article in *Africa*, April 1952.
[2] In Mittwoch, *Traditionelle Aussprache*, p. 9.
[3] Details in *Africa*, 1951, pp. 211–14.

resolve these difficulties; the uninitiated reader will get no assistance from the script.

Finally, words were originally separated from each other by a small perpendicular line which later, in manuscript literature, gives way to two dots (one on top of the other). These dots have retained their function as word-dividers to this day.

Postscript

The widely accepted views on the relationship of the Semitic Ethiopian languages and their classification have now been challenged by R. Hetzron in a characteristically acute study (*Ethiopian Semitic*, Manchester University Press, 1972). This is not the place to discuss Hetzron's thesis which merits the most detailed examination. The present writer, while greatly admiring Hetzron's learning, remains unconvinced in many important respects, particularly in view of some grave historical objections.

VII

LITERATURE

LITERATURE in Ethiopia means Geʿez literature—at least up to
the nineteenth century, when books in Amharic began to
come off the printing presses. Considering the relatively small
number of available studies of detail as well as the peculiar limitations
of the Ethiopic literary *genre*, we are surprisingly well placed for comprehensive sketches of Ethiopic literary history (see Bibliography).
From Ludolf to the present day the main attraction of Ethiopic literature
to European scholars has undoubtedly lain in all that this literature has
preserved, in translation, of earlier and more original literary creations.
Thus the great interest in the Ethiopic version of the book of Enoch[1]
derives, of course, from the fact that in the Ethiopic language alone the
complete text of that work has been preserved. Furthermore, the literary
and cultural relations between Ethiopia and other countries of the
Christian Orient were examined with a view to a clearer understanding
of the origin and development of Oriental Christian Churches and
Oriental Christian literatures. It was for these reasons that the main
attention had hitherto been given to translations rather than to the
original aspects of Ethiopic literature. Only comparatively recently
E. Cerulli[2] has broken fresh ground in redressing the balance and
offering us a *visione d'insieme*: not, of course, to deny the considerable

---

[1] Aramaic fragments of Enoch have been found among the Dead Sea Scrolls
(cf. J. T. Milik in *Revue Biblique*, LXIII, 1, 1956; LXV, 1958). A fresh study of
Enoch in the light of this Aramaic material as well as a new edition of the text are
now being prepared by M. A. Knibb and E. Ullendorff.

[2] *Storia della letteratura etiopica*, Milan, 1956; paperback revised ed., 1968.

influence in Ethiopia of Greek and Christian Arabic literature, but to present a revised estimate of a literature which Cerulli found unexpectedly full of merit.[1]

It has become rather a commonplace, accepted by the expert and the uninitiated alike, to refer to Ethiopian literature somewhat condescendingly as either 'purely ecclesiastical' or 'merely translational'. The present writer must confess that, in working on Ethiopic literary texts, he has frequently been reminded of the great Nöldeke's doubts (expressed à propos of pre-Islamic Arabic poetry)[2] whether the aesthetic pleasure which this study affords is worth the pains one has to take in order to arrive at an understanding of those texts. Yet, as in the similar case of Arabic poetry, such study of Ge'ez literature seems indispensable to a real appreciation of the character of the Ethiopian people. To what extent Cerulli's new and favourable estimate of Ethiopic literature can be sustained, will very largely remain a matter of literary taste, but more artistic merit and historical relevance can certainly be detected in many Ge'ez manuscripts, edited and unedited (and there are still vast numbers of the latter), than has hitherto been conceded.

The formative elements that have contributed to determining the character of Ethiopic literature are manifold: there are, of course, first the Semitic immigrants from South Arabia who inspired the inscriptions on stone and from whom no doubt much more emanated that can now no longer be specifically attributed. Greek influences can readily be discerned in epigraphic documents, in aspects of writing, and literary beginnings, but it is far more difficult to identify those general Oriental currents that were drifting towards the western shores of the Red Sea: Egyptian, Hellenistic, Byzantine. And with the introduction of Christianity into Ethiopia the new religion became the focus and expression of all literary creation; it was also the filter through which every facet of thought, old or new, had to pass—to be accepted, rejected, or modified. How much was suppressed and lost in this process can never be known. Christianity was often projected into pre-Christian times as well, where the principal recipient of this anachronistic treatment is, perhaps, Alexander the Great, who is made to start his letters with the Trinitarian formula.

---

[1] See now also L. Ricci's excellent *Letterature dell' Etiopia*, Milan, 1969.
[2] *Fünf Mo'allaqat* in *SBWA*, 1899, p. 1.

Christianity naturally brought its own allies, political as well as literary, first in Syria (with the influx of Syrian translators and Syriac loanwords) and then in Egypt (with the impact of Christian Arabic, and to a much lesser extent Coptic,[1] literature). Later still, the peripatetics of the Ethiopian community in Jerusalem established connections (investigated in two weighty tomes by E. Cerulli) with the Eastern Mediterranean and, beyond that, with parts of Europe. But Ethiopic literature always maintained its Christian character, the peculiar trait of its indigenous monophysitism, allied to the Ethiopian State, the Court, and the person and institution of the *negusa nagast*.

The 'indigenization' which we have previously observed in other facets of Ethiopian civilization is prominent also in the field of literature —and here in a very tangible form. Many of the works that were rendered into Ethiopic from other languages were 'translated' in the most literal sense of that term: they were conveyed into the spirit and ambiance of Christian Abyssinia, adapted and transformed. Some of them, such as the *Fetha Nagast* ('Legislation of the Kings'), were subjected to such a degree of re-thinking and localization that the resultant metamorphosis bears little resemblance to the original. The relationship between pattern and copy, or model and reproduction, turns out to be so intricate that all the minutiae of research (and who knows how many Ph.D theses!) have to be enlisted to disentangle this complex fabric.

The inscriptions of Yeha, the Akkele Guzay, and finally the great trilinguals of King Ezana, written in South Arabian, Ethiopic, and Greek, are the only literary remnants of Ethiopia's pre-Christian past. The same Ezana also ushers in the Christian era with a further inscription which, under a veneer of Christian invocations, displays in every other respect the lapidary style so familiar from the great Oriental triumphal monuments, be they the annals of Assyrian kings or the victory recital of Mesha the Moabite.

The foremost literary achievement of the Aksumite period was the translation of the Holy Scriptures, which was probably a gradual process extending over a long period, from the late fourth or early fifth century till the seventh. The translators were very largely Syrian monks

---

[1] The Coptic influence was probably not exerted directly but through the medium of Arabic. Cf. Cerulli, *Letteratura*, pp. 31–3.

who had come to Ethiopia in order to escape the Byzantine persecution of the monophysites. For the Old Testament they made use of the Greek version, the Septuagint, but critical examination of the Ethiopic Bible translations is still not sufficiently advanced to establish with certainty that this is true of all the books of the canon of the Old Testament.[1] The rendering of the New Testament is based—as has already been indicated in Chapter V—on the Lucianic recension that was current in Syria. The Aramaic imprint on ecclesiastical Ge'ez, dating not only from this period,[2] is clear and unmistakable, yet it has been so completely absorbed that it has become a characteristic part of the Ethiopic linguistic patrimony.

The translation of the Bible comprises, as we have seen, all canonical and apocryphal books in addition to some pseudepigrapha that were accepted as genuine in Abyssinia. Among these are the Ascension of Isaiah, Jubilees, Enoch, Paralipomena of Baruch, etc., all works for which the Ethiopic text is of paramount importance.

There are one or two other works that belong to this first, Aksumite, period of Ethiopic literature. The monastic *Rules of Pachomius*, of which also Greek, Syriac, and Latin versions are extant, are of considerable practical significance in a country which derives its monastic regulations and institutions from Egypt, but the Ethiopic text has been expanded to cover the special contingencies of monastery life in Abyssinia. The *Kerillos* (Cyril) is a collection of christological writings attributed to several of the Fathers of the Church. It takes its name from Cyril's treatise, *De recta fide*, with which the book opens. Finally, mention must be made of the *Physiologus* (*Fisalgos*), the famous collection of information on animals and plants, a type of natural history, which was very much in vogue during the Middle Ages. This work, liberally expanded with homiletics, was translated into Ethiopic from Greek at this early period. The Syrian monks in whose country the original had been composed no doubt brought this book to Abyssinia, where it attained as much popularity as it achieved in its translations into other oriental and western languages. Later on, when a more scientific approach showed up the legendary character of much of the material contained in this work, the western Church no longer looked with favour on its

[1] See *Ethiopia and the Bible*, chapter I.
[2] Cf. Polotsky in *JSS*, 1964.

propagation, but in Ethiopia it retained its appeal for a long time. Since we now possess only late Greek MSS. of the *Physiologus*, the early Ethiopic version has considerable text-critical value.

The gap of five centuries which follows upon the Aksumite period takes us to the late thirteenth and early fourteenth centuries, to the 'restoration' of the Solomonic dynasty. The interval had seen the decline of the Aksumite Empire, a time of decadence, invasion, and destruction. No literary documents from that period of eclipse have survived, but it would be rash to say that it had been one of utter intellectual sterility. Certainly the chronicles of the early Solomonic kings presuppose at least some measure of literary preparation. The loss of all pre-'Solomonic' manuscripts might be due, in part, to destruction wrought by external foes and internal disorders, but it could also be the partial result of a rigorous censorship and inquisition that were aimed at disposing of all evidence of an un-Solomonic and unorthodox past.

Extremely few Ethiopic manuscripts have been preserved that can securely be attributed to this earliest time of 'Solomonic' literary activity. Most of them are later copies, for it must be recalled that between that period and ours lies the fearful holocaust of Grañ's destructive fury. Also, the dating of Ethiopic MSS. presents considerable problems. The conditions in which MSS. are usually kept in Ethiopia expose them to damp as well as to damage through other causes and thus tend to give them an appearance of greater age than they actually deserve. The most reliable indications in determining the approximate date of MSS. are still furnished by palaeographical criteria,[1] although these have to be employed with much caution and qualification. Fortunately, however, a small number of fourteenth- and fifteenth-century MSS. have survived and can be seen in some of the fine collections in Ethiopia (at the monasteries of Debra Libanos, Debra Bizen, Gunda Gundie, Lake Tana, and others) and in Europe (Bibliothèque Nationale, British Museum, etc.). But Conti Rossini has convincingly shown[2] that Zotenberg's catalogue (see Bibliography) errs in ascribing some of the Paris MSS. to the thirteenth century.

---

[1] Cf. Wright, *B.M. Catalogue*, p. x, and especially the important observations by C. Conti Rossini, *Collection d'Abbadie*, pp. 556–65.

[2] *Collection d'Abbadie*, pp. 555–6.

Ethiopic manuscript art reached a high degree of perfection between the fourteenth and eighteenth centuries, in the writing material itself as well as in calligraphy and illustration. Since then there has taken place a steady decline, though even today one may still on occasion encounter a scribe of exceptional skill and attainment. Manuscripts generally consist of vellum; the best of them, usually prepared for the Court, large churches, or rich monasteries, are written on expensive goatskin, whereas for ordinary purposes sheepskin is used. For some of the largest MSS. as many as 100–150 goats must have been killed to provide the necessary parchment. Quires vary in size, but usually contain ten leaves; each quire has a consecutive number to guard against errors in binding. The number of columns to each page is generally two, but smaller MSS. have one only, while the largest run to three columns. Ink, made of hot-water extract of galls, is black and durable, but the paints used for rubrication are, as a rule, of much less solidity. The pens, or reeds, are ordinarily tried before use, either on the blank pages at the beginning or at the end, where we find the stereotype formulae: *fatina bere'* ('trial of the pen') or *bere' sanay* ('a fine pen'). Ethiopian bindings consist of thick wooden boards, often covered with leather; and the entire volume is then placed into a case with straps, made of rough hide, so that it can be slung over the shoulder. A few MSS. are dated, and the majority include a formula of blessings for the owner and scribe.

Collections of manuscripts were probably kept by monks at very early times. At first they consisted almost exclusively of texts of the Old and New Testaments used in worship. Some of the monastery libraries must have been fairly large, and in a few instances even catalogues of their holdings were kept. The collection of MSS. which King Theodore had intended for the library of the Church of Madhane Alam (the bulk of which is now in the British Museum) was not far short of 1,000 volumes.

The number of Ethiopic MSS. in Europe, in public libraries as well as in private ownership, is considerable. Most of the early travellers returned with a few manuscripts, Bruce brought back an excellent collection, and later expeditions took large hauls of these valuable tomes. No wonder that monks are nowadays reluctant even to show their treasures. Numerically, the Bibliothèque Nationale in Paris (catalogues

by Zotenberg, d'Abbadie, Chaîne, Conti Rossini, Grébaut-Strelcyn)[1]
now possesses the richest collection, and, if the d'Abbadie batch is
included, the grand total approaches 1,000. Though there are some
wonderful MSS. in the Bibliothèque Nationale, the choicest gathering
of Ethiopic manuscript literature is still in Britain. The British Museum
(catalogues by Dillmann and Wright) has some 600 MSS., with the
Magdala collection as their backbone, and the Bodleian Library
possesses just over 100 MSS. (catalogues by Dillmann and Ullendorff),
with the Bruce treasures as their centre-piece. The 67 MSS. in the
Cambridge University Library were catalogued by E. Ullendorff and
S. Wright. There still exist in Britain many uncatalogued collections
of Ethiopic MSS., most of them brought back by members of the
Napier expedition, notably in the John Rylands Library, Manchester
(33 MSS.), the British and Foreign Bible Society, Selly Oak Library,
the National Library, Edinburgh, etc. Six splendid manuscripts are
in the possession of Her Majesty at Windsor Castle (catalogue by
E. Ullendorff). The Vatican Library (catalogue by Grébaut-Tisserant)
comprises some 250 MSS., that in Vienna (Rhodokanakis) about
twenty-five, Berlin (Dillmann) just under 100, Frankfurt (Goldschmidt)
23, Leningrad (Turaiev) over 175, etc.[2]

It was on such manuscripts that Ethiopic literature, as we know it
since the 'restoration' of the Solomonic dynasty in 1270, was written.
By now Ge'ez was no longer spoken by the people; instead, it had
become the exclusive medium of ecclesiastical and literary expression.
Attention was first devoted to a revision[3] of the existing Bible translations. It is interesting to find that in some instances the Ethiopic
translation of the Old Testament adheres more closely to the Hebrew
original than does the Greek version of the Septuagint. This is, however, most unlikely to be due to direct work on the Hebrew text during
the Middle Ages, and it appears that for the revision of Bible translations some Arabic versions were used which might occasionally have
reflected the Hebrew original very closely.

[1] Details in this and the following instances will be found in the Bibliography
under the name of the cataloguer.

[2] S. Strelcyn has recently prepared some important catalogues of MSS. in
Britain and Italy which are currently in the press, including new B.M. MSS., the
Rylands collection, and the Conti Rossini MSS. at the Lincei.

[3] Cf. *Ethiopia and the Bible*, pp. 44, 57-8.

The literary renaissance is connected with King Amda Sion (1314–44) whose reign offered to the country stability as well as prosperity. Amda Sion's victories over his Muslim adversaries are mirrored in the stories and songs composed in honour of this great King. The *Chronicles of the Wars of Amda Sion*[1] were unquestionably written by an eye-witness, and in them we find a vivid account of the King's campaigns against Ifat and other Muslim principalities. What distinguishes this work from the common annalistic compositions are the anecdotes and tales about the King's life—all narrated with a distinct flair and the personal touch.

The greatest work not only of the time of Amda Sion, but the foremost creation of Ethiopic literature generally, is the *Kebra Nagast* ('Glory of the Kings') which has been woven into Ethiopian life in the most intimate manner. It has as its *pièce de résistance* the legend of the Queen of Sheba (based on the narrative in 1 Kings 10: 1–13 and liberally amplified and embellished), how she visited King Solomon, accepted his religion, bore him a son (Menelik I), and how the son visited his father and abducted the Ark of the Covenant, which was taken to Aksum, the new Zion. Apart from numerous quotations and paraphrases from the Old and New Testaments, we find generous borrowings from apocryphal literature, the Book of Enoch, the *Book of the Pearl*, from the christological and patristic writings in Coptic, Syriac, Arabic, and Greek, from the *Testamentum Adami*, from Rabbinical literature as well as the Koran. The legend of Solomon and the Queen of Sheba has had a great vogue in many parts of the ancient East.[2] Details vary, especially the narrative of the King's seduction of the Queen, but all the principal ingredients can be found in the *Targum Sheni of Esther* or the *Alphabet of Ben Sira*, the Koran (Surah xxvii, 15–45), and many other sources. In fact, the main story must have had a very long period of gestation in Ethiopia and elsewhere and have possessed all the elements of a gigantic conflation of cycles of legends and tales.[3] When it was committed to writing, early in the fourteenth

[1] See Perruchon's edition and Dillmann's *Kriegsthaten*.
[2] *Ethiopia and the Bible*, chapter III.
[3] The Literary Sources of the *Kebra Nagast* were examined in a fine doctoral dissertation presented to St. Andrews University in 1956 by David Hubbard. It is to be hoped that this competent work will one day be published.

century, its purpose no doubt was to lend support to the claims and aspirations of the recently established Solomonic dynasty. Its author, the *nebura ed* Yeshaq of Aksum, was thus mainly redactor and interpreter of material which had long been known, but had not until then found a co-ordinating hand, an expository mind, and a great national need.

The *Kebra Nagast* is not merely a literary work, but—as the Old Testament to the Hebrews or the Koran to the Arabs—it is the repository of Ethiopian national and religious feelings, perhaps the truest and most genuine expression of Abyssinian Christianity.

It is not, of course, possible in this context to deal with, or even to enumerate, all the works composed or translated during the reign of Amda Sion. The *Horologium*, *Mashafa Sa'atat*, is a most popular book in Ethiopia and has been printed both in Europe and at Addis Ababa. Its earliest version was based on Coptic-Arabic originals, but there have been later recensions incorporating specifically Ethiopian material. The *Weddase Maryam* is a collection of hymns and laudations dedicated to the Virgin Mary, a work of great liturgical importance since early times, part of the vast literature of Mariolatry, and to this day widespread in Ethiopia.[1] It was translated into Ge'ez from Arabic and is ordered according to the days of the week. Large numbers of MSS. of this work can be found in Ethiopia and in the libraries of Europe. The *Mashafa Genzat* contains a collection of very ancient burial rites, while the *Philoxenus*, which is ascribed to the Syrian Philoxenus of Mabug, offers directions on monastic life in catechetical form.

A significant literary *genre* in Ethiopia are the lives and stories of martyrs and saints of which the *Gadla Sama'tat* 'Acts of the Martyrs' is a representative sample. Such 'Acts' are, of course, ubiquitous in Oriental Christian literature, and a further specimen from this early period is the *Gadla Hawaryat*, the apocryphal 'Acts of the Apostles', translated into English, under the title 'Contendings of the Holy Apostles', by Sir E. A. Wallis Budge. To the end of the fourteenth century belongs the *Senkessar* (Synaxarium), a fundamental work of Ethiopic literature. It is a vast compilation of lives of saints arranged for reading in church on their name-days. The perusal of the appropriate chapter for each day of

---

[1] Cf. Grohmann, *Marienhymnen*, and Cerulli, *Miracoli di Maria* (and p. 142 below).

the year was held to be a religious duty. The narratives, often embellished with short poetic pieces, vary in size and were translated into
Ge'ez from Arabic, with the changes relevant to the requirements of
the Ethiopian Calendar.

The religious life of the Ethiopian is ordered by two works that had
their origin, at least in translation, during the reign of Amda Sion, the
Senodos and *Didascalia*. Their influence in fostering the Semitic concept
of the identity of Church and State must have been very strongly felt.
Early in the fifteenth century the *Fekkare Iyasus* ('Explication of Jesus')
was composed; it is an interesting work of a messianic or eschatological
nature in which the end of the days is discussed. The messianic figure
who will finally restore happiness to tortured mankind is to be a King
by the name of Theodore. It is, therefore, readily understandable how
felicitous was King Theodore's choice of this name in the nineteenth
century, since Ethiopians everywhere would at once appreciate the
allusion. There are several other books of an apocalyptic character
dating from that period, chief among them the *Ra'ya Shenute*, containing ten visions describing the ultimate rewards for the good and the
punishments for the evil.

Finally, we must refer to a secular work that was at this time translated into Ge'ez from Arabic (which in its turn is a rendering from the
original Hebrew), the *Zena Ayhud* ('History of the Jews'), by Pseudo-
Yosippon.[1] While hagiography naturally predominated in the literary
interest of medieval Ethiopia (accurately reflected in the great bulk of
this type of literature), there is no dearth of other writings of a juridical,
historical, apocalyptic, etc., character. As during the Aksumite period
Ge'ez drew its literary strength from Greek models, so during the
Middle Ages Arabic provided the material from which translations and
adaptations were made. Among the Christians of Egypt Coptic had
gradually been replaced by Arabic, and it was in this language that a
fresh blossoming of literary activity occurred in Egypt at a time when
the restoration of the Solomonids had prepared the ground for a high
degree of cultural receptiveness in Ethiopia. No doubt the arrival of the
Coptic Archbishops, accompanied by a suitable retinue, had at times a
salutary effect in keeping Ethiopia in touch with literary trends in
other parts of the Christian Orient; and Coptic monks of the Abuna's

[1] Edited by Murad Kamil, 1937.

suite assisted in the interpretation and translation of such writings. The oral influence of Coptic priests, who acted as 'accoucheurs' in the delivery of these renderings, can be detected—as Guidi and others have recognized—in cases where the Ethiopic version deviates from the Arabic *Vorlage* and approximates more closely to the Coptic original. In those instances the Coptic passage was remembered and interpreted by the Egyptian monks, but the actual text used for the preparation of the Ge'ez paraphrase was almost certainly in Arabic.

The next flowering of Ethiopic literature is naturally connected with the reign of King Zar'a Ya'qob in the fifteenth century. We now reach the culminating point in the development of Ge'ez literary activity. The biographical *genre*, the 'Acts' and 'Lives' of Kings and Saints, had by then become a significant sector of Abyssinian literature occupying a place midway between hagiography and straight historical writing. The zealous personality of Zar'a Ya'qob is reflected in much that was produced at that time, and the King himself turned author and was responsible, directly or indirectly, for a good deal of the politico-religious pamphleteering that was then carried on. The great reformer of the organization of the state and of the religious life of the country stimulated fresh translations from Arabic of all such writings as would lend force to his own endeavours; and he inspired and encouraged polemical tracts that would justify his political and religious innovations.

Among the most important works attributed to Zar'a Ya'qob himself are the *Mashafa Berhan* ('Book of Light') and *Mashafa Milad* ('Book of Nativity').[1] The former in particular embodies admonitions and regulations by the King, who provides an exposition of his ecclesiastical reforms,[2] refutes heresies that had taken root in Ethiopia, attacks magical practices and other un-Christian customs, and in particular reinstates—as we have already seen—the equal observance of Sabbath and Sunday. None the less, magic was far too deeply ingrained in Ethiopia to be suppressed by edicts, and in this epoch as well as in others all forms of magical literature, scrolls, charms, prayers, visions, etc., flourished. The *Lefafa Sedeq*, the burial scroll, has already been

[1] See Wendt's edition in the *CSCO* series.
[2] Details in Dillmann's *Kirchenordnung des Zar'a Jacob* and in the Conti Rossini-Ricci edition.

mentioned. The *Salota Kepryanos* ('the prayer of Cyprian') and the
Salota Keddus Kaleb ('the prayer of King Kaleb of Ethiopia') contain
detailed accounts of the means employed by pagan magicians and have
enjoyed a remarkably wide diffusion.

An original creation of this era is the 'Book of the Mysteries of
Heaven and Earth' (the text has been reproduced and translated into
English by Sir E. A. Wallis Budge) which is divided into four parts
dealing, respectively, with the secrets of the creation and the rebellion
of the angels, St. John's Apocalypse, the mystery of the Divinity, and a
computation of Scriptural cyphers and symbols *à la* Kabbala. Another
literary type which has attained a high degree of development and
popularity in Ethiopia is the *Ta'amer* ('Miracles') *genre* which is, perhaps, the most characteristic aspect of Abyssinian literature. We
possess countless miracles of angels and saints, of Jesus and, above all, of
the Virgin Mary. The *Ta'amra Maryam*, 'the Miracles of Mary', have
been published by Budge in the Lady Meux collection of mammoth
editions. But it was left to Cerulli [1] to examine in detail the Occidental
sources of this vast compilation and to follow its course from France
over many parts of Europe (including Spain, Germany, and Iceland) to
Palestine and thence to Egypt. And once accepted by the Coptic
Church in its Arabic garb, its entry into Ethiopian literature was
assured. Here it was augmented and expanded by local legends and
traditions that were current in fifteenth-century Ethiopia and of which
we would otherwise have no knowledge. With each subsequent
recension the work became increasingly adapted to the Ethiopian
atmosphere and environment until its European provenance was
almost completely blurred.

A direct outcome of Zar'a Ya'qob's reforms was the composition of
immense numbers of homilies, for the newly decreed celebration of
innumerable saint-days and commemorative feasts required a prodigious original production coupled with equally vigorous work of
translation, from Arabic, of homilies in honour of many saints and
patriarchs venerated by the Coptic Church. The most notable representative of this generally repetitious and tedious literary form is the
collection attributed to St. John Chrysostom and entitled *Retu'a
Haymanot* ('The Orthodox').

[1] *Miracoli di Maria*, 1943.

Of much greater interest are several biographies of Zagwe kings, especially the 'Life of Lalibala',[1] which were redacted towards the middle of the fifteenth century. It is obvious that a long interval, nearly 200 years, had to elapse before it was safe to write with appreciation of members of a dynasty of 'usurpers'. In the event, Lalibala, Na'akweto la-Ab, and others turn out to be saints, builders of churches, and staunch defenders of the monophysite Faith. Other 'lives' are those of Gebre Manfas Keddus, St. George, and Tekla Haymanot. Most of these superb manuscripts are accompanied by beautifully coloured paintings, some of which can be seen in the excellent reproductions in Lady Meux's sumptuous editions. Though this hagiographic literature is part of a strongly evolved general trend in all Oriental Christian writing, combining biographical and homiletic elements with collections of miracles wrought by the saints concerned, we yet find here many important matters of specifically Ethiopian interest transcending the limited intent of the authors. Biography introduces us to the historical events of the time, many of which cannot be gleaned from other sources, and it also incorporates numerous place-names which permit us to make a beginning in compiling an historical geography of Ethiopia. At the same time we gain an impression of the political and doctrinal struggles of that period: thus we possess two recensions of the life of Tekla Haymanot, in the divergences of which are reflected religious disagreements as well as the petty jealousies of different monastic institutions.

While the small samples of secular poetry of the age of Zar'a Ya'qob have a great measure of freshness and immediacy, the same cannot be said of the vastly larger volume of religious poetry. The hymnology of that era (and others as well) has an element of artificiality of form and substance wholly absent from the very few specimens of secular poems and songs that have come down to us. Innumerable hymns were composed in honour of Christ, the Virgin, saints, and angels. Many of the hymns to Mary—which form, of course, the largest element—originate from the fifteenth century, but hymnography continued to flourish also during the following centuries. Zar'a Ya'qob himself is the alleged author, though more probably the sponsor, of hymn-collections entitled *Egzi'abher nagsa* ('God has reigned') and *Arganona Maryam*

---

[1] Edited and translated by Perruchon (see Bibliography).

Dengel ('Organ of the Virgin Mary')—both popular and widespread—which, like the *Weddase Maryam*, are ordered according to the days of the week. The principal collection of hymns is the famous *Deggwa* or hymnary which is popularly attributed to Abuna Yared (sixth century) but whose recension dates undoubtedly from the fifteenth century (though there also exist later versions and elaborations). Some very beautiful MSS. of this fine large volume may be found in Ethiopia as well as in several libraries in Europe; nearly all of them contain a form of musical notation, which has still not been studied in sufficient detail, made up of small letters placed over the operative syllables (for further details see Chapter VIII).

We now enter the period of Ethiopic literature which is characterized by three important milestones in the history of Abyssinia: (1) the Muslim invasion under Ahmad Grañ; (2) the Portuguese intervention; (3) the occasional appearance of Amharic in literary documents.

The disastrous effect of the Muslim conquest in the sixteenth century has already been discussed in Chapter IV. That the dire straits in which Christian Abyssinia found herself had the most calamitous consequences for all literary development need hardly be stressed, but it would be wrong to suppose that a great deal of Ethiopic literature perished at that time. Certainly monasteries and churches were burnt, and with them no doubt precious collections of manuscripts, but sufficient numbers of copies of most works must have been distributed and dispersed over many parts of the country to safeguard the essential continuity of Ge'ez literature. Naturally, it is quite possible that a few *unica* were lost, but it would be a gross exaggeration to speak—as has sometimes been done —of a profound break in the transmission of literary documents.

The Jesuits, once the Muslim danger had been averted, wished to address their religious propaganda not only to Court and clergy but to the ordinary Ethiopian as well. This purpose could only be served by writing in Amharic. And even though not much was accomplished at that time, it did at least break the spell and show that Amharic was capable of being used as a literary language. But its use was not entirely confined to religious pamphleteering; there also sprang up a modest activity of translation embracing such popular works as the Psalter, Canticles, *Weddase Maryam*, etc.

V

Ethiopian dwelling

Some of the Aksum obelisks

Apart from a few passages in the so-called 'Abbreviated Chronicles' which deal with the events of the Muslim invasion, our main source for the campaigns of Ahmad Grañ is Shihab ad-Din's 'History of the Conquest of Abyssinia' (*Futuh al-Habasha*). This detailed account (only the first part is extant—it is doubtful if the second part was ever composed) is written in Arabic and looks upon happenings through the eyes of the Imam.

An interesting and very unusual historical work, dating from the time of the Galla penetrations, is Bahrey's 'History of the Galla'.[1] It is a short treatise dealing with the ethnic and political situation of the people and represents a precious document of a time and of events which are otherwise shrouded in darkness and removed from all express historical evidence. The author even introduces a philosophical element in trying to discover the secret of the Galla success against a Christian, well-armed, and generally superior people.

Of King Claudius' spirited exposition of the Alexandrine Faith ('Confessio Claudii') in rebuttal of Jesuit accusations we have already heard. Other similar writings followed, all re-asserting Ethiopian determination to remain faithful to their historic religion and the special forms it had taken on Abyssinian soil: the *Sawana Nafs* ('Refuge of the Soul') and *Fekkare Malakot*[2] ('Exposition of the Divinity') are apologetic writings which, in Ethiopian eyes, have become classic statements of the monophysite doctrine. To the same *genre* belongs the important *Haymanota Abaw* ('Faith of the Fathers') which is a collection, based on an Arabic original, of homilies by the Fathers of the Church, pastoral letters, and especially discussions of an abstruse theological character on the nature of the Trinity, the incarnation of Christ, and the special claims of monophysitism. Also a translation from Arabic is the *Mashafa Tomar* ('Book of the Letter'), which relates the story of the missive that fell from heaven at Rome in the presence of priests and dignitaries of the Church. The letter deals with Christian doctrines in the broadest sense, but directs particular attention to the importance of Sabbath observance.

[1] Translated by I. Guidi, *CSCO*, Vol. 21; Budge, *History*, II, pp. 603 seq.; Beckingham-Huntingford, *Records*.
[2] Cerulli, *Scritti teologici*, vols. I and II, where both these works are edited, translated, and explained.

F

Another result of the monophysite-Jesuit controversies is the *Mazgaba Haymanot*[1] ('Treasure of the Faith') which is highly polemical in tone and was clearly composed at a time when the dispute had reached a peak of acrimony and vituperation, though even now there is no trace of personal attacks and insinuations. The *Mazgaba Haymanot* naturally drew a flood of Jesuit replies and refutations, including a letter by King Susenyos himself defending the Roman Faith and trying to persuade the Ethiopian people to accept the teachings of the Church of Rome—with what success we have already seen.

Ascribed to this period are two philosophical treatises of a very singular character entitled *Hatata Zar'a Ya'qob* ('Examination of Zar'a Ya'qob') and the similar examination or investigation by that same Zar'a Ya'qob's pupil, Walda Heywat. The work is inspired by profound scepticism and a distaste of barren theological disputation and advocates a rationalistic and philosophical approach. It was edited and translated by E. Littmann (*CSCO*, Vols. 18 and 19) and generally enjoyed considerable attention by scholars—until C. Conti Rossini proved that the two booklets were written in the mid-nineteenth century by Padre Giusto da Urbino, a great Italian connoisseur of Ge'ez who, succumbing to theological doubts and uncertainties in his Ethiopian exile, gave vent to his spiritual frustration by writing philosophical treatises in Ge'ez.

Another work of a pseudo-philosophical character, though of genuine ascription, is the *Mashafa Falasfa Tabiban*, or 'Book of Philosophers', which contains a collection of the sayings and epigrams of philosophers and wise men of many nations.

One of the last great theological works translated into Ge'ez from Arabic is the *Faws Manfasawi* ('Spiritual Medicine') whose authorship is attributed to Michael, Bishop of Atrib and Malig in Egypt.

Hymnography and prayer-book literature have a second blossoming in the seventeenth century. The *Weddase Amlak* ('Laudations of God') is modelled on the *Weddase Maryam* and is similarly ordered according to the days of the week. The book is also called *Baselyos*, after St. Basil, Bishop of Caesarea, whose portion is recited on the first day. The *Mazmura Krestos* ('Psalter of Christ') and *Mazmura Dengel* ('Psalter of the Virgin') are usually appended to the canonical Psalter; they have

[1] Op. cit., vol. II.

enjoyed immense popularity and are to this day every Ethiopian's spiritual mainstay. The manuscript literature of hymns, *salam* ('salutations'), is truly prodigious. These hymns vary in size from a few lines to compositions of considerable length and are devoted, first and foremost, to the Virgin Mary, but also to Christ, angels and saints, the Trinity, bishops and Abunas, etc.

A special form of Abyssinian hymn is the *kene* (collected in the *Mazgaba Kene*) whose rhyme and metre have still not been sufficiently studied and whose proper understanding can only result from a thorough investigation of Ethiopian literary culture.[1] For a few additional observations on the *kene* see the next chapter.

One of the most fundamental works of Ethiopic literature is the *Fetha Nagast* ('Legislation of the Kings'), which has retained its value and practical importance in Ethiopia to the present day.[2] It forms the basis of a good deal of the customary law in some regions and has also inspired some of the civil and penal law that has been enacted in Ethiopia over many years. The compiler of the *Fetha Nagast* was Ibn al-Assal who wrote this large work for the use of Coptic Christians living in Muslim Egypt. It deals with canon law as well as civil and penal legislation. In the latter respect it was originally of rather limited relevance to conditions in Ethiopia, and Guidi has shown many instances in which the Ge'ez translator misunderstood the original—not so much on linguistic grounds as for its basic incompatibility with local circumstances.

A very active figure in Ethiopic literature was a certain Embakom (Habakkuk) who flourished in the sixteenth century and had a most adventurous career. An Arab by birth, he came to Ethiopia during the Grañ wars, was converted to Christianity and entered the monastery of Debra Libanos. Through his piety and exceptional learning he rose to the position of Prior and thus became Etchege—a feat no other foreigner has achieved. Embakom distinguished himself principally by a series of translations from Arabic (though he was also the author of an original work, the *Ankasa Amin*, 'Gate of Faith',[3] an anti-Islamic

---

[1] The Addis Ababa Institute of Ethiopian Studies has initiated a series of *Kene* collections. Ethiopian scholars, such as Ato Alamayahu Mogas, have made very valuable contributions.

[2] Cf. Guidi's masterly edition and translation (Bibliography).

[3] Cf. van Donzel's model edition (Bibliography).

polemical tract) among which the novel 'Baralam and Yewasef' is of particular interest. This historical romance, of Indian origin, has had a most chequered career in Asia and Europe and has been translated into Syriac, Hebrew, Arabic, Greek, Latin, and several other languages. Of a similar character, though of much greater originality in its Ethiopic garb, is the *Zena Eskender* ('History of Alexander') which is part of the oriental cycle of Alexander legends, based on the Pseudo-Callisthenes, but with remarkably fresh offshoots in its Ge'ez form. Both the Alexander and Baralam and Yewasef romances have been translated and published by Sir E. A. Wallis Budge; yet the Ethiopic text and its literary ramifications will require further examination.

Historiography is the principal branch of original literature in Ethiopia. We have already mentioned some of the Royal Chronicles; to these must now be added the history of Sarsa Dengel (published by Conti Rossini), of Claudius (published by Conzelman), of Minas (published by Pereira), the annals of Iyasu I, of Tekla Giyorgis, and others. Their historical yield has been sketched in Chapter IV, their geographical and sociological interest is considerable, but their literary value must be judged rather low. There exist, of course, many other writings which have a direct bearing on the history of the country, such as historical legends, biographies, etc., too numerous to be mentioned here; and though to the student of literature their worth may be limited, the historian cannot afford to neglect any of those precious indications which, cumulatively, offer us a picture of Ethiopia that is becoming increasingly fuller and more distinct.

By way of a postscript to this short outline of Ge'ez literature some brief notes ought to be added about Falasha literature and the development of philological writing in Ethiopia. We have already seen that the Falashas share part of their literature with their Christian compatriots, but there exist a few works which are peculiar to them. Despite the valiant spade-work by Halévy, Aešcoly, and other scholars, Falasha literature is only now beginning to receive the detailed examination it deserves, both for its own sake and for the investigation of historical, literary, and sociological connections and ramifications. Among original Falasha works are the 'Commandments of the Sabbath', the 'Book of Abba Elijah', and many of their prayers. Books which have

received at least an original and specific elaboration by the Falashas
include the Apocalypses of Gorgorios and Ezra, the 'Book of Disciples',
the Lives of Adam and Moses, the 'Death of Moses', the 'Testament of
Abraham', etc. It has already been stated that all this literature has been
produced in Ge'ez; the Falashas are entirely innocent of Hebrew, and
their Agaw vernacular is not employed for literary purposes.

Philological studies have never been keenly cultivated in Ethiopia,
although we encounter the occasional *Sawasew* ('ladders'—a literal
rendering from the Arabic). The *Sawasew* are a kind of omnibus study
of vocabulary, grammar, and rhetoric. A modest beginning has been
made in evolving an indigenous grammatical terminology, and in
recent times more than a few works of this type, covering Ge'ez,
Amharic, and Tigrinya, have been published. Several scholars have
studied the methodology of the Sawasew; the most valuable results
have been attained by H. Brauner-Plazikowski and especially by M. M.
Moreno (see Bibliography).

While Amharic literature achieved full emancipation only during
the reign of King Theodore in the nineteenth century, we have already
discussed some of its fitful beginnings in the seventeenth century. Of
those early writings, many Amharic glosses in MSS., Amharic com-
mentaries, and short theological tracts have been preserved. Among the
latter the *Senna Fetrat* ('Beauty of the Creation') is probably the best
known.

It was, however, King Theodore who gave the greatest impulse and
encouragement to Amharic literature as a plank in his general programme of Imperial unification, and this has remained an aim of
Ethiopian policy (with the short interval only of the Tigrean Emperor
John IV) to this day. Theodore's Chronicles (extant in three different
versions) are written in a terse and vigorous Amharic which almost
reflects the personality of its subject. Since then enormous progress has
been made in the development of Amharic literature, and Ge'ez is now
completely relegated to the liturgical sphere (and even there Amharic is
making some inroads). The day when the Emperor Menelik II established a printing press at Addis Ababa, though only two generations
ago, seems an echo from a different age altogether, for now a dozen or
more well-equipped printing establishments at Addis Ababa and

Asmara turn out books, pamphlets, periodicals, and newspapers at a steadily mounting pace. Much of this acceleration has occurred since the last war and provides eloquent testimony to the vitality of modern Ethiopian life. Hundreds of books have been published in the past quarter of a century. Naturally, standards are very uneven: there are some excellent translations of European literature, some interesting fresh trends in Amharic poetry have come to light (one need only think of such different authors as Ato Kebbede Mika'el and Ato Mangestu Lemma), and countless books on education, health, administration, social problems, etc., have been printed. Some good novels and plays have had reasonably large sales, and even work whose intrinsic literary value may be slight will frequently still be of interest to the student or the linguist.

It would be impossible to convey an impression of this new and rapidly developing literature in these summary notes; some very general remarks must suffice.[1]

Among the last generation of writers three in particular stand out: Aleka Tayye whose 'History of the People of Ethiopia' is of some interest; Afework whose 'Life of Menelik II' and *Lebb Walad Tarik*, the first Amharic novel, broke entirely fresh ground in presentation as well as style. His work on Amharic grammar is of considerable value on account of its terminology and conception; and Heruy Walda Sellasie whose study of the reign of King John IV, biographical sketches of notable Ethiopians, together with his political reflections, amount to a considerable and distinguished literary output.

Blatta Mars'e Hazan, among contemporary writers, has given us a valuable Amharic grammar in which not the least interesting aspect is the employment of Amharic grammatical terminology; and Ato Ba'emnat Gebre-Amlak has produced a linguistic work on the origin and growth of Amharic.

Many collections of proverbs, fables, and songs have been published —a precious source for otherwise greatly neglected folkloristic studies. Ras Bitwodded Makonnen Endalkatchew (for many years Prime Minister of Ethiopia), Germatchew Tekla-Hawaryat, and Kebbede

[1] Cf. the valuable article and bibliography by Albert Gérard in *JES*, July 1968, as well as his 1971 book (Bibliography). See also L. Ricci's and P. Comba's contributions in *JSS*, 1964.

Mika'el have devoted their considerable talents to the theatre and the novel. That their steps are at times still somewhat groping can hardly be surprising, for every advance in this field is a pioneering effort.

Some Ethiopian writers have helped to bring before their fellow-countrymen the best of European literature and civilization: there are essays on, as well as renderings of works by, Shakespeare, Goethe, and Zola. Aesop's fables, *The Arabian Nights*, *Pilgrim's Progress*, Dr. Johnson's *Rasselas* (in an excellent version by Blatta Sirak Heruy), *Pinocchio*, and many religious tracts have been translated into Amharic. Alexander the Great, Mahatma Gandhi, and other great figures of world history have been made the subjects of valuable interpretative essays.

Ato Mangestu Lemma's poetry, plays, and biography of his father have demonstrated originality in language as well as subject, while Ato Tsegaye Gabre-Medhin's writings have been characterized by stylistic vigour and a sense of urgency.

Exhortations and panegyrics are, perhaps, still the most voluminous sector of modern Amharic poetry. Laudatory songs and poems in honour of His Imperial Majesty's birthday anniversaries somehow continue a trend which began in the fourteenth century with the first Imperial songs in Amharic. Some of these compositions have been collected and published by Murad Kamil (see Bibliography). Not all of the rhymes and verses produced for those occasions can be called 'literature', but they are genuine and spontaneous effusions of respect and affection for a great King.

Finally, mention must be made of Amharic newspapers and periodicals: *Aimero* was the first, if I am not mistaken, to be followed by *Berhanenna Salam*. The official gazette is *Negarit Gazeta*, while *Addis Zaman* and *Ya-Ityopya Dems'* are at present the daily newspapers of Addis Ababa. All of these are of some historical and linguistic interest. We are, however, approaching the time when not everything printed in Amharic will be classed as 'literature', when competitive claims will impose more severe standards, and output will become more selective. The linguist might then regret the disappearance of some of this 'unfiltered' material, but Amharic literature will benefit and flourish on a higher plane.

VIII

ART AND MUSIC

———∿∿∿∿∿(◎)∿∿∿∿∿———

NO COMPREHENSIVE study of Ethiopian art or music has yet been attempted, though in recent years the situation has markedly improved: we now possess many studies of detail which, cumulatively, amount to a collection of data of great value.[1] The extent of the summary observations proffered in this chapter has been circumscribed by the requirements of an overall balance and by the present writer's limited competence in this field.

In its art Ethiopia displays the same syncretistic traits which we have observed in other facets of its civilization. Coupled with the usual Semitic hesitations over representational art we find here the complex effects of the confluence of Byzantine, Syrian, and Coptic stylistic currents as well as many of the elements of Christian Oriental art. Yet, in the growth of art or civilization we can presumably only speak of a greater or lesser degree of syncretism, for no civilization and no form of

---

[1] Apart from vols. II and III of the *Deutsche Aksum Expedition* (written by Krencker and von Lüpke, respectively) dealing in minute detail with ancient and medieval buildings in Northern Ethiopia, we have of course long had some of the magisterial incidental observations by such scholars as Conti Rossini and Cerulli. More recently David Buxton and Miss Beatrice Playne (see bibliography) have studied aspects of architecture and painting. And during the last few years there has been a steady flow of valuable work which the present writer is too ignorant to assess in detail. See especially Leroy's and Mordini's contributions to painting and architecture, respectively, in *Christentum am Nil*; Leroy's *La pittura etiopica*; Gerster's *Kirchen im Fels* (with its magnificent photographs and the relevant chapters by Leclant, Buxton, Leroy, and Schneider); Bianchi Barriviera's articles on the rock churches of Lalibela in *RSE*, XVIII and XIX; Chojnacki's short introduction to Ethiopian painting in *JES*, II, 2; Pankhurst's notes for a history of Ethiopian secular art in *Ethiopia Observer*, X, 1.

art are born in a void: all possess antecedents which have left their indelible imprint upon aspects of development determining a particular bias, slant, or direction. But it is the autochthonous moulding to which foreign influences have been subjected and their eventual emergence as a new style which are the hall-mark of a fresh and characteristic artistic expression—frequently not readily definable, but usually not hard to recognize.

The Semitic, and specifically Syrian, element in Ethiopian art accounts for a certain directness, almost crudity, and for a distinct lack of elegance. Vividness and the urge to convey an idea seem more pronounced than the desire to give pleasure. These traits find expression in the almost universal frontal pose (see, however, below) and in the distortion of proportions in order to underline the importance of particular persons or features. Such Semitic elements would have entered Ethiopia by way of South Arabia and through the influx of Syrian monks. It was due to Ethiopian contacts with Alexandria that the Coptic style became established in the realm of the Negus. It is made up of features known from the art of ancient Egypt and the stylized forms of the Hellenistic *genre*. The most potent influence in Ethiopia was no doubt exerted by Byzantine art, the perfect fusion of classical and oriental strands, whose elegance and delicacy can be discerned especially in manuscript art and metal work. From Byzantium also originates (or at least receives strong support) the curious ambivalence between the Semitic aversion to depicting the divine figure and the uninhibited anthropomorphism of the classical world.

Both Byzantine art and the indigenous Ethiopian tradition were deeply transfused with Christianity which imbued the two civilizations with an almost unparalleled exclusiveness and dominance of religious matter. Literature, art, music, and most facets of organized expression were virtually wholly ecclesiastical, and the religion of the state determined the scope of all artistic creation. Christianity was thus not only the source of Byzantine and Ethiopian art, but it also moulded it and prescribed its task and purpose.

With the exception of the great obelisks and some thrones of Kings and judges, Ethiopian architecture is primarily ecclesiastical. No secular buildings of note have survived apart from the castles at Gondar. As

Ethiopian Emperors had no permanent capital (excepting again only the Gondar period), no royal palaces were built. The old and new palaces at Addis Ababa are essentially European edifices.

A characteristic aspect of old Abyssinian architecture is the use of stone and wood in alternate layers. That was the case in ancient Aksumite building and is prominently attested in some of the early medieval churches (especially at Debra Damo and in the old church at Asmara) as well as in many modern structures.[1] The protruding horizontal beams (called 'monkey-heads' by Ethiopians) are so distinctive a feature of this type of building that they are even symbolically carved into the great obelisks whose designs represent old Ethiopian building fashions. K. A. C. Creswell has shown[2] that the man responsible for the reconstruction of the Ka'ba at Mecca, in A.D. 608, must have been an Abyssinian. His name was Bakum (=Embakom, i.e. Habakkuk) and he used the wood of a ship which had been wrecked, thus building the new Ka'ba with a course of stone alternating with a course of wood up to the roof, altogether sixteen layers of stone and fifteen of wood. The close resemblance to the characteristic Abyssinian style need scarcely be stressed.

The Ethiopian stelae, whose development through various stages of refinement can still be followed thanks to the examples of different styles that have been preserved, are perhaps the most notable achievement of indigenous art. They are pre-Christian and served as gravestones and memorials. The perfection reached by the largest of these monoliths is expressed not only in the immense technical skill required in working, moving, and erecting these colossal single blocks of granite, but especially in their beautiful sculpturing and rich decoration as well-proportioned multi-storeyed towers. The largest obelisk still standing at Aksum is nearly 70 feet high (21 metres), while the biggest of all, though broken through the enormous force of its fall, measures about 110 feet (a little over 33 metres) in height and is thus the largest (at one time upright) monolith in the world (exceeding the height of the Lateran obelisk by just over four feet). An Aksum obelisk of 24 metres was taken to Rome in 1937 and has been erected at the Piazza di Porta Capena.

---

[1] See especially *Aksum Expedition*, Vol. II, p. 9, Abb. 14.
[2] *Encyclopaedia of Islam* (new edition), I, p. 609.

Four types of stelae can be distinguished: (1) the crude pieces of shapeless rock are probably waste material left over from the quarrying in the adjacent mountains; (2) stones with strongly pointed forms and carefully smoothed surfaces; (3) obelisk-shaped monoliths with varying head-shapes, at times with inscribed surfaces;[1] (4) obelisks of the kind found at Aksum, provided with delicately executed ornamental designs of the storey or window type.

The stele at Aksum which is still erect is sunk some nine feet into the ground, so that its overall height, below and above the surface, approaches 80 feet. Front and both sides are covered with relief designs, while the back is blank—save for five small circles enclosed by a larger ring near the apex of the stone.[2] Some other obelisks are fully ornamented at the back as well. The front part has, at the bottom, the image of a door complete with lock. Above the door are nine storeys between each of which are five round 'imitation beams' or 'monkey-heads'. The sides possess no door, but are otherwise similarly adorned—making allowances, of course, for the much smaller surface available. The Church of Debra Damo shows the window formations and the alternating stone and wood layers (with the protruding beam-heads) which appear as relief motifs on the obelisks. The multi-storey representation on these monoliths is no doubt a reminiscence of the high and many-storeyed palaces and dwellings of South Arabia.

Another, though much less spectacular, feature of the Aksumite remains is the large number of thrones which have been preserved. According to Ethiopian tradition, one of these thrones belonged to the King, another to the Abuna, and the remainder were occupied by the judges. At the top of the flight of stairs leading to the Zion's Church at Aksum we still find a throne consisting of a seat and foot-stool. Several attempts were made by Krencker (*Aksum Expedition*, II, pp. 66–7) to reconstruct such thrones, and in the light of the actual remains, supplemented by some scant literary sources, these reconstructions must be judged highly successful.

Church architecture has already been alluded to in Chapter V where we have also discussed the interior arrangement of Ethiopian churches. By far the most beautiful as well as the oldest church is that of Debra

[1] The Obelisk of Matara (*JRAS*, 1951) is of this type.
[2] Drawing and photographs in *Aksum Expedition*, II, pp. 20 seq.

Damo[1] which dates back to the early Middle Ages and is the finest and best preserved example of the old rectangular style. This Tigrean monastery is situated on the summit of an *amba* and can only be reached by a rope-ascent. That its style of construction reflects the earliest methods of building known in Ethiopia is apparent from the close resemblance (already referred to before) which this church bears to the multi-storeyed stelae. The narthex of Debra Damo has an exquisite (and probably in present-day Ethiopia unparalleled) panelled ceiling. Some of the panels are now empty, as the ceiling is in a state of disrepair (very recently reconstruction work is reported to have been carried out), but the majority contain beautifully executed designs of animals, floral and geometrical patterns, and delicately carved crosses. Coptic and Byzantine models spring to mind at once, but this connection cannot detract in any way from the rare and superb craftsmanship of the Ethiopian woodcutters who produced such exquisite beauty in so remote and inaccessible a place. Almost equally remarkable is the carved entrance-door to the church of the northern (i.e. Eritrean) Debra Libanos with its arabesque-like patterns displaying an elegance and delicacy quite untypical of the main current of Abyssinian art.[2]

The round church which is now much more common is of later date, and I would doubt that there is any connection with the circular buildings which were in fairly general use as pagan mausoleums, both at Rome and in the East (one need only think of the Pantheon at Rome or some of the large circular structures at Constantinople). Reminiscent of Byzantine models is the atmosphere of almost total darkness inside churches which scarcely permits inspection, let alone contemplation, of some of the elaborately decorated interiors, paintings, and icons.

Of a different kind altogether and undoubtedly among the great marvels of the world are the justly famous rock-hewn churches[3] of the village of Lalibala in the province of Lasta. Until recently they were fairly inaccessible in their splendid mountain isolation, but a rough air-strip a few miles away has now brought them within reach of the

[1] Cf. op. cit., pp. 168 seq., where some excellent photographs and sketches are reproduced. See also Buxton, *Travels*, plates 74–81; Gerster, pp. 71 ff.

[2] See Buxton, op. cit., photograph 84.

[3] Cf. the photographs and descriptions in the books by Monti della Corte, Findlay, Buxton, and Gerster (Bibliography).

enterprising tourist. There are altogether eleven, of which that of Madhane Alam is the largest (110 by 77 feet and 35 feet high). These churches are hewn out of the solid rock and display a remarkable variety of styles. While the temples of Abu Simbel on the Nile are larger, they remain caves within the rock; in contrast, the Lalibala churches are almost invariably completely freed from the rock from which they were hewn. Generally big trenches were excavated on all sides of a rectangle, thus isolating in the centre a huge block of granite. This rock was then shaped and formed internally as well as externally. In part, these decorations, carvings, and pillars display workmanship of great delicacy and of the highest standard.

The Church of Madhane Alam in particular betrays at once its connection with the storeyed stelae of Aksum and thus appears to support the view that these fine and elaborate structures were metaphorically as well as literally cut out of the native soil of Ethiopia. The Church of St. Mary is distinguished by its extremely elaborate interior and a courtyard of very considerable dimensions whose excavation must have presented a formidable task. A different type is represented by the Church of St. George which has been cut out of the rock in the shape of a cross. The Church of Abba Libanos is severed from the rock on all four sides, but its roof forms part of the overhanging mountain. Very striking is the temple-like building of the Genete Maryam Church, not far from Lalibala, whose columns and general appearance convey the impression—at least from a distance—of a structure in the classical tradition. On closer inspection, however, one notices the rather crude forms in contrast to the accomplished workmanship on the churches at Lalibala itself.

The rock-hewn churches of Lalibala, though almost unique in their medium and some of their stylistic features, are yet an elaboration of an indigenous style which was already apparent in the Church of Debra Damo—as had, indeed, been recognized by the members of the German Aksum Expedition in the early years of this century and has more recently been proved by Mr. David Buxton.[1] Since 1967 a number of other rock churches have been found in the Tigrai (Gerster, pp. 79 ff.), thus confirming earlier views about the existence of such structures in Northern Ethiopia.

[1] Op. cit., pp. 197 seq.

We must conclude this cursory inspection of Ethiopian architecture with a brief look at the singular phenomenon of a great vogue of secular building at Gondar. Fasiladas' castles[1] represent certainly a strange episode in the history of Ethiopia. Portuguese craftsmen, who had remained after the expulsion of the Jesuits, were almost certainly employed in the building of these remarkable structures, but there is no evidence that they were concerned in the planning of either the castles or their large precincts. Nor can the style be said to be Portuguese. Some have professed to find European models, while others have been reminded of the palaces of South Arabia, but I would doubt that the hybrid, yet not unpleasing, aspect of these castles lends itself to neat stylistic classification. Fasiladas' palace is the centre-piece of the huge compound of buildings which is enclosed by thick walls. The palace was tall and rectangular, built in grey stone, with four round turrets at the corners. The wooden balconies lend a most incongruous touch to the whole structure. The grounds surrounding the castle and its ancillary buildings and pavilions were spacious and planted with trees and bushes. Twelve gates, constructed over a long period, gave access to the interior of the compound. Fasiladas died before the ambitious programme of building had been completed, but his successors persevered, and the growth of the Imperial enclave (including forts and churches) continued unabated for some time. At one period the circumference of the precinct was said to have been a mile, and the great audience hall, 120 feet long, was reported to have been luxuriously furnished and covered with fine carpets and silks. Yet the castles of Gondar have remained as detached from Ethiopia and its traditional architecture as have most of the Emperors who resided in them and whose dominion became ever more restricted and removed from the main stream of Ethiopian history.

The earliest known specimens of pictorial art in Ethiopia are the rock carvings found in some northern parts of the country.[2] Their workman-

---

[1] Photographs in op. cit., plates 64, 65; also in Pankhurst, *Cultural History of Ethiopia*, plates 81–95; Ursin, plates 86–7.

[2] See Conti Rossini, *Storia d'Etiopia*, plates LI, LII; *idem*, in *RSE*, III (1943); Dainelli and Marinelli in *R. Ist. di Studi Superiori*, 1912; A. Mordini in *RSE*, I (1941); P. Graziosi, *ibidem*; S. Drew in *Man*, 1951, 155; D. J. Duncanson, *ibidem*, 1952, 117.

ship varies from crude and hasty incisions to beautifully accomplished
carvings and delicate colour paintings of human and animal figures on
the rock face. It is almost impossible to give any indication of their
date, especially as there is no certainty that they all belong to the same
period and are part of a uniform inspiration. But it seems probable that
they are either contemporaneous with the Aksumite epoch or even
antedate it. In any event they must be very much earlier than even the
oldest paintings in manuscripts, for they belong to a completely different type of art form and to a mode of contemplation that is far removed
from everything else that is known to us of Abyssinian pictorial
representation. And even though further specimens of this art may yet
lie hidden and concealed,[1] it must be judged an urgent desideratum to
have those rock carvings and paintings subjected to a comprehensive
study in which all the scattered information, photographs, and sketches
could be brought together.

Of particular elegance are the rock drawings at Kohaito which are
worked on the perpendicular cliff faces; they depict animal scenes and
movements of great delicacy. Of a very singular type is the carving of
the figure of a lioness on a rock at Gobedra.[2] This exquisitely beautiful
and life-like contour-cutting reminds one of the White Horses which
have been cut in the chalk in Berkshire and Wiltshire.

By far the most representative and ubiquitous branch of Ethiopian
art is painting on canvas and walls in churches and on vellum in manuscripts. At the same time, one should not neglect the considerable
development, attained in early MSS., of the art of writing and illumination.[3] The beautifully shaped letters, distinguished by attention to
minute detail, reached, in the fourteenth and fifteenth centuries, a
standard of perfection that has never been surpassed; they are a delight
to the eye—even to an eye unfamiliar with Ethiopic writing. Colour
and illumination were often generously applied; ornamentation and
vegetal designs and borders gave free rein to the imaginative powers of
artists.

It is here in particular that the attachment of Ethiopian art to Byzantine models—no doubt in the wake of the Coptic example—can be

[1] See V. Franchini in *RSE*, XX, 1964.
[2] Cf. von Lüpke in *Aksum Expedition*, II, pp. 73–4, plate XV.
[3] Cf. Leroy, Wright, Jäger, *Ethiopia: Illuminated MSS.*

recognized. At the same time, direct or indirect European influence cannot be excluded. We know that Europeans, Italians in particular, could be found at the Ethiopian Court as early as the fifteenth century. In one case at least the help of a Roman illustrator is expressly acknowledged.[1] In other instances we may well suppose that works like the 'Miracles of Mary', whose European antecedents are clearly established, will also have introduced European *Vorlagen* for the illustration of the text. Naturally, it must not be assumed that there was direct copying (save for a few attested cases), but Ethiopian artists drew inspiration, both in subject-matter and in style, from certain European models. Yet these models were transformed, adapted, and imbued with the authentic artistic expression of Ethiopia. One need only compare some of the Copto-Byzantine and European designs and stylistic forms with the elaboration they received in Ethiopia (in the physiognomy of the people, in the characteristically Abyssinian landscape, or other features peculiar to Ethiopia) in order to convince oneself that artistic impact is an infinitely subtle process that is far removed from mere dependence or borrowing. One such peculiarly Ethiopian stylistic facet is the unparalleled custom (at least so far as I know) of reserving the presentation of the face in profile to enemies and evildoers.

When the force of Byzantine, Syrian, and Coptic influences had been spent, occidental elements—after a period of transition—made themselves increasingly and directly felt. Since the sixteenth century, with the arrival of the Jesuits and the discovery of new maritime routes, the introduction of Western iconographic types became systematic and fairly widespread. Yet receptiveness in Ethiopia never meant slavish adherence, and indigenous traditions of painting were still sufficiently vigorous and flexible to assimilate these fresh influences and to adapt them to the local environment. E. Cerulli has investigated the instructive case of the representation of the head of Christ, the *Gesù percosso*, and its origins in fifteenth-century Europe.[2] Here, in a safely attested instance, we may observe the transformations which Ethiopian art has

---

[1] Conti Rossini, *Collection d'Abbadie*, pp. 567 seq.

[2] *RSE*, VI (1947), pp. 109–29 (with 10 plates). This particular example can be studied in an Ethiopic MS. in the Royal Library, Windsor Castle; cf. E. Ullendorff, *RSE*, XII, 1953, p. 77, where further references may be found. The original from which this head was copied is a Flemish painting, probably of the Bruges school.

brought about in an occidental theme and the specific and idiosyncratic use it made of such a model. Thus Ethiopia has her artistic roots also in the civilization of the Mediterranean and, through it, in contacts with the Occident, for Christianity deflected her from Africa and maintained her civilization, her art, and her entire life as part of the great Mediterranean culture.

Ethiopian painting may be divided into two great periods which are separated by the Muslim invasion in the sixteenth century. Those who painted—like those who wrote and produced manuscripts—were naturally priests and monks. They inserted pictures into their books to render the message more vivid, more colourful, and more widely comprehensible. Since the fourteenth century, the beginning of the period of manuscript illustration (earlier examples no doubt existed, but none have been preserved), painting has been as much in the service of Abyssinian Christianity as any other cultural manifestation in the country; and it is only in recent times that some secular art has begun.

The period of the fourteenth and fifteenth centuries is characterized by paintings with a biblical theme, especially the Evangelists, and some angels and saints. Colours are strong, proportions are large, and the entire style is one of great expressiveness rather than of elegance or delicacy of form.

With the defeat of Ahmad Grañ the rebuilding of churches and monasteries began, and associated with many of these institutions were sizeable libraries of manuscripts which had to be restocked after the devastations and depletions of the Muslim attacks. Painting thus received a vigorous stimulus in the late sixteenth century and throughout the seventeenth, for the decoration of the interiors of newly built or reconstructed churches needed as many artists as did the illustration of manuscripts. At the same time there also occurred a perceptible change in the subject-matters which appealed to these artists: biblical themes were increasingly displaced by, first and foremost, the attention given to the Virgin Mary and, in the second place, by the lives and acts of saints. The extreme veneration accorded to Mary in Ethiopia has, of course, long been recognized as a distinctive feature of Abyssinian Christianity and finds expression in countless pictorial representations. These pictures vary a good deal and show the Virgin at times as a delicate and rather frail young girl, while in other instances she appears as a strong woman who is capable of leading the Ethiopian people, protecting them, and punishing their enemies.

Scenes of martyrdom lack nothing in realism, which is the keynote of Ethiopian painting in this post-Grañ period. There is nothing fragile or shy in these miniatures; they express everything with vigour and extreme directness. Saints have an earthy rather than spiritual aspect, and the supernatural seems to have vanished from religious painting after the cataclysm of the mid-sixteenth century.

Of the semi-secular paintings the traditional scenes of King Solomon and the Queen of Sheba have long enjoyed considerable favour, while during the past century or so battle pictures have been much in vogue. All these paintings are highly stylized and leave comparatively little room for the individual artist's initiative. Conventions have been established within which there is generally latitude for greater or lesser technical talent only; personal and imaginative treatment is severely curtailed. But just as the conventionalized forms in poetry have recently been breached, so also in art: among young Ethiopian artists, who combine a healthy regard for their own traditions with the enrichment and broadening which occidental methods and themes may offer, there have been quite a few of considerable talent. Some are self-taught, such as Gebre-Krestos Desta or Mangestu Lemma, while others, among whom Afework Tekle is undoubtedly the best known, are graduates of Art Colleges.[1]

Ethiopians have long excelled in metal, especially silver, work. To this day one can watch silversmiths engaged in this traditional art producing finely wrought crosses of the Byzantine-Coptic type: tall stems with leaved and looped crosses and balancing patterns at the sides. Some of the large churches and monasteries possess precious processional crowns, giant crosses, prayer-sticks with intricately patterned handles, beautifully ornamented censers, processional umbrellas, sistra as well as metal book-covers. Excellent reproductions of these tools and vessels can be seen in *Aksum Expedition*, III, pp. 93–105, Plates VIII–XI.[2]

[1] For examples of this work see Pankhurst, *Cultural History*, plates CXXXVII–CLIII, and *Ethiopia Observer*, VI, 3. Afework Tekle has meanwhile attained considerable eminence as an artist, both inside Ethiopia and in other parts of Africa (cf. *Menen*, Sept.–Oct. 1968, pp. 14 ff.; *Ethiopia Mirror*, Jan. 1969, pp. 20 ff.).

[2] See also *Ethiopian Processional Crosses*, Addis Ababa, 1971.

Ethiopian music and hymnography have not yet received the detailed study which they deserve.[1] Research into the history of Ethiopian music and examination of its contemporary manifestations will require the co-operation of a trained musicologist and a competent *éthiopisant*. While the musical notation of the *deggwa* can be studied in Europe (where some excellent manuscripts of this work exist), much of the material will have to be gathered and recorded in Ethiopia.[2]

In the circumstances it might be of value to the reader to preface the summary remarks which are to follow with a brief survey of the existing bibliographical material.

Already Marianus Victorius had appended to the first printed grammar of Geʿez (1552) a brief excursus, *De musica Aethiopum*, in which he offers some musical transcriptions which have never since been examined. Ludolf, in his *Commentarius* (1691), gives the musical notation of the Ethiopian call to the Sovereign (*Janhoy*) and some very

---

[1] The following works are relevant: Marianus Victorius appended an excursus *De musica Aethiopum* to his 1552 *Chaldeae seu Aethiopicae linguae institutiones* in which he offered some musical transcriptions which have, to my knowledge, never been properly examined; Ludolf, *Commentarius*, pp. 263, 380–1; Guidi, *Vocabolario*, cols. 265, 607–8; C. Mondon-Vidailhet's *Musique éthiopienne* (see bibliography) remains the most detailed account of Ethiopian music hitherto published; M. Cohen, 'Couplets Amhariques du Choa', *JA*, 1924; *idem*, 'Sur la notation musicale éthiopienne', *Levi Della Vida Festschrift*, Rome, 1956; E. Wellesz, 'Studien zur aethiopischen Kirchenmusik', *Oriens Christianus*, 1920; *New Oxford History of Music*, vols. i and ii; A. M. Rothmüller, *The Music of the Jews*, London, 1953; Guidi, 'Qene o Inni Abissini', *RAL*, 1900; E. Cerulli, 'Di alcune varietà di inni della chiesa etiopica', *Orientalia*, 1934; *idem*, 'Canti popolari amarici', *RAL*, 1916; Conti Rossini, *Proverbi, Tradizioni e Canzoni Tigrine*, Verbania, 1942; E. Littmann, *Abess. Klagelieder*, Tübingen, 1949.

Michael Powne's *Ethiopian Music* is an introduction to existing knowledge rather than an independent study.

[2] J. Tubiana (*Journal of African History*, ii, 1961) refers to German Odeon recordings, taken just before the Second World War, and to the records of the Collection Universelle de Musique Populaire de l'Unesco. In recent years quite a number of recordings have been made of both secular and ecclesiastical Ethiopian music, though not in any systematic form. Miss Jean Jenkins of the Horniman Museum, London, is now aiming at a collection of records covering as wide a geographical area of Ethiopia as possible and as full a typological representation as can be arranged. Some records, including 'Music of the Ethiopian Coptic Church', have been published since 1967 by the UNESCO collection.

general remarks on musical instruments (pp. 263 and 380–1, respectively).

The first competent study of oriental music was undertaken by Villoteau in his *Description de l'Égypte* (1799), where a section is devoted to Ethiopian music, including lists of neumes and interlinear notation. The results of I. Guidi's studies in the Ethiopian *zema* (liturgical chant) have been included in his *Vocabolario Amarico* (especially cols. 265 and 607–8).

The most detailed account of Ethiopian music hitherto published[1] we owe to C. Mondon-Vidailhet (see Bibliography), though the author relied only in part on a study carried out in Ethiopia itself. Mondon-Vidailhet's article includes an examination of the chant, musical instruments, *zema*, a translation into French (which could in parts be improved) of the Synaxarium passage concerning Yared, the putative father of Ethiopian church music; and there is also a brief investigation of modes, notation (together with a specimen passage), and the *kene*. Useful information is contained also in M. Cohen's '*Couplets Amhariques du Choa*' (*Journal Asiatique*, 1924) and in the same author's '*Sur la notation musicale éthiopienne*' (*Levi della Vida Festschrift*, Rome, 1956).

Among three works by a musicologist of international repute, one has a direct bearing on Ethiopian music, while the other two are of great importance for an understanding of the general musical setting of which Abyssinian musical expression forms part: E. Wellesz, '*Studien zur aethiopischen Kirchenmusik*' (*Oriens Christianus*, 1920); *Byzantine Music and Hymnography* (Oxford, 1949); and *Ancient and Oriental Music* (London, 1957) of which Wellesz is the editor and in which H. G. Farmer's 'The Music of Ancient Egypt', C. H. Kraeling's 'Music in the Bible', and E. Werner's 'Music of Post-Biblical Judaism' are of particular relevance. Of great value in this context is also A. M. Rothmüller's *The Music of the Jews* (London, 1953).

While the importance of music, song and dirge, dance as well as instruments, is common to most peoples of the East, we are, I suggest, able to recognize specifically Hebraic-Old Testament elements in the musical manifestations, largely of a religious character, of the Ethiopians. The fact as such had been recognized by scholars as long ago as

[1] On Michael Powne's introduction see the penultimate footnote.

Ludolf (*Commentarius*, pp. 380–1) and as recently as Rathjens (*Juden in Abessinien*, p. 48), but their statements were based on impression rather than detailed evidence.

Professor Gavino Gabriel, an authority on music, says (in an unpublished note): 'The Abyssinian talks and sings in falsetto or "*voix de tête*" which represents a considerable economy of breath, so that he can sing all his life without showing signs of weariness.' A similar tireless capacity seems to be implied with regard to the Levites in 1 Chron. 23:30, and the same falsetto element probably applied to the vocal parts in the Hebrew Temple services, though it would appear that the occasional indications to that effect in the Old Testament may not always have been properly understood.[1]

The Levites had been set apart for the service of the Ark and for choral functions. The twofold division of the Israelite priesthood is paralleled in Ethiopia by the categories of *kahen* and *debtera*. The office of the latter is in most respects comparable to the tasks entrusted to the Levites, particularly in their role as cantors and choristers. That had already been recognized by B. Tellez and by Ludolf (*Lex. Aeth.*, col. 504).

The *debtera* occupies in the Ethiopian Church an 'intermediate' position 'between the clergy and laymen'.[2] 'Though the *debtera* are not ordained . . . , no service can properly be held without their presence. It is their chief duty to chant the psalms and hymns.'[3] According to 1 Chronicles 23:3–5, David's census established that Levites were employed as Temple-supervisors, as clerks and judges, as orderlies, and as musicians and singers. Similarly, the *debtera* look after the administration of the larger churches and their musical and liturgical requirements. They are trained in the study of Amharic and Ge'ez, but their attainments in the latter in particular are apt to vary widely. They undergo instruction in *kene* 'poetry or sacred hymns', *zema* 'song', *aqwaqwam* 'dancing and rhythmical movements', and, at least in theory, also in Bible, *Fetha Nagast*, and canon law.

The main musical manifestation of Abyssinian women is trilling, an immensely effective tremulous vibration which can be heard on all

---

[1] Cf. *Ethiopia and the Bible*, pp. 89–97.
[2] Hyatt, *Church of Abyssinia*, p. 59.
[3] *Ibidem.*

solemn occasions within the church and outside it. This ululating sound had already been connected by Isenberg with certain musical utterances in the ancient Hebrew worship: Hebrew *hallel* (Halleluyah), Ethiopic *ellel*.

Among musical instruments the Abyssinian *kerar* 'lyre' of six or ten strings has its counterpart (probably also etymologically) in the Hebrew *kinnor* played by David. The *bagana* 'harp' of eight or ten strings corresponds to the *nebel* in the Old Testament. A most effective and very popular instrument is the one-stringed *masanko*, while the *kabaro* ('tambourine') is probably the earliest and most widespread instrument. Its primary function is to indicate rhythm and it may thus be compared to the Hebrew *tof* ('drum'). The sistrum, *sanasel*, corresponds to Hebrew *mena'an'im*, though etymologically it is presumably *selselim* 'cymbals' that is related to *sanasel*.

And no Ethiopian musical occasion is complete without the prayer-stick (*makwamiya*) which plays so prominent a part in marking the beat, accompanied by rhythmic hand-clapping, at all religious ceremonies. As in 2 Sam. 6:5, so still in Ethiopia today there is the dancing, the beating of drums, the rattling of sistra—a truly biblical scene with its bright colours and almost hypnotic musical accompaniment.

In the Ethiopian *Deggwa* or Hymnary we find an elaborate system of musical notation which, in many ways, seems reminiscent of the biblical *te'amim* and *neginoth* or τρόπος. These signs consist of letters as well as dots and circles placed above the relevant syllable; they indicate the raising or lowering of the voice as well as other modes of voice production, but in the absence of proper investigation it would be hazardous to be more specific. The system arose during the early Middle Ages—just as Hebrew cantillation appears to derive its origin, at least in part, from the neume notation of the Greek Gospels current at that time. There are nine or more Ethiopic signs, and the present writer has suggested elsewhere[1] very tentatively how some of these might be set against their Hebrew equivalents, both in meaning and musical significance. As far as can be judged at present, the Ethiopian signs do not possess any of the syntactical and hermeneutical significance which the biblical *te'amim* display; their object seems to be purely the indication of the correct liturgical chant.

[1] *Ethiopia and the Bible*, p. 96.

Three modes of *zema* are being distinguished in Ethiopia: (1) *ge'ez*, for weekdays, is the ordinary and basic mode and probably also the oldest; (2) *ezel* for Lent, days of fasting, and funeral ceremonies; and (3) *araray* is reserved for feasts and days of joy. A similar division exists also in the case of the Hebrew *niggunim* which vary in very much the same manner.

Many of the existing uncertainties about musical patterns that were used by singers and instrumentalists in biblical times could be removed by a thorough study of the Ethiopian liturgical chant and the musical instruments still in use. But time is pressing, for the day is approaching when jazz and rock 'n roll present a serious challenge to the survival of traditional musical forms in Ethiopia.

Postscript

Among recent studies on Ethiopian music the following may be noted:

Ashenafi Kebede, *ya-muziqa sawasew*, Addis Ababa, 1967; *idem*, 'The Krar' in *Ethiopia Observer*, XI, 3; *idem* and Kurt Suttner, *Äthiopien: Musik der Koptischen Kirche*, Berlin, 1969.

Balint Sarosi, 'Melodic patterns in the folk music of the Ethiopian peoples', in *Proceedings, 3rd Int. Conf. of Ethiopian Studies*, vol. II, Addis Ababa, 1970.

IX

DAILY LIFE AND CUSTOMS

⟿⟿⟿⟿⟲⟳⟿⟿⟿⟿

I N WRITING of the life and customs of the Ethiopians, I am thinking of traditional Ethiopia, within whose atmosphere, both mental and material, the overwhelming majority of the people are still living. At times traditional Abyssinia reaches within a few yards of the small urbanized and partially Westernized minority who govern the country or are engaged in those administrative and commercial duties which have become the outward manifestations of our modern bureaucratic civilization. Some of these urban officials and administrators remain throughout within the grasp of this new, foreign, and imported way of life, while many of them every evening re-cross the frontier into the Ethiopia of old—often only a few paces away, even in the modern and bustling capital of cosmopolitan elegance and American cars.

Naturally, there are many different ways of life and many different sets of customs within the political confines of the large Ethiopian state, but we shall again only be concerned with the life of the people of historic Abyssinia, the monophysite Christian majority of the central and northern highlands, since they alone embody and represent traditional Ethiopia, internally as well as in the eyes of the outside world.

The elaborate architecture depicted on the Aksum monoliths or exemplified in the Church of Debra Damo was, of course, exclusively that of a number of ecclesiastical and royal prestige buildings. Even in the heyday of Aksumite power and prosperity the ordinary Abyssinian lived in a modest hut—as indeed he still does today. The usual type of house in Ethiopia is the round *tukul* or *agdo* with a cone-shaped roof. It appears that circular structures and conical thatched roofs stand up more successfully to winds and heavy rain, and the roof in particular can more easily be made watertight. In smaller houses the roof is supported by a big pole, while larger buildings usually have an inner concentric circle of props. The round skeleton of such huts is made of tree trunks and branches tied together with bundles of straw and then frequently cemented and plastered over. The interior is usually similarly treated with a mixture of mud, clay, and ash. There is one fairly low door and no windows or other openings; light and air have to enter by the door. The 'hearth' consists either of a hole in the ground or is made in the form of a small earthen elevation. The beds, placed by the walls, are similarly built of a ridge of earth on which hides and blankets are spread out.

That is, of course, the simplest and humblest type of dwelling, without any internal divisions—except, on occasion, a small compartment for animals. Larger *tukuls* of more prosperous owners can be a good deal more elaborate: the cylindrical wooden structure is often strengthened by stones either inserted or superimposed in layers, but the large amount of wood needed for the building and not infrequent reconstruction of these huts has, incidentally, caused serious deforestation of the Abyssinian uplands, especially in the north. As prosperity increases, internal divisions, generally of wood, sometimes of stone, become more common. These internal walls are concentric, so that little round corridors enclose the central part of the house. In such cases we would also be likely to find one or more windows placed fairly high in the outer wall.

The villages of the Tigrai and Eritrea are of a less uniform type. Houses may be either round or rectangular (the latter kind is, perhaps, more common and is called *hedmo*) and are at times of substantial size. They are usually built of stone, rough blocks, in some cases held together by a sort of mud-mortar and in others ingeniously stacked without any such binding substance. As rainfall in the north is somewhat lighter, roofs here are almost invariably flat—as is, of course, also the case in the adjacent and sun-baked regions of Semitic western Asia. These flat roofs usually protrude a few feet and are supported by large poles which are secured in the ground in front of the house and form a sort of portico (called *gebela*). The roof itself consists of layers of twigs and branches and earth. Very frequently whole villages are perched along the slopes of hills and *ambas*, at times so steep that the mountain forms the back wall of the house. This type of building is so perfectly adapted to the landscape, with its mud-coloured contours, that it represents the most effective kind of camouflage and is scarcely visible from the air. The interior of the humbler houses is marked by haphazardly distributed wooden columns which help to support the roof. There is ordinarily no walled division, but frequently grain-jars separate the living quarters from the 'kitchen' and stores. The space near the entrance serves, throughout the rainy and cold seasons, as a sitting-room during the day and by night as a stable for animals.

The layout of villages is generally irregular and quite haphazard, yet at times the overall effect is far from displeasing. Village and district chiefs (*chikka* and *meslenie*, respectively) and other important personages usually live in larger and more elaborately constructed houses (at times with an upper storey) which often possess a sizeable reception hall (*addarash*). In the towns officials, ministers, and other well-to-do people live in European-type houses, often of great spaciousness, which are in every way comparable to dwellings in the materially most advanced countries. Yet even in the insanitary conditions of the humble huts in remote villages, without the most rudimentary means of plumbing and often far away from brooks or streams, disease is not as prevalent as one might fear. But one must hope that the steady advance of Ethiopia will in time also improve housing conditions and raise the level of hygiene in even the most distant and inaccessible parts of the country.[1]

Furnishings in the majority of huts are extremely limited and usually consist of a couple of low stools, a large stone serving as a table (sometimes baskets or wooden tables are available), and kitchen utensils. Hooks are liberally distributed all over the interior of houses to hang up clothes, hides, water containers, knives, and anything else that need not occupy the restricted floor-space.[2]

The national dress of Ethiopians is the toga-like white *shamma* which is a rectangular shawl, exceeding 3 yards in length, hand-woven and

[1] A detailed treatment of private and public buildings, though limited to the Aksum region, will be found in Vol. III of the *Aksum Expedition* (with photographs and drawings).

[2] Op. cit., photographs 76 and 120.

made of cotton.[1] Both men and women wear the *shamma*, but the manner in which it is draped by women differs from that of men. If this garment has a wide red stripe not far from the hem, it is called *jano* and is worn on feast days; it is then also differently folded. Underneath the *shamma* men will be dressed in cotton trousers or white jodhpurs which are tight-fitting from knee to ankle, while women have shirt-like dresses with very full skirts of ankle length. These dresses are often made of beautifully coloured materials.

Men of distinction wear a silk tunic (*kamis*), magnificently embroidered and coloured according to their rank. Both men and women may wrap a cloak (*barnos*) over their shoulders, especially in the cool evenings. These garments are often richly ornamented and lined with leather. Most of the people walk barefoot, but some wear sandals. Very few Ethiopians cover their heads, though a hood is ordinarily attached to the *barnos*, and recently European headgear has been gaining ground among men. Small umbrellas, woven from grass or reeds, are sometimes carried as a protection against rain or sun.[2] At church ceremonies highly colourful or intricately ornamented brocade umbrellas are carried by the great dignitaries. In the towns European dress has been spreading at a rapid pace.

The Ethiopian national dish is *injera* (bread) and *wat* (*zegeni* in Tigrinya), a kind of curried stew made of beef, mutton, or chicken, often with some hard-boiled eggs, and most liberally seasoned with red pepper (*berbere*) and other spices. It is an excellent and most delicious dish, but the uninitiated foreigner will at first suspect that his alimentary channels have been set on fire. He will, therefore, have generous recourse to the extremely tasty and potent *tedj* (*mies* in Tigrinya), a sort of honey-mead, or *talla*, the Ethiopian beer.

Injera is a type of unleavened bread made of *teff* (millet) or barley; it is circular, generally 18 inches in diameter and less than $\frac{1}{4}$ inch in height. It is baked in a large earthenware or iron pan (called *mogogo*) over the open fire. The meat (beef or mutton) is either eaten raw (*berundo*), especially at large and usually most colourful banquets, or in the form of *wat* (or *zegeni*) and also as *fetfet*, i.e. small pieces of meat cooked in a sauce of butter and pepper.

[1] Cf. Messing in *Anthropos*, 1960.
[2] Cf. the novel by Dana Faralla, *The Straw Umbrella*.

Tedj is made of honey and water and then fermented with the leaves and bitter roots of the *saddo* (*Rhamnus saddo*) or *gesho* (*Rhamnus pauciflorus*) trees. It is not only a delicious but also a highly inebriating drink, and is invariably kept in an attractive, round-bellied bottle with a very tall neck of decanter shape (called *berille*). While *tedj* is prepared by men, *talla* or beer is usually made by women. The main ingredient is barley, and the leaves of the *gesho* are used for fermentation; *talla* is drunk out of horn-shaped vessels.

Except by the well-to-do, fruit is not widely eaten, nor sweets or sugared dishes. The excellent Ethiopian coffee is usually drunk bitter; it is served in double-handled pottery jugs of carafe shape. In the major towns European cuisine is gaining ground rapidly.

The *Fetha Nagast*[1] contains a sizeable section dealing with the laws of marriage. Polygamy is forbidden by the Ethiopian Penal Code, but divorce is relatively easy; and though there exists undoubtedly a good deal of promiscuity, relations between the sexes appear unstrained and free from the elements of dissimulation and pretence, so often present in western society. Sexual morals, in any event, have to be seen in their natural and indigenous context and must not be judged by alien and inapplicable criteria.

Three forms of marriage are current in Ethiopia:

(1) *Damoz* is a limited and 'salaried' matrimonial arrangement by which a woman agrees with a man to cohabit for a specified time (a month or longer), renewable or terminable at the wish of either party, and at a specified remuneration. This is a purely contractual arrangement, and unless her salary has been in arrears the woman has no claim against her partner's estate. On the other hand, any issue from such a union is regarded as legitimate with the same rights of inheritance as children born in lawful and full wedlock. Neither the Church nor the 'Establishment' looks with favour upon such temporary unions.

(2) The most common form of marriage in Ethiopia is called *kal kidan* or *serat*, a binding civil marriage contract entered into by the parents of the prospective bride and bridegroom. This is usually, though

[1] Ethiopia now possesses a penal code (1957) and a civil code (1960). Cf. Moreno in *RSE*, XX (1964) and G. Krzeczunowicz in *JES*, I (1963).

not invariably, preceded by a long engagement until the bride reaches the age of puberty and is declared by her parents fit for marriage. During the period of the engagement, the bridegroom is not supposed to meet his betrothed or any of her female relations. When the marriage is finally celebrated, without any ecclesiastical intervention and purely as a civil ceremony, there are several days of feasting on a very lavish scale which usually far exceeds the financial resources of the two families. After the wedding the bride follows her husband to his parents' house, but in many cases she returns again to her own home for a limited period. Upon consummation of the marriage, the young couple will join the household of the husband's parents and only after about two or three years will they request a plot of land from the village community and build on it their own house. Modern practice, especially in the larger urban centres, may vary perceptibly and increasingly follows the European pattern. 'Registry Office' marriages without previous engagement can be solemnized by a *danya* ('magistrate') at the municipal offices.

(3) The civil marriage does not require, and in the majority of cases does not receive, the additional sanction of the Church. A small number of people prefer, however, to celebrate their marriage in a religious ceremony as well, which consists of joint communion (*kwerban*); hence this type of marriage is called *kal kidan bekwerban* or just *bekwerban*. Such marriages are, strictly speaking, indissoluble and are therefore frequently chosen by elderly people who have long been united in civil marriage and now feel sure that divorce can safely be ruled out in their case. Church ceremonies are customary also among the ruling classes and are compulsory for the clergy.

While the Monophysite Church does not ordinarily admit dissolution of unions blessed by religious celebration, there are some rare cases in which a divorce has been granted by both the High Court and the Ecclesiastical Courts.[1] Civil marriages can be dissolved at the request of either party, the woman having equal rights with regard to divorce proceedings. Negotiations leading to a dissolution are frequently accompanied by long discussions about the division of the property. Customary law decrees, as a rule, that each spouse retains such property as he or she has contributed to the common pool, but codes diverge as

[1] Cf. Marein, *Federation and Laws*, p. 162.

to the question of forfeiture by the guilty partner and the division of property acquired since the beginning of the marriage.

A woman's rights with regard to divorce are symptomatic of the comparatively favourable legal position of women in Ethiopia. While women in traditional society may still occupy a subordinate, though by no means oppressed or unprivileged, place, emancipation of women in the towns and among the wives of senior officials has, in recent times, progressed at an astonishing and most gratifying pace. Ethiopian women today lend charm and grace to social life, and with the spread of education among women they become increasingly able to hold their own with their menfolk.

Ethiopian personal onomastics is an intricate subject that requires comprehensive investigation,[1] having regard to considerable regional variations and the influence of modernization. In the Tigrinya-speaking areas of the north children generally receive a baptismal name and take their father's name in addition: e.g. child's name Yohannes, father's name Gebre-Maskal ('servant of the cross'); the next generation will now be named, say, Walda-Sellasie ('son of the Trinity') Yohannes, and so forth. Among the Tigre tribes children are usually given two names, of which one is used by men, the other by women.

Among the peoples of Amharic speech customs are not uniform, but ordinarily Amharas bear their father's name as the second element (though there are many exceptions to this statement), and receive, in addition, a secular and a baptismal name. If one child has died or some other disaster has befallen the family, the new-born baby will often be called *Kassa* ('compensation', *Ersatz*). Among common secular names for men are *Hagos* ('joy'), *Desta* ('pleasure'), *Mebrahtu* ('light'), *Tesfaye* ('my hope'), etc., and for women *Ababa* ('flower'), *Terunesh* ('you are pure'), *Hagosa* (see above), *Zawditu* ('crown'), *Belainesh* ('you are superior'), etc. Typical Christian names are compounds with *Gebre*- ('servant of'), *Walda*- ('son of'), *Amete*-('maid of'), *Walatta*- ('daughter of'), *Tesfa*- ('hope of'), *Tekla*- ('plant of'), *Haile*- ('power of'), *Habte*

---

[1] A few observations with regard to parts of the Amharic-speaking area may be found in M. Cohen's notes in *Proceedings and Transactions, Third International Congress of Toponymy and Anthroponymy* (Louvain) 1951, pp. 774–7. See also Ricci in *RSE*, XXI (1966), pp. 111–61.

('gift of'), etc. Examples are: Gebre-Yesus ('servant of Jesus'), Amete-Maryam ('maid of Mary'), Walatta-Sion ('daughter of Zion'), Habte-Mika'el ('gift of Michael'), Walda-Ab ('son of the Father'), etc.

Death is followed by the most vigorous manifestations of mourning. Men and women will lament and cry, recite dirges and sing the praises of the departed. All this will be punctuated with the shrill notes of ululating women. Relatives will tear their clothes, throw themselves to the ground, and appear in sackcloth and ashes. The body of the deceased is then washed, wrapped in a white sheet, and taken to church, where it receives the blessing of the priest. The burial, usually in rather shallow graves, takes place a few hours after death has occurred, but the performance of the funeral rites and prayers may be prolonged. There are generally no inscribed headstones, and graves are variously marked by small piles of stones in pyramid shape or by one large stone or even by indicating the outline of the grave by a neat row of pebbles distinguishing the burial-place from the surrounding ground.

Similar to Hebraic customs is the daily assembly of relatives and friends in the house of the deceased throughout the first week of mourning, when prayers are said, laments are recited, and—as in some parts of Europe—generous hospitality is dispensed to all and sundry. On the twelfth, fortieth and eightieth days after death memorial services (*tezkar*) are held in church, and these are frequently followed by sumptuous banquets, which may at times impose a heavy financial burden on the bereaved.

The canons of Ethiopian etiquette are strict and well regulated, and there exists a good deal of punctiliousness in Ethiopian life which is far removed from empty ceremoniousness. Ethiopians are generally wonderfully polite to each other and show consideration and respect even to the humblest among them. Quarrels in public or undignified scenes are rare. Unhappily, urban life and not infrequently the bad example of Europeans have in recent times contributed to a slight lowering of these high standards, but it must be hoped that Ethiopians will be able to maintain their own codes of polite behaviour in the face of outside influences.

When people meet on the road (apart, of course, from the larger urban centres), they will inquire after each other's health even if they are strangers. While the formulae employed in this elaborate exchange of greetings are stereotyped, it would be wrong to infer that they are meaningless or insincere. The type of greeting will, of course, vary with the importance and position of the person concerned. A low bow is *de rigueur* in almost all instances. If the *shamma* covers one's head, hood-like, it will be lowered, and at times also the shoulders may be uncovered. Frequently the ground is touched with the right hand which is then brought to the lips. Children will often prostrate themselves completely before their father or grandfather and kiss his feet. Genuflexion by adults is nowadays generally reserved for the Emperor and persons of high rank.

On encountering a friend or acquaintance, the exchange of the formulae of greetings may take fully a minute or two, and if neither of them has time or occasion to stop, the pronouncements will continue long after the two persons have passed each other and are some distance apart:

'How are you?' or 'How have you passed the night?'

'Thanks be to God. I am well. How are you?'

'Thanks be to God. I am well.'

'How are your sons?'

And this will be followed by inquiries after other members of the family, animals, harvest, etc. It is only after this unhurried exchange of courtesies (and the same, incidentally, applies to epistolary etiquette) that one speaks of matters of substance. And convention demands that the replies to all the questions during the initial interchange are in the affirmative: 'Well, thanks be to God'—whatever the real position may be. Bad news is communicated only later on after the requirements of etiquette have been satisfied.

The handshake is customary only among equals, though there has been some relaxation in this respect. But when hands are joined, they remain in this position throughout the entire greeting. Kissing among relatives, friends, and acquaintances of either sex is very common, the only exception being husband and wife who will scarcely ever be seen exchanging kisses in public. Among relatives kisses on the mouth are the usual practice, both among persons of the same and the opposite sex, but kisses are never single—they always come in a prolonged series

(a) *Ethiopian manuscript*

(b) *Bizen Monastery*

(a) *The Church remains the centre of Ethiopian life*

(b) *Modern Addis Ababa*

and are punctuated with the formulae of greeting previously described. Friends and acquaintances are kissed repeatedly on the cheek. Persons of seniority or members of the clergy are embraced in such a way that they can kiss and be kissed on the right shoulder, always repeatedly and interrupted by the exchange of courtesies. Before one approaches one's parents for the familiar kisses, the usual bows and prostrations due to a person of rank or regard are performed. The collective greeting of women, especially in honour of chiefs and notables, is the sound of ululating. On receiving a gift, one stretches out both hands; offering one hand only connotes reluctance on the part of the recipient.

The Ethiopian year[1] consists of 365 days distributed over twelve months, each of thirty days, plus one additional month, at the end of the year, containing five days only (six days in leap years). The incongruities between the Ethiopian calendar and ours arise from those of the Julian and Gregorian computations, respectively. From 11 September till 31 December the Ethiopian era is seven years behind ours, while for the remainder of the year the gap amounts to eight years. This difference originates from a divergence between the Roman and Ethiopian Churches as to the date of the creation of the world.

The Ethiopian New Year falls on 11 September (the 12th in leap years which, incidentally, precede ours by one year) in the month of *Maskaram. Tekemt* lasts from 11 October to 9 November; *Hedar* (10 November to 9 December); *Tahsas* (10 December to 8 January); *Ter* (9 January to 7 February); *Yakatit* (8 February to 9 March); *Magabit* (10 March to 8 April); *Miyazya* (9 April to 8 May); *Genbot* (9 May to 7 June); *Sane* (8 June to 7 July); *Hamle* (8 July to 6 August); *Nahase* (7 August to 5 September); *Pagwemen* (6–10 or 11 September). Thus 1 Maskaram 1951 (Ethiopian era) corresponds to 11 September 1958. These computations are no idle theory, for the traditional calendar is in universal use in Ethiopia and is referred to as *Amata Mehrat* ('Era [or 'Year'] of Mercy') in contrast to the Gregorian calendar.

The years are classified by the names of the Evangelists: Matthew, Mark, Luke, and John, the extra day of the leap year always being added in St. Luke's year. The names of the days of the week betray an

[1] Cf. Conti Rossini, *Tabelle Comparative del Calendario Etiopico col Calendario Romano*, Rome, 1948.

G

Hebraic origin; and the beginning of the day of twenty-four hours is
reckoned—in Semitic fashion—from sunset (=6 p.m. European =12.00
Ethiopian; sunrise =6 a.m. European =00.00 Ethiopian). Thus, if an
Ethiopian wishes to meet you at, say, 4 a.m. (Ethiopian time), he
will expect you at 10 a.m. (European reckoning). Yet, whether he will
actually be there is somewhat doubtful, for Ethiopia remains a country
of timelessness, where time, this overvalued commodity, is still in ample
supply; and it is only the impatient and unacclimatized European to
whom this attitude of largesse is the bane of his life.

While the *Fetha Nagast* retains a measure of importance in ecclesiastical circles and while the central courts administer the new legal codes,
in day-to-day life regional customary law[1] is, of course, of primary
relevance. As this quasi-legal system is essentially parochial and usually
of rather limited territorial concern and is also, with some exceptions,
neither properly codified nor written down, it will in this context only
be possible to offer a few general observations of fairly wide applic-
ability, especially to the northern parts of the Abyssinian tableland.

The main political units of Ethiopian peasant society are the district
and particularly the village. In many cases the district represents a
traditional entity, though certain districts have been re-defined or
newly created in recent times. Each district is administered by a chief
styled *meslenie*. But among the highland population which is concentrated in large settlements the village is the traditional focus of social
life. It is governed by a village chief (*chikka*) who is elected by the village
or at times nominated by the district chief. The basic kinship unit is the
enda which consists of the offspring of a common ancestor, many
generations back, by whose name the *enda* is known. Historically it has
grown out of the individual family; fully crystallized, it embraces a
greatly varying number of family units who often live together in the
same or adjacent houses, work together, and share the fruits of their
labour. An understanding of the status of the *enda* and village organiza-

[1] See especially Ostini, *Diritto Consuetudinario; Adkeme Melga Law Code*
(Tigrinya and Italian), Asmara, 1944; *Consuetudini Giuridiche del Serae* (Tigrinya
and Italian), 2 vols. (edited by C. Conti Rossini and L. Ricci, respectively), Rome,
1948, 1953; *Logo Tchwa Law Code* (in Tigrinya), Asmara, 1946. For general
principles see C. Conti Rossini, *Principi di diritto consuetudinario dell' Eritrea*, Rome,
1916; also Brit. Mil. Admin. of Eritrea, *Glossary of Tigrinya terms in law, custom,
and land tenure*, Asmara, 1943.

tion is essential to a proper appreciation of customary law and land tenure.

The material which constitutes the juridical basis of customary law (called *wag*) is generally collected and defined at meetings of elders, notables, and chiefs. These assemblies establish general principles, they do not (at least not until recently) reduce the law to writing. The sole effective repository of customary law is thus the individual and collective memory of all those who were present at such councils. Much of this legal material is expressed in the form of maxims which are frequently ascribed to a specific author, usually a tribal ancestor or some outstanding chief.

On the whole, the system of justice dispensed by the traditional courts works admirably. From the arbitrator (*danya*) and the village chief to proper tribunals, presided over by senior district chiefs and assisted by assessors, we find a well integrated legal structure which inspires confidence among all those who have witnessed its performance. As has already been mentioned at the end of Chapter III, every Ethiopian takes the closest interest in litigation and in the work of the lower courts. Most Ethiopians possess an astonishing knowledge of customary law enhanced by clear thinking, memory, and a wonderful facility of eloquent exposition. It is, therefore, not surprising that Abyssinians generally conduct their lawsuits in person, for they usually derive much pleasure from the sheer presentation of their case which encourages in them the feeling that justice is being done. The act of pleading has been elevated to a minor art, and as long as the litigant is allowed virtually unlimited time for the leisurely exposition of his grievance, he will be content with the final verdict. Advocates (*tebeka*), i.e. experts in customary law and procedure, are employed only in cases of exceptional intricacy.

Most of the minor cases come before a *danya* who is at once arbitrator and magistrate. Anyone can act as a *danya* if both parties agree that his qualifications are adequate. A common form of arbitration is also that which is exercised by three arbitrators appointed *ad hoc* by the litigants. The *danya* or the arbitrators must hold the hearing in public and are usually assured of a large crowd who will almost invariably be found at the assembly place in the village. There are two interesting procedural points: the two parties can at any stage agree to make a wager (*werdi* in

Tigrinya, *wererred* in Amharic) that they are able to prove the truth of a given assertion (the amount of the bet is customarily fixed by bidding). The value of the wager is later handed over to the *danya* by the losing party. The other point is that one of the litigants can apply for a restraint or a type of injunction to be placed upon the other contestant, in order to prevent him from interfering with witnesses or interrupting the public proceedings by irrelevancies.

There is no trial by ordeal or torture, but an interesting custom is sometimes practised in the southern regions. It is called *liebasha* and is meant to identify the perpetrator of a theft or robbery. A suitably qualified person, known for special aptitude in such matters, is placed in a trance or under a form of hypnosis, often induced by inhaling the smoke of burning herbs, and he will then somnambulate to the house of the thief or his hide-out. The verdict of the *liebasha* is generally accepted.

Of greater importance is a form of customary oath (*fetm* in Amharic, *fesmi* in Tigrinya) which is pronounced at the acceptance of certain obligations, promises, renunciations, etc. The solemn formula used for this oath or injunction is *negus yemut* 'may the King die if. . .'. The force of the formula lies in the fact that the defaulter will have threatened the life of the King. A heavy fine is imposed for the breach of *fetm* (it used to be 120 Maria Theresa thalers). Another type of injunction, used particularly in the north, is that called *zeban negus*, literally 'by the back of the King'. It is a formula that can be applied in the most diverse circumstances: to subpoena witnesses, to prevent access to persons or chattels, to command or hinder a certain action. This formal injunction (*gezzi*) has legal validity and continues in force until removed by the court. The object of these injunctions is to prevent the commission of wrongs in conditions where no police or other agents of enforcement are readily available and when it is essential that any potentially harmful action should be stayed till a competent court has had occasion to pronounce on the matter.

Most litigation in the highland provinces of Ethiopia arises from land-rights. The principles of land tenure vary, at least to some extent, from province to province and are so involved and complicated that only the most general aspects can be rehearsed here. It had long been accepted in Ethiopia that all land was owned by the Emperor, so that in theory at least every cultivator of land (*gabbar*) was a tenant of the Emperor. The practical implication of this constitutional theory was that the collectivity of *gabbar*, through their work on the land, had to provide for the maintenance of the government, both central and provincial, for the Army, and for the Church.

By far the most important form of land tenure is family or group ownership (*rest* in Amharic, *resti* in Tigrinya). *Rest* is 'hereditary' possession of the land and is deeply rooted in the social structure of Ethiopia. It refers more commonly to ownership by a kinship group rather than by an individual, but historically *rest* is conceived as being derived from an originally clearly defined single notion of ownership— that founded on the first occupation of land by an individual family. With the natural growth of the family of the original occupants the title to the land changed from an individual to a collective right. The council of elders of each village group will assign the land to individual families and lay down a strict system of rotation. *Rest* is, however, much more than an economic benefit; it lends to each *restenya*, each holder of *rest*, social status based on the permanent and inalienable possession of land.

Crown lands comprise such property as was either abandoned or of which the original title had become extinct through the dissolution of the hereditary kinship group or any other cause. Apart from that there exist large territorial fiefs (*gult* in Amharic, *gulti* in Tigrinya) conferred upon chiefs, troops, or the Church. The feudal landlord (*gultenya*) became the owner of all land so granted, and the peasants on his domain, whatever their original title to the land may have been, were reduced to tenant status. Unlike all other land, *gult* was free of tribute.

Monasteries and churches used to own large territorial fiefs. A portion of the land is generally worked by the monks themselves, the rest is hired out to the peasants of neighbouring villages. Much of the wealth and power of the Church is based on these possessions, and considering the enormous number of churches in Ethiopia one might almost give credence to the legend according to which King Menelik I, on his return from King Solomon, divided the land into three equal parts: one for the Crown, one for the Church, and one for the people.

Schemes for the reform of some aspects of land tenure are now being contemplated and are, in fact, in the forefront of current political thinking in Ethiopia. The Emperor has already provided for the distribution of public land to farmers and for the amelioration of their legal position, since as owners rather than tenants they would gain an added interest in the improvement and care of their land.

Postscript

The following works are relevant to the problems of land tenure in Ethiopia:

Ambaye Zekarias, *Land tenure in Eritrea* (Ethiopia), Addis Ababa, 1966.

British Military Administration, Eritrea, *Land tenure on the Eritrean plateau*, Asmara, 1944.

Ethiopian Government, *Report on land tenure survey of Tigre province*, Addis Ababa, 1969.

Hoben, A., 'Land tenure and social mobility among the Damot Amhara' in *Proceedings, 3rd Int. Conf. of Ethiopian Studies*, vol. III, Addis Ababa, 1970.

Lambton, A. K. S., 'Ethiopia: an approach to land reform' in *BSOAS*, XXXIV, 2 (1971).

Mann, H.S., *Land tenure in Chore (Shoa)*, Addis Ababa, 1965.

Moreno, M. M., 'La terminologia dei nuovi codici etiopici' in *RSE*, XX, 1964.

Pankhurst, Richard, *State and land in Ethiopian history*, Addis Ababa, 1966.

X

ETHIOPIA TODAY

━━━∿∿∿∿∿◖Ⓞ◗∿∿∿∿∿━━━

O NE of the first things the Emperor Haile Sellasie did after
his Coronation in 1930 (see end of Chapter IV) was to offer
his people a written Constitution. This was an entirely
voluntary act for which there had been no public clamour in the
country, but it has always been the Emperor's particular strength to
judge the right moment and to grant the right measure of advance.
True, the 1931 Constitution was a modest affair in that the two delibera-
tive chambers (the members of the Senate being appointed by the
Emperor from among the dignitaries, and the members of the Chamber
of Deputies being chosen by the dignitaries and chiefs) could in effect
only advise the Emperor; yet the real significance did not lie in the
powers of the new parliament but in the Emperor's injunction to his
people that 'it is necessary for the modern Ethiopian to accustom himself to take part in the direction of all departments of the State' and 'to
share in the mighty task which Ethiopian Sovereigns have had to
accomplish alone in the past'.[1]

There then followed the appointment of Ministers and foreign
advisers, the distribution of duties, the organization of security forces,
of financial administration and customs services, and all the paraphernalia of modern government. But all this could only be carried out with
the help of a reliable cadre of educated men. Education, in fact, was the
key to most achievements, and the Emperor has always been profoundly conscious of the overwhelming need of a properly integrated

[1] Speech by the Emperor on the occasion of the signing of the 1931 Constitution, English version p. 2.

educational system. Until 1960 he was his own Minister of Education, so as to underline the paramount importance attached to these endeavours. Ethiopian students who were pursuing their studies abroad used to do so on Ministry of Education grants, but many of them are nowadays supported by scholarships which are financed by non-Ethiopian sources. They were generally expected to appear before His Majesty upon their departure and return. Health services had to be initiated, and roads and communications needed urgent improvement. The reform of provincial administration, which previous Emperors throughout the centuries had found a Sisyphean task, could not be long delayed if the cohesion of the Empire was to be maintained and strengthened and if advance and newly created services were not to be limited to a small urban minority.

In the early 1930s, as indeed to some extent still now, the Emperor was the inspirer of most and the executant of many of the policies of government, diverse and intricate even at the stage of development in which Ethiopia found herself then. At that time the volume of work carried by the King of Kings virtually single-handed was immense, but the burden was made the heavier by the clouds of war that were unmistakably gathering on the horizon.

There is no need to go once more over the terrible episode of Fascist aggression in 1935–6 following upon a prolonged period of provocations, instigated by Mussolini, and all the, by now familiar, concomitants of a war of nerves. The story has so often been told and retold,[1] and many of us have retained such vivid and painful memories of those anxious days that want to be soothed rather than be stirred afresh. But amidst the holocaust of bombing and poison-gas raids as well as the futile debates of an impotent and frightened League of Nations there stood out the lonely, slight, and noble figure of the Emperor who, in 1936, came to Geneva to plead the cause of his people. There could have been no more dramatic or moving scene in the history of the League of Nations, and among the delegates there must have been many who knew in their hearts that the words of the prophet from Africa's oldest

---

[1] Never more effectively than in G. L. Steer's *Caesar in Abyssinia*, London, 1936. Cf. also the Earl of Avon, *The Eden Memoirs, Facing the Dictators* (1962), *passim* (Lord Avon, who, as Mr. Anthony Eden, had been so closely concerned with Ethiopia's fate, is now President of the Anglo-Ethiopian Society).

Christian Kingdom were bound to be fulfilled—as indeed they were within less than half a decade.

When the Emperor arrived in Britain, in 1936, he came as an exile, as the first victim of Fascist aggression. Many people will recall the spontaneous demonstrations of public sympathy which greeted him then. The painful journey from his own brutally conquered country to Jerusalem, London, Geneva, and Bath had stirred the imagination of a world that had become increasingly disturbed by the dictators' successful policy of aggression. But the way back in 1940–1, via Khartoum, was shorter and quicker than anyone had expected, and, after a campaign brilliantly conducted by Generals Platt, Cunningham, Wingate, and Sandford in the face of the most incredible odds and vigorously supported by Ethiopian patriots,[1] the first victim became the first monarch restored to his rightful throne.

There were two things which the Emperor especially stressed in a moving speech on that great day in 1941 when he re-entered his capital: reconstruction, development of education, agriculture, and commerce; and restraint and mercy towards the defeated enemy: 'Do not reward evil for evil. Do not commit any acts of cruelty like those which the enemy committed against us.' And it will for ever redound to the honour and glory of the Ethiopian people that in fact no Italian, man, woman, or child, was harmed in those days of excitement and victory. Since then, thousands of Italians have left the country, but thousands have remained in Eritrea and Ethiopia, and one must be glad that the bitterness of the past has been forgotten and that normal and indeed friendly relations have been resumed.

Yet all the elation of victory could not conceal the stark realities of the situation as it presented itself in 1941: the return to peace and normality of a people that for six years or more had lived through war, upheaval, and guerrilla fighting with all the attendant weakening of moral restraints; the accumulation of arms left behind by the retreating enemy; the confusion of loyalties and the disintegration of administration over so far-flung an empire; the dislocation of communications, the lack of transport, and the complete standstill of trade and commerce; the shortage of food and clothing; the elimination of the

[1] See the Ministry of Information's excellent *The Abyssinian Campaigns*, London, 1942.

educated *élite* whom the Emperor had carefully nursed before the invasion and the consequent lack of trained personnel; the delicate relations between patriots and 'collaborators', the guerrilla fighters who had to be rewarded, and the great Rases and chiefs who had to be reconciled to a new situation; and, finally, the British military authorities whose primary aim, and rightly so, was the successful prosecution of the war, then only in its beginning (Russia and America had not yet come in), and who could at times be impatient with a self-willed and strange ally.

It is against this sombre background that the achievements of the Emperor and the Ethiopian people have to be judged. The stability and relative prosperity which have been attained within so short a time are eloquent witnesses to the ability and resilience of the people and the foresight and enlightenment of their leadership. The greatest change has probably taken place in the post–1955 period, and especially since 1961, when the pace of reform and modernization have gained added momentum.

What does Ethiopia look like today, when during the reign of the present Emperor greater advance has taken place within the space of fifty years than during the 3,000 years between Menelik I and Menelik II; when Ethiopia has leapt from the early Middle Ages right into the atomic era of the twentieth century?

In trying to answer this question it is important to remember that Ethiopia, like any other developing country, is in a state of rapid change and transformation and that any assessment offered today is likely to have been overtaken by events tomorrow. It might be best to begin with a quick glance at the formal machinery of government. On the occasion of the twenty-fifth anniversary of his Coronation, in 1955, the Emperor promulgated a revised Constitution to supersede the one granted in 1931. This new Constitution has since been put into action and several General Elections were held for Parliament. It would be easy to dismiss these as so much window-dressing, but such facile comment would completely misjudge the Emperor's principal purpose of bringing the people at large into a gradual partnership of government. That cannot happen overnight, and, for the present, many Ethiopians seem content to leave all great decisions in the hands of the man who, in the eyes of his own people and of the world as a whole, is the very embodiment of Ethiopia. But the time will come, probably with the advent of the present Emperor's successor, the able and frequently underrated Crown Prince Asfa Wossen, when a constitutional monarchy, perhaps in the western sense or perhaps in some other form, will be established in the country. Ministers will then show a greater measure of independence and personal responsibility, and the people will be ready and willing to undertake their democratic duties. And, in the last resort, the Emperor's judgement has been proved right by the comparative absence of political agitation and upheaval, rife in many other parts of Africa, by which the careful evolutionary and gradual processes in Ethiopia have been characterized.

This judgement has not been materially impaired by the unsuccessful *coup d'état* of December 1960 nor by a measure of restiveness among young westernized Ethiopian civil servants and students. A certain loosening of the traditional fabric of Ethiopian society, at least in the larger urban centres, can now be discerned and is unquestionably one of the direct effects of the events of 1960; but the basic situation in the country as a whole remains one of fair stability and confidence.

The 1955 Constitution lays down that 'the Imperial dignity shall remain perpetually attached to the line of Haile Sellasie I, descendant of King Sahela Sellasie, whose line descends without interruption from the dynasty of Menelik I, son of the Queen of Ethiopia, the Queen of Sheba, and King Solomon of Jerusalem' (Article 2). It is interesting to note here the connection with Sahela Sellasie, King of Shoa, rather than with the last Emperors at Gondar. Equally significant is the continued insistence, and here in the cold terms of legal phraseology, on the *mystique* of a direct descent from King Solomon and the Queen of Sheba, a powerful reminder of the enduring efficacy of the *Kebra Nagast*. There also seems to adhere something of the idea of sacral kingship[1] to the conception of the Ethiopian monarchy: 'By virtue of His Imperial Blood, as well as by the anointing which He has received, the person of the Emperor is sacred, His dignity is inviolable and His power indisputable. . . .' (Article 4).[2] Under Article 13 of the Constitution the Imperial Crown can pass to a male descendant only, which means that under the law as it stands now the arrangement by which Zawditu

[1] Cf. A. R. Johnson, *Sacral Kingship in Ancient Israel*[2], Cardiff, 1967.
[2] See *Ethiopia and the Bible*, pp. 131–2.

became Empress could no longer operate. The Emperor must be the Defender of the 'Holy Orthodox Faith based on the doctrines of St. Mark of Alexandria' (Article 21).

As to the powers of the Emperor, Articles 27 and 28 provide that he appoints, promotes, transfers, suspends, and dismisses the officials of all ministries and departments as well as mayors of municipalities.[1] But war can only be declared by the Emperor 'with the advice and consent of Parliament' (Article 29). He alone exercises the supreme direction of the foreign relations of the Empire, but any modifications of the territory of the Empire or any financial undertakings laying a burden on his subjects require the approval of both Houses of Parliament before ratification by the Emperor (Article 30). He may initiate legislation and proclaim laws after they have been passed by Parliament (Article 34).

The rights of the people include the free exercise of the rites of any religion or creed 'provided that such rites be not utilized for political purposes' (Article 40). Freedom of speech and of the press is guaranteed, correspondence shall not be subject to censorship, and no one may be deprived of life, liberty, or property without due process of law (Articles 41–3). No suits can be brought against the Emperor, but legal action may be taken against any ministry or department of government (Article 62). It is clear that these and other provisions represent an ideal rather than the reflection of present conditions, though one may be confident of the speed with which the letter and spirit of the Constitution will be translated into living practice.

The Council of Ministers consists of the Prime Minister and the departmental Ministers, all of whom are appointed or dismissed by the Emperor (Article 66)[1] and are individually responsible to him (Article 68). At the time of writing the Prime Minister is *Tsahafe Te'ezaz* Aklilu Habte-Wald; he succeeded, after an interval of some years, the late Ras Bitwodded Makonnen Endalkatchew. Ministers are not members of Parliament, but they may attend the meetings of either

---

[1] The 'Ministers (Definition of Powers) Order' of March 1966 changes the position in so far as the Prime Minister may now select ministers and submit their names for approval by the Emperor. The practical effect of this provision will only become apparent when the Prime Minister himself has gained an adequate measure of independence of the Crown. (For the text of the Order see *Ethiopia Observer*, X, 1 (1966).)

Chamber and they shall be obliged to answer, orally or in writing, questions concerning legislation (which is presented to Parliament by the Prime Minister after approval by the Emperor) or the conduct of their Ministries (Articles 72-3). There are seventeen Ministries (Interior, Pen, Foreign Affairs, Education, National Defence, Finance, Justice, Commerce and Industry, Agriculture, Communications and Public Works, Post and Telegraph, Public Health, Information, Pension and Supply, National Community Development, Mines and State Domain, Imperial Court)[1] which are centralized at Addis Ababa but may have representatives in the provinces. Provincial administration, under Governors of districts and provinces, is carried out under the authority of the Ministry of Interior which is also charged with the preservation of law and order and with responsibility for the police forces.

The two Chambers of Parliament meet together at the beginning and end of each session and, if required, on certain other occasions. The meetings of the two Houses are open to the public. Members of Parliament receive a salary. Proceedings in Parliament are privileged, and members cannot be arrested on a criminal (as opposed to civil) charge, unless their immunity has been waived by leave of the Chamber. Laws may be proposed either by the Emperor or by at least ten members of either house, except that financial Bills shall first be presented to the Chamber of Deputies (Articles 76-86). When Parliament is in recess the Emperor may proclaim decrees which will become law if subsequently approved by both Houses; otherwise such decrees cease to have legal force (Article 92).

The Chamber of Deputies is elected by direct franchise, for which purpose the country is divided into electoral districts of about two hundred thousand inhabitants each (there are slightly more favourable conditions for towns), every such district returning two deputies. All Ethiopian subjects aged twenty-one or more may elect and, if aged twenty-five or over, may be elected to the Chamber of Deputies. The term of service of each deputy is four years and he is eligible for re-election (Articles 93-100).

Senators are appointed by the Emperor for six years. Their number must not exceed one half of the total number of deputies and they are

---

[1] The titles by which these ministries are known and the functions which they discharge are at times subject to minor variations.

selected from among princes, dignitaries, former senior government officials and other persons of high attainments. A senator's minimum age is thirty-five (Articles 101–3).

Addis Ababa is the official capital city of the Empire (Article 123) whose flag is green, yellow, red in horizontal bands (Article 124). The official language is Amharic (Article 125), and the Established Church of the Empire is the Ethiopian Orthodox Church based on the doctrines of St. Mark (Article 126).

Judges are appointed by the Emperor, and the Constitution guarantees their independence in the administration of the law. Trials are in public, except when the requirements of public order or morals make it necessary to conduct proceedings *in camera*. All legislation must be published in the official gazette (*Negarit Gazeta*) before coming into force. Apart from the village courts administering customary law (discussed in the preceding chapter) and Muslim *shari'a* courts dealing with matters of personal status, there are District Courts in many parts of the country. Provincial Courts have been established in each provincial capital with competence in both criminal and civil jurisdiction. The Imperial High Court is represented in the capital of each Governorate General. There are fourteen divisions of the Addis Ababa High Court (including land, probate, criminal, civil, and appeals). The Supreme Imperial Court is the ultimate tribunal of appeal in criminal and civil suits. Among the judges of the highest Courts in Ethiopia there used to be a few foreigners of several nationalities.

Death sentences require confirmation by the Emperor, who retains the prerogative of mercy. The volume of legislation that has been needed since the restoration (including that connected with the former federation of Eritrea) has been immense and has made heavy demands upon the combined talents of foreign and indigenous lawyers. Some time ago European jurists were engaged to prepare drafts of criminal, civil, and commercial codes, and these new Ethiopian legal systems have since been enacted. The Haile Sellasie I University now possesses a Faculty of Law with a sizeable enrolment of students.

Ethiopia is at present divided into fourteen provinces, each with a provincial capital and a Governor General:

Arussi is situated to the south of Addis Ababa. It is a province of fertile farmlands, mountain slopes, and valleys. A good all-weather road leads from Addis Ababa via Nazareth to Asela, the provincial capital.

Bale adjoins Arussi in the south-east. It is a large province extending to the borders of Somalia. The capital is Goba.

Begemder, in the north-west of the country, is one of the historic provinces of Ethiopia. It includes Lake Tana, and its capital is the medieval city of Gondar.

Eritrea is the northernmost province of Ethiopia and extends to the boundaries of the Sudan in the north and west, and as far south as Assab in the east. Its capital is Asmara, and Massawa is the principal sea port of the Ethiopian Empire.

Gemu-Gofa is situated in the extreme south-west of Ethiopia and is one of the most fertile regions of the country, with its coffee plantations and herds of buffalo and other game. The capital is Arba Minch.

Gojjam is Ethiopia's Blue Nile province and one of the most beautiful and spectacular areas of the Abyssinian Alps. The provincial capital is Debra Markos.

Hararge, with historic Harar as its capital, is the largest province in the country. It stretches from the Dankali desert to the southern borders of Somalia. Dire Dawa is the most important business centre.

Ilubabor is the most westerly of Ethiopia's provinces. Gore, the capital, is served by Ethiopian Airlines, and the river Baro/Sobat is the only navigable waterway in the country.

Kaffa, with its capital at Jimma, is a densely wooded, fertile, and beautiful part of the Ethiopian Empire. It is the principal coffee-producing area.

Shoa, once in the extreme south of the country, is now, in the wake of Menelik's conquests, situated in the heart of Ethiopia. Addis Ababa, the capital, is also the most populous city in Ethiopia.

Sidamo is located on the borders of Kenya and is being developed as a safari region. Lake Abaye, or Margherita, is the home of the hippopotamus and crocodile. The capital is Yerga Alem.

Tigrai is the area of the old Aksumite Empire. It has some of the finest archaeological sites in Ethiopia and includes, of course, the

ancient capital of Aksum. The modern administrative headquarters is
Makalle.

Wollega, to the west of Shoa, has a rich soil and rivers bearing gold
and platinum. Coffee is the chief crop, but there are also vast forests
and large timber reserves. The provincial capital is Lekemt.

Wollo, on the Addis Ababa–Asmara highway, includes such spectacular sites as the Lalibela rock churches; it has some of the highest
mountains in the west and some of the deepest depressions, along the
Dankali coast, in the east. Dessie is the provincial capital.

One of the Emperor's main triumphs in the field of foreign and
internal policy alike was the federation of Eritrea with Ethiopia under
the sovereignty of the Ethiopian Crown. Eritrea was never a viable unit
economically, and culturally and ethnically it was artificially severed
from the Tigrai province of Ethiopia of which its highland regions
formed an integral part. While the Italians could never really be
content with this unproductive colony from which they made repeated
forays southwards till decisively checked by Menelik at Adwa in
1896 (see Chapter IV), Eritreans and Ethiopians were bound to engage
in irredentist activities. For nearly forty years this uneasy arrangement
worked remarkably well, but when the Italians occupied Ethiopia in
1936 they welded the Tigrinya-speaking Tigrai and Eritrea into one
province. The pre-1936 international frontiers were, however, re-
established after the liberation of Ethiopia in 1941, and Eritrea came
under a British Military Administration. The United Kingdom
Government encountered considerable difficulties, after the war, in
disposing of the burden it had to assume by virtue of military conquest.
Under the terms of the 1947 Peace Treaty, Italy renounced her title to
her former African colonies, but the Four Power Commission of
Investigation (France, Soviet Union, U.K., and U.S.A.) failed to agree
on a solution for the future of Eritrea. Among the many schemes can-
vassed by Eritrean and foreign opinion were full independence or
complete union with Ethiopia, partition of the Christian highlands and
Muslim lowlands, return to Italy, United Nations Trusteeship, and
several other proposals. But when the matter was referred to the United
Nations and after a further commission of inquiry, the General
Assembly finally decided, in December 1950, that Eritrea should be

self-governing in domestic affairs but that foreign affairs and trade, defence and communications were to be vested in the Federal Government of Ethiopia.

From 1952 to 1962 Eritrea had her own Parliament and Administration, presided over by a Chief Executive who was responsible to the Eritrean Assembly. Both Parliament and Administration, drawing inspiration from British models, worked with exemplary efficiency. Many improvements, especially in the field of education, were carried through, but nothing could alter the fact that, apart from her interesting history, her attractive people, and wonderful climate and scenery, Eritrea was a poor country with very inadequate resources. It was a poignant experience to go back there only a decade after the war and find that the young clerks and interpreters of yesterday, who so recently knew little or no English, had become directors-general of government departments or other senior executives, writing minutes and memoranda with almost equal facility in English, Tigrinya, and Amharic. Their adaptability and competence were encouraging and they were deeply conscious of a sense of adventure and achievement. Yet, Eritrea's separate Administration was flying in the face of economic and political realities alike, and in 1962 her Parliament voted to dissolve itself and to dismantle the federal structure. Eritrea then became an integral part of Ethiopia and now constitutes the northernmost governorate-general.

The Emperor's first representative in Eritrea was his son-in-law, Bitwodded Andargatchew Massai, who, with the Princess Tenagne Work Haile Sellasie, presided over the Imperial Palace at Asmara. He was followed by General Abiye Ababa. The next Governor-General was His Highness Ras Asrate Kassa who lent dignity as well as a sense of purpose to Eritrean affairs. He was succeeded, in 1971, by a military governor.

In recent years, stagnation at Asmara has been replaced by growth and considerable economic and cultural activity. Some Italians have returned, and many are engaged in important agricultural schemes. Asmara remains an attractive town with some fine buildings and excellent facilities. The Eritrean people as a whole need a period of quiet after the upsets of the past eighty years. Yet, if some of the pressing economic and political problems can be solved—as no doubt they will be—the future of this northernmost and ancient part of historic Abyssinia might be as bright as was its remote past. At present the political situation in parts of Eritrea is tense owing to the activities of the (largely foreign inspired and financed) Eritrean Liberation Front.

Eritrea's educational system, set on its course during the British caretaker administration by an exceptionally able and enthusiastic Director of Education, has taken great strides forward during the past few years. The Haile Sellasie Secondary School at Asmara is a fine institution, both in terms of bricks and mortar as well as in educational facilities, and the same is true of the large Comboni School, formerly under the direction of the gifted and scholarly Father Gasparini. Of late, even a university has been established at Asmara, but inevitably it will take time for standards to evolve and for professors of the requisite calibre to come forward.

Of course, this is only a small sector of the entire educational system of Ethiopia. Traditionally, the nucleus of Ethiopian education is formed by the ancient institution of church schools. The priests would gather groups of small boys outside the many thousands of village churches and drill them in the rudiments of the Ethiopic syllabary. From there they would pass on to the Psalms and to the Gospels in Ge'ez, and though teachers and pupils will have little more than the vaguest idea of what they are reading, the discipline is wholesome and the art of reading and writing might stand the boys in good stead later on. Since early this century mission societies have notably contributed to educational work in Ethiopia, and here it is, perhaps, the Swedish Evangelical Mission that deserves to be singled out for praise, for many of Ethiopia's outstanding men received their early training in its schools.

In 1908 the Emperor Menelik opened a large school at Addis Ababa, and during the regency of the present Emperor the Tafari Makonnen school was established. Ethiopia thus possessed two great educational institutions which were the focus for the best talent from all parts of the realm. Some of the ablest of the alumni were then sent abroad for higher education, and it was unhappily this trained intelligentsia that suffered the most grievous decimation in the 1937 massacres. But despite the restrictions and difficulties of war these schools were re-opened shortly after the restoration, and it was not long before they were joined by the Haile Sellasie I and Orde Wingate Secondary Schools as well as by others elsewhere. The teachers are drawn from many nationalities, and the language of instruction is English which has taken the place of French since the liberation. Standards are said to be good, and many pupils take the London University General Certificate of Education examination. Mention should also be made of the Lycée Franco-Éthiopien and the English and German schools whose contribution to modern education has been considerable. The largest contingent of foreign teachers at one time consisted of the American Peace Corps. These public-spirited volunteers taught in almost every secondary school and were stationed in many remote places. Their number approached 500, and their devotion did honour to their country.

Apart from the main type of secondary school, there also exist commercial, technical, agricultural, and teacher-training establishments, as well as the Empress Menen School for girls. Education is free, and so is boarding accommodation for pupils from distant regions of the country.

The backbone of the educational system is naturally the network of primary schools throughout the country. There are some 1,400 such establishments (government, missionary, private, church and community development) in which the language of instruction is Amharic (now also beginning to replace English in secondary schools). Handicrafts and agriculture play an important part in the curriculum of these schools.

Elementary education is financed from the proceeds of a national land educational tax that is collected by provincial boards of education which, under the authority of the Ministry of Education, prepare local school budgets and are responsible for the control of expenditure. Secondary and higher education is a direct charge on the national exchequer.

At the apex of the education system stands the Haile Sellasie I University which confers its own degrees and which consists of ten Colleges (University College, including the Faculties of Arts, Science, and Education, Colleges of Law, Business Administration, Public Health, Agriculture, Theology, Engineering, Building, Medicine, and Social Work). The Emperor is the Chancellor, and the University is run by an Ethiopian President and two Vice-Presidents, one academic and the other administrative. The University was officially inaugurated in 1961 in the premises of the former Imperial Palace. It developed from the University College which had been functioning since 1951. The teaching staff includes members of many nationalities. The excellent campus of Science, Arts, and administrative buildings, including a rapidly expanding Library (under the able and dynamic direction of Mrs. Rita Pankhurst), can bear comparison with academic buildings anywhere in the world. Standards are being gradually raised, and the day is not far off when the University of Addis Ababa will take its place in international academic life and make its distinctive contribution.

That contribution has now begun to embrace the study of Ethiopian languages, history, civilization, ethnology, and archaeology—all fields in which Ethiopian scholars have been trained during the last few years. In fact, the Institute of Ethiopian Studies, under the Directorship of Dr. Richard Pankhurst, is beginning to make its impact felt also in European and American centres of Ethiopian studies.

The University's Imperial Charter guarantees academic independence, and the Board of Governors includes several Ministers who can be trusted to uphold this assurance. The language of instruction is English. Close to the great Trinity Church is the Theological College which has just completed a series of excellent modern buildings. The board of management is presided over by His Beatitude the Abuna Theophilos, and the Director is a member of the Christian Church of St. Thomas in India. It is intended that the College should become the main theological centre for the oriental Apostolic Churches, consisting of the Coptic, Ethiopian, Syrian, and Armenian Orthodox Churches in the Middle East and India.

Apart from the students who make use of the educational opportunities now existing in Ethiopia, about a thousand young Ethiopian men and women are pursuing their studies abroad, especially in the United States, Britain, Canada, Russia, France, and Germany. Many have returned to their country with degrees in Arts, Science, Law, Engineering, Agriculture, and Medicine. Among these are quite a few who now hold senior appointments in the central government as well as in the provinces.

In planning her educational development, Ethiopia has taken pains not to imitate the system of one particular country but to employ teachers from many lands and to send her students to different environments, so that in the end she will be able to select what appears most appropriate to her national genius—even if this process involves a degree of dispersal of effort and of unevenness of standards.

Finally, mention must be made of the National Library at Addis Ababa which has greatly added, though inevitably not always purposively, to the nucleus of mainly Italian books which it possessed when it was opened in 1944. Attached to the Library are a museum and an archaeological section.

Apart from its ancient civilization, most things in Ethiopia are new. At the beginning of this century there were virtually no health services in the country. Today seventy hospitals and sixty health centres as well as some 500 provincial health stations are in existence and serve most parts of the Empire. Several dozen Ethiopian physicians have completed their medical studies abroad and have returned to their country. There are at present thirteen provincial health departments and some 500 Ethiopian registered nurses in addition to malarial workers and dressers. There are regular broadcasts on health and hygiene, and leaflets and posters in schools, camps, and community centres explain the most important precautions against disease. The old Menelik Hospital has been largely reconstructed, and the Haile Sellasie Hospital and Princess Tsahai Memorial Hospital (named after the Emperor's younger daughter who had been trained at Guy's Hospital) have been built and include much of the equipment expected of a modern hospital. The Russian Government have staffed and furnished the Dejatch Balcha Hospital, while St. Paul's Hospital, in the poor district of Addis Ababa, is largely maintained from the Emperor's privy purse. Among the most modern hospitals are the Duke of Harar Memorial Hospital at Addis Ababa and the Hospital of the Wonji sugar factory. But in a country of the size of Ethiopia, with an overwhelming proportion of the population still poorly housed, the back of the problem has scarcely been broken.

The size of Ethiopia is no doubt also a constant worry to the Ministers of Communications and Public Works. Ethiopia possesses virtually no navigable internal waterways, and access to the sea has been gained only recently with the incorporation of Eritrea. The ports of Massawa and Assab serve the northern and central hinterland, respectively, and Assab has undergone considerable development which has now been largely completed. Road development before, during, and since the Italian occupation has been encouraging, but even the maintenance of existing roads is a formidable task, financially as well as technically. The alternation of mountains and valleys, the steep escarpment, the torrential rains of the summer and the dryness of the winter, the constant crossings and tramplings by animals, all contribute to an inordinate degree of wear and tear, probably quite out of proportion to the actual density of traffic. Vast sums of money, both from Ethiopian sources and the International Bank, have been, and are being, expended on the upkeep and improvement of existing roads and the construction of new highways. Of some 22,000 km. of primary and secondary roads in Ethiopia, over 7,000 km. are all-weather primary roads.

There are two railway systems, the 500-mile stretch from Jibuti to Addis Ababa, owned by the Compagnie du Chemin de Fer Franco-Éthiopien, and some 200 miles of government-operated track from Massawa to Asmara-Keren-Agordat. New rolling stock has recently been introduced into both systems. Though the railways have been of some value for freight transport, the roads remain the main arteries of communication in Ethiopia.

The inauguration of Ethiopian Airlines in 1946 was a milestone in the improvement of internal communications in particular. There are at present four airfields capable of handling jet airliners: Addis Ababa, Asmara, Dire Dawa, and Harar. DC-3 aircraft and Convairs are now mostly confined to internal traffic, while Boeing 707s and 720Bs are used for international routes. EAL flight operations extend to Rome, Madrid, Frankfurt, Delhi, Paris, London, Accra, Dar-es-Salaam, etc. Air traffic has revolutionized internal communications in Ethiopia, and modern aircraft now ply between many places, within an hour or two, which it takes weeks to reach by mule or on foot. Their human and animal cargo, when disgorged at modern airports, are a most picturesque sight—yet another reminder, in that country of no transitions, of the leap from mule to jet. Ethiopian Airlines have an admirable record of safety over national and international routes. American pilots are gradually being replaced by Ethiopians. A flight over the mountains, gorges, and lakes of Ethiopia, her fields, plantations, and round churches, is a memorable experience.

Progress in most fields has, of course, only been possible because Ethiopia possesses a relatively sound economy with a favourable balance of trade and considerable foreign reserves. There has been growing prosperity among some of the people, and generous foreign loans, investments, United Nations and United States development projects, have aided economic growth and financial stability. Agriculture remains the backbone of the Ethiopian economy, but small industrial enterprises, often run by foreigners, have recently been established. In trade and commerce Asians and Europeans have long been predominant, for Ethiopians have always displayed a traditional reluctance, which is now beginning to break down, to engage in commercial and financial activities. At the same time, the gap between the rich and the poor, the privileged and the deprived, remains uncomfortably wide and troubles the conscience of some of the best men in Ethiopia.

Basketry, woodwork, jewellery, leather goods, and animal husbandry are the principal aspects of indigenous industry, followed by the preparation of beeswax, distilling of alcohol, and miscellaneous other minor industrial activities. Coffee is Ethiopia's principal export and her main dollar-earner. Coffee cultivation has been steadily increased, and most of the produce is being shipped to the United States where Ethiopian coffee is used for the blending of high quality mixtures. Hides and live cattle, some textiles and leather goods are among other valuable exports.

Although coins were known in Ethiopia in the earliest times, nearly all trade was carried on by barter, blocks of salt or lengths of cloth. The Maria Theresa thaler was introduced into Ethiopia in the mid-nineteenth century and remained the only acceptable form of currency till 1945. Neither the coinage of Menelik II nor that of Haile Sellasie, before 1935, was able to replace the widespread use of, and indeed attachment to, this thaler whose decorative design and high silver content were greatly valued and trusted by the Ethiopian population. Italian lire and East African shillings were mere episodes till currency reform in 1945 established the Ethiopian paper dollar as the only legal tender. One dollar is worth 40 U.S. cents, and there are 5.5 Ethiopian dollars to the pound sterling. The right of issue is vested in the State Bank of Ethiopia, the principal banking concern in the country, which maintains a currency fund consisting of gold, silver, and foreign bank balances. Exchange control is fairly strict, but it has contributed to the welcome accumulation of Ethiopia's foreign reserves.

Military prowess in Ethiopia does not date from the days of Adwa but has been a characteristic feature since ancient times. An Ethiopian battalion acquitted itself with great honour in the Korean War. The Ethiopian Government sent a contingent to the Congo, and United Nations forces in the Congo fought under the command of several Ethiopian generals. The police force now consists of some 30,000 men, many of whom had fought with the patriots during the Italo-Abyssinian War and the campaign of liberation. A British Military Mission was in charge of the training of the Ethiopian Army from 1942 till 1950, but since American military assistance became available on an increasing scale an American advisory group has assumed the training of the Ethiopian forces in the use of modern weapons. The Imperial Body-Guard, a splendid corps of some 5,000 men, continues to be helped by Swedish officers. A military training college is located at Holeta, and the Military Academy at Harar is largely staffed by Indian officers.

The Air Force, trained by American advisers, maintains a training centre at Bishoftu (Debra Zeit). A number of fully qualified pilots, radio operators, and ground crews have already graduated. Norwegian officers assist in naval training at Massawa, while the United States is responsible for the supply and repair of equipment. Commodore Alexander Desta, a British-educated grandson of the Emperor and a man of considerable gifts, is the senior Ethiopian officer of this young force.

Ethiopia is a country of great natural beauty, and the Ethiopians are a people of profound interest and fascination to all who take the trouble to study their past and their present. Of their future one feels confident when one watches the enthusiasm and pride with which Ethiopians, led by a remarkable King, are building their country and developing its resources. The dynamism of our technological age, the paraphernalia of the twentieth-century concepts of progress have firmly gripped all those who are now determining the country's future course. Here indeed are forces at work that are inevitable and incapable of being halted. The sympathetic student of Ethiopia feels at times an almost schizophrenic urge of wanting to preserve historic Abyssinia as a relic of an ancient, yet still living, civilization which has no need of aeroplanes or water-closets; and, at the same time, he wishes Ethiopia to be healthy and educated—but he then realizes that hospitals and schools, by a strong inner logic, attract Cadillacs and television sets. Ethiopia—as one of her Ambassadors recently said—possessed the wireless almost before she knew a piece of wire.

To the urban centres, inevitably, are now coming all the strains and stresses of our age, the subversion from outside and the repression from inside, the student troubles, the propaganda, the injustices of the bureaucracy, and the frustrations of the new urban proletariat—and all the loosening of traditional restraints.

Yet outside the bustling towns Ethiopia remains a haven of peace where priests are dancing before the ark and the courtesies of the ancient Orient continue to live. It will always be the Emperor Haile Sellasie's greatest glory that for so long he was able to bring these two worlds into harmony: gently to restrain the impatient and quietly to urge on the tardy, to preserve and also to discard without loss of Ethiopia's ancient and historic identity.

SELECT BIBLIOGRAPHY

◦──◦◦◦◦◦·◦◦·◦/◦\◦·◦◦·◦◦◦◦──◦

d'Abbadie, A., *Catalogue raisonné de Manuscrits Éthiopiens*, Paris, 1859.

—— *Douze ans dans la Haute Éthiopie*, Paris, 1868.

Abir, M., *Ethiopia: the era of the princes*, London, 1968.

Abraham Demoz, 'European loanwords in an Amharic daily newspaper' in *Language in Africa*, Cambridge, 1963.

—— 'Emperor Menelik's phonograph message to Queen Victoria' in *BSOAS*, 1969/2.

Abu Sālih, *Churches and monasteries of Egypt and some neighbouring countries* (translated and edited by B. T. A. Evetts, with notes by A. J. Butler); Oxford, 1895.

Abul-Haggag, Y., *A contribution to the physiography of Northern Ethiopia*, London, 1961.

Accademia Nazionale dei Lincei, *Atti del Convegno Internazionale di Studi Etiopici*, Rome, 1960.

Aešcoly, A. Z., 'The Falashas' (bibliography) in *Kiryath Sepher* XII, XIII (1935–7).

—— *Sefer Ha-Falashim* (in Hebrew); Jerusalem, 1943.

—— *Recueil de textes Falachas*, Paris, 1951.

Alvarez, F., *Narrative of the Portuguese Embassy to Abyssinia* (translated and edited by Lord Stanley of Alderley); Hakluyt Society, London, 1881.

Andrzejewski, B. W., 'The position of Galla in the Cushitic Group', *Ethiopian Studies*, *JSS*, IX, 1, Spring 1964.

Anfray, F., 'Aspects de l'archéologie éthiopienne' in *JAH*, IX, 3, 1968.

Armbruster, C. H., *Initia Amharica*, Part I, Grammar, Cambridge, 1908.

—— *Initia Amharica*, Part II, English-Amharic Vocabulary, Cambridge, 1910.

Armbruster, Stephana, *Life and history of John Bell and his descendants*, Palma de Mallorca, 1966.

Baars, W., and Zuurmond, R., 'The project for a new edition of the Ethiopic Book of Jubilees', *JSS*, IX, 1, Spring 1964.

Baeteman, J., *Dictionnaire amarigna-français*, Dire Daoua, 1929.

Bassano, F. da, *Vocabolario tigray-italiano e repertorio italiano-tigray*, Rome, 1918.

—— *Old Testament* in Ge'ez (4 vols.); Asmara, 1922–6.

Basset, R., *Histoire de la conquête de l'Abyssinie* (*XVIᵉ siècle*), Paris, 1897–1901.

—— 'Études sur l'histoire d'Éthiopie', *JA*, 1881.

Beaton, A. C., and Paul, A., *Grammar and vocabulary of the Tigre language* (as spoken by the Beni Amer); Khartoum, 1954.

Beccari, C., *Rerum Aethiopicarum Scriptores Occidentales Inediti a saeculo XVI ad XIX*, Rome, 1903–17; Brussels, 1969 (reprint).

Beckingham, C. F., 'A Note on the topography of Ahmad Grāñ's campaigns in 1542', *Journal of Semitic Studies*, October 1959.

—— 'The "Itinerario" of Jeronimo Lobo' in *JSS*, X, 2, Autumn 1965.

—— *The Achievements of Prester John* (Inaugural Lecture); School of Oriental and African Studies, London, 1966.

Beckingham, C. F., and Huntingford, G. W. B. (translators), *Some records of Ethiopia, 1593–1646* (Manoel de Almeida and Bahrey); Hakluyt Society, London, 1954.

—— *The Prester John of the Indies*, 2 vols, Hakluyt Society, London, 1961.

Beeston, A. F. L., 'ABRAHA' in *Encyclopaedia of Islam*, 2nd ed., 1965.

—— *A Descriptive grammar of epigraphic South Arabian*, London, 1962.

Beke, C. T., 'On the languages and dialects of Abyssinia and the countries to the South', *Proceedings of the Philological Society*, London, 1845.

—— 'Map of the languages of Abyssinia and the neighbouring countries', *Edinburgh New Philosophical Journal*, vol. 47, Edinburgh, 1849.

Bent, T., *The sacred city of the Ethiopians* (With a chapter by D. H. Müller on the Yeha and Aksum inscriptions); London, 1893.

Bezold, C., *Kebra Nagast*, Munich, 1909.

Brauner-Plazikowski, H., *Ein aethiopisch-amharisches Glossar* (*Sawasew*), Berlin, 1914.

Boyd, O., *The Octateuch in Ethiopic, according to the text of the Paris Codex, with the variants of five other MSS* in *Bibliotheca Abessinica*; Part I: Genesis, Leiden and Princeton, 1909; Part II: Exodus and Leviticus, Leiden and Princeton, 1911.

Breasted, J. H., *History of Egypt*, 2nd ed., London, 1948.

British Military Administration, Eritrea, *Races and tribes of Eritrea*, Asmara, 1943.

Brown, L., *Ethiopian episode*, London, 1965.

Bruce, J., *Travels to discover the Source of the Nile* (1st ed., 5 vols, Edinburgh, 1790; 3rd ed., 8 vols., Edinburgh, 1813).

Buchthal, H., 'An Ethiopic miniature of Christ being nailed to the Cross' in *Atti del Conv. Internaz. di Studi Etiopici*, 1960.

Budge, Sir E. A. Wallis, *The life and exploits of Alexander the Great*, 2 vols., London, 1896.

—— *Life of Hanna* (Lady Meux MSS. 2–5; text and trans.); London, 1900.

—— *A History of Ethiopia*, 2 vols., London, 1928.

—— *Book of the Saints of the Ethiopian Church*, 4 vols., Cambridge, 1928.

—— *The Queen of Sheba and her only son Menyelek*, London, 1932.

—— *The contendings of the Apostles*, London, 1935.

—— *The Book of the Mysteries of the Heavens and the Earth*, London, 1935.

—— *Amulets and talismans*, New York, 1961.

Burton, Sir Richard, *First footsteps in East Africa*, 2 vols., London, 1894.

Butler, A. J., *see* Abu Sālih.

Buxton, D. R., 'Ethiopian rock-hewn churches', *Antiquity*, 1946.

—— *Travels in Ethiopia*, London, 1949.

Caquot, A., 'La Reine de Saba et le bois de la croix' in *Annales d'Éthiopie*, I, 1955.

—— 'La royauté sacrale en Éthiopie' in *Annales d'Éthiopie*, II, 1957.

Castanhoso, *The Portuguese expedition to Abyssinia* (translated and edited by R. S. Whiteway); Hakluyt Society, London, 1902.

Cerulli, Enrico, 'Canti popolari amarici' in *RRAL*, 1916.

—— *Etiopia occidentale*, Rome, 1933.

—— 'Di alcune varietà di inni della chiesa etiopica' in *Orientalia*, 1934.

—— *Studi Etiopici:*
    I. *La Lingua e la storia di Harar*, Rome, 1936.
    II. *La Lingua e la storia dei Sidamo*, Rome, 1938.
    III. *Il Linguaggio dei Giangero, etc.*, Rome, 1938.
    IV. *La Lingua caffina*, Rome, 1951.

—— 'Il Sultanato dello Scioa nel secolo XIII secondo un nuovo documento storico', *RSE*, 1941.

—— *Il Libro etiopico dei Miracoli di Maria e le sue fonti nella letteratura del medio evo latino*, Rome, 1943.

—— *Etiopi in Palestina*, 2 vols., Rome, 1943–7.

—— 'Il "Gesù percosso" nell'arte etiopica e le sue origini nell'Europa del XV secolo' in *RSE*, VI, 2, 1947.

—— *Storia della letteratura etiopica*, Rome, 1956; 3rd ed., Milan, 1968.

—— *Somalia*, Rome, 1957–1964, 3 vols.

—— *Scritti teologici etiopici dei secoli XVI–XVII*, Città del Vaticano, 1958–1960, 2 vols.

—— 'L'Islam en Ethiopie: sa signification historique et ses méthodes', *Correspondance d'Orient*, No. 5, 1961.

—— *Les Vies éthiopiennes de Saint Alexis l'Homme de Dieu*, CSCO, Louvain, 1969.

Cerulli, Enrico, 'L'Islam etiopico', *L'Islam di ieri e di oggi*, Rome, 1971.

—— 'Harar, centro musulmano in Etiopia', *L'Islam di ieri e di oggi*, Rome, 1971.

Cerulli, Ernesta, *Peoples of south-west Ethiopia and its borderland*, London, 1956.

Chaîne, M., *Catalogue des manuscrits éthiopiens de la Collection Antoine d'Abbadie*, Paris, 1912.

—— *Catalogue des manuscrits éthiopiens de la Collection Mondon-Vidailhet*, Paris, 1913.

—— *Grammaire éthiopienne*, Beyrouth, 1938.

Chamber of Commerce, *Guide Book of Ethiopia*, Addis Ababa, 1954.

—— *Trade directory and guide book to Ethiopia*, Addis Ababa, 1967.

Charles, R. H., *The Ethiopic version of the Hebrew Book of Jubilees*, Oxford, 1895.

—— *The Book of Jubilees or the Little Genesis* (translated from Ethiopic text; introduction; notes); London, 1902.

—— *The Ethiopic version of the Book of Enoch* (Anecdota Oxoniensia); Oxford, 1906.

—— *The Book of Enoch*, English translation, 2nd ed., Oxford, 1912.

—— *The Apocrypha and Pseudepigrapha of the Old Testament*, 2 vols., Oxford, 1913.

Cheesman, R. E., *Lake Tana and the Blue Nile*, London, 1936.

Chojnacki, S., 'Short introduction to Ethiopian traditional painting' in *JES*, II, 2, 1964.

Church of Ethiopia, A panorama of history and spiritual life, Addis Ababa, 1970.

Cohen, M., 'La prononciation traditionelle du Guèze', *JA*, Paris, 1921.

—— *Études d'éthiopien méridional*, Paris, 1931.

—— *Traité de langue amharique*, Paris, 1936.

—— *Nouvelles études d'éthiopien méridional*, Paris, 1939.

—— *Essai comparatif sur le vocabulaire et la phonétique du Chamito-Sémitique*, Paris, 1947.

—— 'Sur la notation musicale éthiopienne' in *Levi Della Vida Festschrift*, Rome, 1956.

Clapham, C., *Haile Selassie's government*, London, 1969.

Comba, P., 'Le Roman dans la littérature éthiopienne de langue amharique' in *JSS*, IX, 1 (*Ethiopian Studies*), 1964.

Conti Rossini, C., 'Note per la storia letteraria abissina', *RRAL*, 1899.

—— 'Sugli Habašat', *RRAL*, 1906.

—— *Liber Axumae*, *CSCO*, 1909.

—— 'Un Documento sul Cristianesimo nello Iemen ai tempi del Re Šarahbil Yakkuf' in *RRAL*, 1910.

—— 'L'itinerario di Beniamino da Tudela e l'Etiopia' in *ZA*, XXVII, Leipzig, 1911-12.

Conti Rossini, C., 'Sul Metropolita Salama d'Etiopia' in *ZA*, XXVII, Leipzig, 1911–12.

—— *La Langue des Kemant en Abyssinie*, Vienna, 1912.

—— 'Notice sur les manuscrits éthiopiens de la Collection d'Abbadie', *JA*, 1912–15.

—— 'Expéditions et possessions des Habašat en Arabie', *JA*, 1921.

—— 'Le Lingue e le letterature Semitiche d'Abissinia', *OM*, 1921–2 (pp. 38–48, 169–76).

—— 'La Caduta della dinastia Zague e la versione amarica del Be'ela Nagast' in *RRAL*, 1922.

—— 'Leggende Geografiche Giudaiche del IX Secolo (Il Sefer Eldad)' in *Bollettino della R. Società Geografica Italiana*, 1925.

—— *Storia d'Etiopia*, Bergamo, 1928.

—— *L'Abissinia*, Rome, 1929.

—— *Etiopia e genti d'Etiopia*, Florence, 1937.

—— *Lingua Tigrina*, Milan, 1940.

—— 'Le Sorgenti del Nilo Azzurro e Giovanni Gabriel', *Boll. R. Soc. Geogr. Ital.*, 1941.

—— *Proverbi, tradizioni e canzoni Tigrine*, Verbania, 1942.

—— 'La regalità sacra in Abissinia e nei regni dell'Africa centrale ed occidentale' in *Studi e materiali di storia delle religioni*, XXI, Bologna, 1948.

—— *Historia Regis Sarsa Dengel*, CSCO, 1955 (reprint).

Conti Rossini, C., and Ricci, L. (ed.), *Mashafa Berhan: Il Libro della Luce del Negus Zar'a Ya'qob* (text and translation; 4 parts); CSCO, 1964–5.

Conzelman, W. E., *Chronique de Galawdewos*, Paris, 1895.

Cook Book, Ethiopian-American, Asmara (no date).

Cosmas, *Christian topography* (translated by J. W. McCrindle); Hakluyt Society, London, 1897.

Crawford, O. G. S., *Ethiopian itineraries, circa 1400–1524*, Hakluyt Society, London, 1958.

Dillmann, A., *Catalogus Codicum MSS Aethiopicorum qui in Museo Britannico asservantur*, London, 1847.

—— *Catalogus Codicum Manuscriptorum Bibliothecae Bodleianae Oxoniensis*, pars VII, Oxford, 1848.

—— *Liber Henoch Aethiopice*, Leipzig, 1851.

—— *Liber Jubilaeorum*, Kiel, 1859.

—— *Chrestomathia Aethiopica Edita et Glossario Explanata*, Lipsiae, 1866.

—— *Lexicon Linguae Aethiopicae*, Lipsiae, 1865.

—— *Ascensio Isaiae*, Leipzig, 1877.

Dillmann, A., *Verzeichniss der Abessinischen Handschriften*, Königliche Bibliothek, Berlin, 1878.

—— 'Zur Geschichte des Axumitischen Reichs im vierten bis sechsten Jahrhundert' in *Abh. d. Königl. Akad. d. Wissensch. zu Berlin*, 1880.

—— *Über die Regierung, insbesondere die Kirchenordnung des Königs Zar'a-Jacob*, Berlin, 1884.

—— 'Die Kriegsthaten des Königs 'Amda-Sion gegen die Muslim' in *Sitzungsberichte d. K. Preuss. Akad. d. Wissensch.*, Berlin, 1884.

—— *Biblia Veteris Testamenti Aethiopica:*
Bd. I (1853): Oct.; Bd. II, Fasc. 1 (1861): Reg. I, II; Fasc. 2 (1871): Reg. III, IV; Bd. V (1894): Libri Apocr.; Leipzig, 1853–94.

—— *Ethiopic grammar* (translated by J. A. Crichton); London, 1907.

Donzel, E. J. van, *Enbaqom's Anqasa Amin*, Leiden, 1969.

Doresse, J., *Au pays de la Reine de Saba; L'Éthiopie antique et moderne*, Paris, 1956.

—— *L'Empire du prêtre Jean*, 2 vols., Paris, 1957.

Drewes, A. J., *Inscriptions de l'Éthiopie antique*, Leiden, 1962.

Driver, G. R., *Semitic writing*, London, 1948.

Duchesne-Fournet, J., *Mission en Éthiopie* (1901–3), 2 vols. and atlas, Paris, 1909.

Epstein, Abraham, *Eldad Hadani*, Pressburg, 1891.

Ethiopia Observer, Journal published in Ethiopia and Britain; December 1956–.

Ethiopian Studies: Proceedings of the International Conference of Ethiopian Studies at Manchester University, 1963, edited by E. Ullendorff and C. F. Beckingham, *JSS*, Spring 1964.

Etiopia and *Eritrea* (in *Enciclopedia Italiana*, vol. XIV, pp. 220–34, 459–92).

Faitlovitch, J., *The Falashas*, Philadelphia, 1920.

Faralla, D., *The straw umbrella*, London, 1968.

Findlay, L., *The monolithic churches at Lalibela in Ethiopia*, Cairo, 1944.

Flad, J. M., *The Falashas of Abyssinia*, London, 1869.

—— *60 Jahre in der Mission unter den Falaschas*, Giessen, 1922.

Flemming, J., 'Hiob Ludolf—Ein Beitrag zur Geschichte der orient. Philologie' in *Beiträge zur Assyriologie*, I and II, 1890, 1894.

—— *Das Buch Henoch* (Aeth. Text); Leipzig, 1902.

Frend, W. H. C., *The rise of the Monophysite movement in the 5th and 6th centuries*, Cambridge, 1972.

Fumagalli, G., *Bibliografia etiopica*, Milan, 1893.

Fusella, L., 'Breve raccolta di neologismi amarici', *Ann. ist. univ. orient. di Napoli*, 1949.

—— 'La Cronaca dell' Imperatore Teodoro II di Etiopia' in *Ann. ist. univ. orient. di Napoli*, 1957–9.

Gaguine, M., 'The Falasha Version of the Testaments of Abraham, Isaac and Jacob', Manchester University Ph.D. thesis, 1965.

Gamst, F. C., *The Qemant. A Pagan-Hebraic peasantry of Ethiopia*, Stanford, 1970.

Gankin, E., *Russian-Amharic: Amharic-Russian dictionary*, Moscow, 1965, 1969.

Gérard, A., 'Amharic creative literature: the early phase' in *JES*, VI, 2, 1968.

—— *Four African literatures: Amharic*, Univ. of California Press, 1971.

Gerster, G., *Kirchen im Fels*, Zürich and Stuttgart, 1968.

Giglio, C., *L'articolo XVII del Trattato di Uccialli*, Como, 1967.

—— *L'Italia in Africa;* volume primo: *Etiopia—mar rosso*, Rome, 1958–72.

Glaser, E., *Die Abessinier in Arabien und Afrika*, Munich, 1895.

Gleave, H. C., *The Ethiopic version of Song of Songs*, London, 1951.

Gobat, S., *Journal of three years' residence in Abyssinia*, 1851; New York, 1969 (reprint).

Goldenberg, G., 'The Amharic tense-system' (Ph.D. thesis, in Hebrew); Jerusalem University, 1966.

Goldschmidt, L., *Das Buch Henoch* (translated from Ethiopic into Hebrew); Berlin, 1892.

—— *Die Abessinischen Handschriften der Stadtbibliothek zu Frankfurt a/M* (Rüppellsche Sammlung); Berlin, 1897.

Graf, G., *Geschichte der Christlichen Arabischen Literatur*, 5 vols., Città del Vaticano, 1944–53.

Grébaut, S., *Catalogue des manuscrits éthiopiens de la Collection Griaule*, 3 vols., Paris, 1938, 1941, 1944.

Grébaut, S., and Tisserant, E., *Codices Aethiopici Vaticani et Borgiani*, 2 vols., 1935–6.

Grohmann, Adolf, *Aethiopische Marienhymnen*, Leipzig, 1919.

Guebre Sellassie, *Chronique du règne de Ménélik II*, translated from Amharic, 2 vols. and atlas, Paris, 1930–2.

Guida dell' Africa orientale italiana, Milan, 1938.

Guidi, I., *Il Fetha Nagast* (Eth. text, Italian translation); 2 vols., Rome, 1897 and 1899.

—— *Vocabolario amarico-italiano*, Rome, 1901.

—— *Historia gentis galla*, *CSCO*, 1907.

—— 'La Chiesa Abissina' in *Oriente Moderno*, Rome, 1922.

—— 'Contributi alla storia letteraria di Abissinia' (I. Il Ser'ata Mangest); in *RRAL*, 1922.

—— 'Il Be'la Nagast' in *Festschrift Paul Haupt*, Leipzig, 1926.

—— (*Breve*) *Storia della letteratura etiopica*, Rome, 1932.

—— *Grammatica elementare della lingua amarica*, Rome, 1936.

Guidi, I., 'Le Synaxaire éthiopien' (Sane, Hamle, Nahase, Paguemen); in *Patrologia Orientalis*, IX, 4, Paris.

Guidi, I., and others, *Supplemento al vocabolario amarico-italiano*, Rome, 1940.

Haberland, E., *Galla Süd-Äthiopiens*, Stuttgart, 1963.

—— *Untersuchungen zum Äthiopischen Königtum*, Wiesbaden, 1965.

Hackspill, L., 'Die äthiopische Evangelienübersetzung' in *ZA*, XI, 1896.

Halévy, J., *Prières des Falashas*, Paris, 1877.

—— *Te'ezaza Sanbat*, Paris, 1902.

—— 'La Légende de la Reine de Saba' in *Annuaire de l'École des Hautes Études* (Section des sciences historiques); 1905.

Hammerschmidt, E., *Studies in the Ethiopic Anaphoras*, Berlin, 1961.

—— 'Kultsymbolik der koptischen und äthiopischen Kirche' in *Orthodox. und orient. Christentum*, 1962.

—— *Stellung und Bedeutung des Sabbats in Äthiopien*, Stuttgart, 1963.

—— *Symbolik des Orientalischen Christentums*; *Tafelband*, Stuttgart, 1966.

Hammerschmidt, E., and Jäger, O. A., *Illuminierte Äthiopische Handschriften in Deutschland*, Wiesbaden, 1968.

Harden, J. M., *The Ethiopic Didascalia*, Soc. for Promoting Christ. Knowledge, London, 1920.

Harris, W. Cornwallis, *The Highlands of Æthiopia*, 3 vols., London, 1844.

Heider, A., *Die äthiopische Bibelübersetzung* (Ihre Herkunft, Art, Geschichte, und ihr Wert für die alt- und neutestamentliche Wissenschaft); Leipzig, 1902.

Hetzron, R., *The verbal system of Southern Agaw*, Univ. of California Press, 1969.

—— *Ethiopian semitic; studies in classification*, Manchester, 1972.

Heyer, F., *Die Kirche Äthiopiens*, Berlin, 1971.

Hirschberg, H. Z., *Yisra'el ba'Arab*, Tel Aviv, 1946.

Höfner, M., *Das Feteh Mahari*, Wiesbaden, 1952.

—— 'Das Südarabische der Inschriften und der lebenden Mundarten', *Handbuch der Orientalistik*, III, 2–3, Leiden, 1954.

—— 'Über sprachliche und kulturelle Beziehungen zwischen Südarabien und Äthiopien im Altertum' in *Atti del Conv. Internaz. di Studi Etiopici*, 1960.

Holland, T. J., and Hozier, H., *Record of the expedition to Abyssinia*, 3 vols., London, 1870.

Honeyman, A. M., 'The letter-order of the Semitic alphabets in Africa and the Near East', *Africa*, 1952.

Howard, W. E. H., *Public administration in Ethiopia*, Groningen, 1956.

Hubbard, D. A., 'The literary sources of the Kebra Nagast' (as yet unpublished Ph.D. thesis), St. Andrews University, 1956.

Huntingford, G. W. B., *The Galla of Ethiopia*, London, 1955.

Hyatt, H. M., *The Church of Abyssinia*, London, 1928.

SELECT BIBLIOGRAPHY   211

Illustrated London News, 'The Abyssinian expedition and the life and reign of
King Theodore', history by R. Acton, London, 1868.

Irvine, A. K., 'HABASHAT' in *Encyclopaedia of Islam*, 2nd ed., 1965.

—— 'On the identity of Habashat in the South Arabian Inscriptions' in *JSS*,
X, 2, Autumn 1965.

—— 'Ethiopic literature', *Guide to Eastern Literatures*, London, 1971.

Isenberg, C. W., *Dictionary of the Amharic language*, London, 1841.

—— *Grammar of the Amharic language*, London, 1842.

Isenberg, C. W., and Krapf, J. L., *The journals of Isenberg and Krapf*, London,
1968 (reprint).

Jäger, O. A., *Aethiopische Miniaturen*, Berlin, 1957.

Jamme, A., *Sabaean inscriptions from Mahram Bilqis*, Baltimore, 1962.

Jensen, Ad. E., Haberland, E., Pauli, Elisabeth, and Schulz-Weidner, W.,
Völker Süd-Äthiopiens, vol. I, Altvölker Süd-Äthiopiens, Stuttgart, 1959.

Jesman, C., 'The tragedy of Magdala' in *Ethiopia Observer*, X, 2, 1966.

Jowett, W., *Christian researches in the Mediterranean*, London, 1822.

Kammerer, A., *Essai sur l'histoire antique d'Abyssinie*, Paris, 1926.

—— *La mer Rouge, l'Abyssinie et l'Arabie depuis l'antiquité*, Cairo, 1929.

Klingenheben, A., *Deutsch-Amharischer Sprachführer*, Wiesbaden, 1966.

Kolmodin, J. A., 'Meine Studienreise in Abessinien, 1908–10', *MO*, Uppsala,
1910.

—— 'Traditions de Tsazzega et Hazzega, textes tigrigna', Rome, Uppsala,
1912–14 (*Archives d'Études Orientales*, vol. 5: 1, 2, 3).

Krapf, J. L., *Reisen in Ostafrika*, Stuttgart, 1964 (reprint).

Kromrei, E., *Glaubenslehre und Gebräuche der älteren abessinischen Kirche*, Leipzig,
1895.

Lantschoot, A. van, 'Abbā Salāmā, métropolite d'Éthiopie (1348–1388) et son
rôle de traducteur' in *Atti del Conv. Internaz. di Studi Etiopici*, 1960.

Leclant, J., 'Le Musée des Antiquités d'Addis-Ababa', *Bulletin de la Société
d'Archéologie Copte*, xvi, 1962.

Lefevre, R., 'Documenti pontifici sui rapporti con l'Etiopia nei secoli XV e
XVI', *RSE*, V, 1946.

Leonessa, M. da, *Grammatica analitica della lingua tigray*, Rome, 1928.

Leroy, J., Wright, S., Jäger, O., *Ethiopia—illuminated manuscripts*, UNESCO,
1961.

Leroy, J., *La pittura etiopica*, Milano, 1964.

Leslau, W., *Documents tigrigna*, Paris, 1941.

—— *Short grammar of Tigré*, *JAOS*, 1945; and *Supplementary observations*, 1948.

—— 'The influence of Cushitic on the Semitic languages of Ethiopia. A problem
of substratum', *Word*, I, New York, 1945.

Leslau, W., *Ethiopic documents: Gurage*, New York, 1950.

—— *Falasha anthology*, New Haven, 1951.

—— *Étude descriptive et comparative du Gafat*, Paris, 1956.

—— *Coutumes et croyances des Falachas*, Paris, 1957.

—— *Etymological dictionary of Harari*, Univ. of Calif. Press, 1963.

—— *An Amharic conversation book*, Wiesbaden, 1965.

—— *Ethiopians speak—I. Harari*, Univ. of Calif. Press, 1965.

—— *Ethiopians speak—II. Chaha*, Univ. of Calif. Press, 1966.

—— *Amharic textbook*, Wiesbaden, 1967.

—— *An annotated bibliography of the Semitic languages of Ethiopia*, The Hague, 1965.

Levine, D. N., *Wax and gold*, University of Chicago Press, 1965.

Lewis, I. M., *The modern history of Somaliland*, London, 1965.

Lifchitz, D., *Textes éthiopiens magico-religieux*, Paris, 1940.

Lipsky, George A., *Ethiopia (its people, its society, its culture)*, New Haven, Conn., 1962.

Littmann, E., 'Die Pronomina im Tigré', *ZA*, 1897, vol. 12.

—— 'Das Verbum der Tigré-Sprache', *ZA*, 1898-9, vols. 13, 14.

—— 'Geschichte der äthiopischen Litteratur' in *Geschichte d. christlichen Litteraturen des Orients*, 2nd ed., Leipzig, 1909.

—— *Publications of the Princeton expedition to Abyssinia; tales, customs, names and dirges of the Tigre tribes*, Leyden, 1910-15.

—— *Deutsche Aksum Expedition*, Berlin, 1913.

—— *Abessinien*, Hamburg, 1935.

—— 'Altamharisches Glossar', *RSO*, XX.

—— *The chronicle of King Theodore of Abyssinia*, Princeton, 1902.

Littmann, E., and Höfner, M., *Wörterbuch der Tigre-Sprache*, Wiesbaden, 1956-62.

Lobo, J., *A voyage to Abyssinia* (translated into French by Le Grand and into English by Dr. Samuel Johnson); London, 1735.

—— *Itinerário e outros escritos inéditos*, edited by M. Gonçalves da Costa, Barcelos (Portugal), 1971.

Löfgren, O., *Die Äthiopische Übersetzung des Propheten Daniel*, Paris, 1927.

—— 'Die äthiopische Bibelausgabe der Katholischen Mission' (Mit einer Kollation des Danieltextes) in *MO*, XXIII, 1929.

—— *Jona, Nahum, Habakuk, Zephanja, Haggai, Sacharja und Maleachi äthiopisch, unter Zugrundelegung des Oxforder MS. Huntington 625 nach mehreren Handschriften herausgegeben*, Uppsala, 1930.

—— Review of S. A. B. Mercer's *The Ethiopic text of the Book of Ecclesiastes* (London, 1931) in *MO*, XXVII, 1933.

Löfgren, O., 'The necessity of a critical edition of the Ethiopian Bible', paper submitted to 3rd Int. Conf. of Eth. Stud., vol. II, Addis Ababa, 1970.

Longrigg, S. H., *A short history of Eritrea*, Oxford, 1945.

Ludolf, H., *Grammatica Aethiopica*, Frankfort, 1661.

—— *Historia Aethiopica*, Frankfort, 1681.

—— *Commentarius ad suam Historiam Aethiopicam*, Frankfort, 1691.

—— *Grammatica Linguae Amharicae*, Frankfort, 1698.

—— *Lexicon Aethiopico-Latinum²*, Frankfort, 1699.

—— *Psalterium Davidis aethiopice et latine cum duobus impressis et tribus MSStis codicibus diligenter collatum et emendatum*, Frankfort, 1701.

McCrindle, J. W. (trans. and ed.), Cosmas, *Christian topography*, Hakluyt Society, London, 1897.

Marein, N., *The Ethiopian Empire, federation and laws*, Rotterdam, 1954.

Marianus Victorius, *Chaldeae seu Aethiopicae linguae institutiones*, Rome, 1552.

Markham, C. R., *A history of the Abyssinian expedition*, London, 1869.

Mathew, D., *Ethiopia: study of a polity 1540–1935*, London, 1947.

Mérab, 'Docteur', *Impressions d'Éthiopie (L'Abyssinie sous Ménélik II)*, 3 vols., Paris, 1921, 1922, 1929.

Mercer, S. A. B., *The Ethiopic liturgy*, London, 1915.

—— *The Ethiopic text of the Book of Ecclesiastes*, London, 1931.

Merid Wolde Aregay, 'Southern Ethiopia and the Christian Kingdom, 1508–1708—with special reference to the Galla migrations and their consequences', unpublished London Ph.D. thesis, 1971.

Mesfin Wolde Mariam, *Atlas of Ethiopia*, Addis Ababa, 1970.

—— *An Introductory Geography of Ethiopia*, Addis Ababa, 1972.

Messing, S. D., 'The non-verbal language of the Ethiopian Toga' in *Anthropos*, 1960, 3–4.

Missione Cattolica dell' Eritrea, *Grammatica della lingua tigre*, Asmara, 1919.

Mittwoch, E., *Die traditionelle Aussprache des Aethiopischen*, Berlin, 1926.

Mondon-Vidailhet, C., *Chronique de Théodoros II*, Paris, 1904.

—— 'La musique éthiopienne', *Encyclopédie de la musique et dictionnaire du Conservatoire*, 1ᵉʳ part, pp. 3179–96, Paris, 1922.

Monneret de Villard, U., *Aksum*, Rome, 1938.

Monti della Corte, A. A., *Lalibela*, Rome, 1940.

—— *I castelli di Gondar*, Rome, 1938.

Mordini, A., 'Il Convento di Gunde Gundiè', *RSE*, 1953.

—— 'Appunti di numismatica aksumita', *Annales d'Éthiopie*, III, 1959.

—— 'L'Architecture religieuse chrétienne dans l'Éthiopie du Moyen Age: Un Programme de recherches', *Cahiers d'Études Africaines*, II, 1961.

Moreno, M. M., *Grammatica della lingua Galla*, Milan, 1939.

—— 'La Cronaca di Re Teodoro attribuita al Dabtara Zanab' in *RSE*, 1942.

—— 'L'Azione del cuscitico sul sistema morfologico delle lingue semitiche dell' Etiopia', *RSE*, 1948.

—— 'Struttura e terminologia del Säwasew', *RSE*, VIII, 1950.

—— *Il Somalo della Somalia*, Rome, 1955.

Mosley, L., *Haile Selassie*, London, 1964.

Munzinger, W., *Vocabulaire de la langue tigre*, 1863 (Appendix to Dillmann's *Lexicon*).

—— *Ostafrikanische Studien*, 2nd ed., Basel, 1883.

Murad Kamil, Josippon's *History of the Jews*, New York-Berlin, 1937.

—— *Amharische Kaiserlieder*, Wiesbaden, 1957.

Negarit Gazeta, Official Ethiopian Gazette, published in Addis Ababa (in Amharic and English).

—— An order to provide for the establishment of a national Academy of the Amharic Language, Addis Ababa, 27 June 1972.

Nesbitt, L. M., *Desert and forest (first journey through Danakil country of Eastern Abyssinia)*, Penguin, 1955.

Nicholson, T. R., *A toy for the lion*, London, 1965.

Nielsen, D., *Handbuch der alt-arabischen Altertumskunde*, Copenhagen, 1927.

Nöldeke, T., 'Theodorus, König von Abessinien' in *Orientalische Skizzen*, Berlin, 1892.

—— *Neue Beiträge zur Semitischen Sprachwissenschaft*, Strasbourg, 1910.

Obolensky, S., and others, *Amharic basic course*, 2 vols., Dept. of State, Washington, 1964.

Offeio, F. da, *Grammatica della lingua tigrai*, Asmara, 1935.

Ostini, F., *Trattato di Diritto Consuetudinario dell' Eritrea*, Asmara, 1956.

Pais, P., *Historia da Etiopia*, 3 vols., Porto, 1945.

Palmer, F. R., *The Morphology of the Tigre noun*, Oxford, 1962.

Pankhurst, R., *An introduction to the economic history of Ethiopia from early times to 1800*, 1961.

—— *Travellers in Ethiopia*, London, 1965.

—— 'Some notes for a history of Ethiopian secular art', in *Ethiopia Observer*, X, 1, 1966.

——*Economic history of Ethiopia, 1800–1935*, Addis Ababa, 1968.

Pankhurst, Rita, 'The library of Emperor Tewodros II at Magdala', *BSOAS*, 1973.

Parkyns, Mansfield, *Life in Abyssinia*, London, 1966, reprint of 2nd ed. 1868 (1st ed. 1853).

Paul, A., *A history of the Beja tribes of the Sudan*, Cambridge, 1954.

Perham, M., *The government of Ethiopia*, London, 1948, new ed., 1969.

Periplus of the Erythraean Sea (translated by W. H. Schoff), New York, 1912.

Perruchon, J., *Les chroniques de Zar'a Ya'qob et de Ba'eda Maryam*, Paris, 1893.

—— 'Histoire des guerres d'Amda Syon', *JA*, 1889.

—— *Vie de Lalibala*, Paris, 1892.

Pétridès, S. P., *Le Héros d'Adoua—Ras Makonnen, Prince d'Éthiopie*, Paris, 1963.

Platt, T. P., *Biblia sacra amharice, sub auspiciis D. Asselini in linguam amharicam vertit Abu Rumi*, London, 1840.

Playne, B., *St. George for Ethiopia*, London, 1954.

Pollera, A., *Lo Stato Etiopico e la sua Chiesa*, Rome-Milan, 1926.

—— *Le popolazioni indigene dell' Eritrea*, Bologna, 1935.

—— *L'Abissinia di ieri*, Rome, 1940.

Polotsky, H. J., 'Études de grammaire gouragué', *BSL*, 1938.

—— *Notes on Gurage grammar*, Jerusalem, 1951.

—— 'Aramaic, Syriac and Ge'ez' in *JSS*, IX, 1 (*Ethiopian Studies*), 1964.

Poncet, C. J., *A voyage to Ethiopia 1698–1701*, Hakluyt Society, 1949.

Portal, G. H., *My Mission to Abyssinia*, London, 1892.

Potken, J., *Alphabetum seu potius syllabarium literarum Chaldaearum, Psalterium Chaldaeum*, Rome, 1513.

Powne, M., *Ethiopian Music*, London, 1968.

Praetorius, F., *Fabula de regina Sabaea apud Aethiopes*, Halle, 1870.

—— *Grammatik der Tigriñasprache in Abessinien*, Halle, 1871.

—— *Die Amharische Sprache*, Halle, 1879.

—— *Aethiopische Grammatik*, Leipzig, 1886.

—— *Zur Grammatik der Gallasprache*, Berlin, 1893.

Rabin, C., *Ancient West Arabian*, London, 1951.

Rahlfs, A., 'Nissel und Petraeus, ihre aethiopischen Textausgaben und Typen' in *Nachrichten von d. Königl. Gesellschaft der Wissenschaften*, Göttingen, 1917.

—— 'Die äthiopische Bibelübersetzung' in *Septuaginta Studien* (pp. 659–81), Göttingen, 1965.

Rassam, H., *Narrative of the British Mission to Theodore*, 2 vols., London, 1869.

Rassegna di studi etiopici, Rome, 1941–.

Rathjens, C., *Die Juden in Abessinien*, Hamburg, 1921.

Reale Società Geografica Italiana, *L'Africa Orientale*, Bologna, 1936.

Reinisch, L., *Bilin Sprache*, Vienna, 1882.

—— *Wörterbuch der Bilin Sprache*, Vienna, 1887.

—— 'Die Bedauye Sprache', *SBWA*, 1893–4.

—— *Die Somali Sprache*, Vienna, 1903.

Rennell of Rodd, Lord, *British military administration of occupied territories in Africa*, London, 1948.

Rey, C. F., *The romance of the Portuguese in Abyssinia*, London, 1929.

Rhodokanakis, N., *Die äthiopischen Handschriften der K.K. Hofbibliothek zu Wien*, Vienna, 1906.

Ricci, Lanfranco, 'Pubblicazioni in amarico di questi ultimi anni', *OM*, October–December 1950.

—— 'Romanzo e novella: due esperimenti nella letteratura amarica attuale' in *JSS*, IX, 1 (*Ethiopian Studies*), 1964.

—— *Mashafa Berhan* (*see under* Conti Rossini, C.).

—— *Letterature dell' Etiopia* (Botto, *Storia delle letterature d'Oriente*), Milan, 1969.

Rinck, F. T., *Macrizi historia regum Islamiticorum in Abyssinia* (Arabic text and Latin translation), Leiden, 1790.

Rochet d'Héricourt, *Voyage de la côte orientale de la Mer Rouge dans le pays d'Adel et le Royaume de Choa*, Paris, 1841.

Roden, K. G., *Le tribù dei Mensa* (Tigre text and Italian trans.); Asmara and Stockholm, 1913.

Rodinson, M., 'Sur la question des "influences juives" en Éthiopie', in *JSS*, IX, 1 (*Ethiopian Studies*), 1964.

—— 'GHIDHĀ' in *Encyclopaedia of Islam*², vol. II (pp. 1057–72).

—— Review of *The Ethiopians*, *Bi Or*, 1964.

—— *Magie, médecine, possession en Éthiopie*, Paris, 1967.

—— 'Les Interdictions alimentaires éthiopiennes', *Proceedings, 3rd Internat. Conf. of Ethiopian Studies, Addis Ababa 1966*, vol. III, Addis Ababa, 1970.

—— Review of *Ethiopia and the Bible*, *JSS*, 1972.

Rönsch, H., *Das Buch der Jubiläen oder Die kleine Genesis* (lateinische Fragmente der Ambrosiana sowie eine von Dillmann aus 2 aeth. MSS gefertigten lat. Übertr.); Leipzig, 1874.

Rösch, G., 'Die Königin von Saba als Königin Bilqis' in *Jahrbuch für Protestantische Theologie*, VI, 1880.

Rosen, B. von, *Game Animals of Ethiopia*, Stockholm and Addis Ababa, 1953.

Rosen, F., *Eine deutsche Gesandtschaft in Abessinien*, Leipzig, 1907.

Rothmüller, A. M., *The music of the Jews*, London, 1953.

Rubenson, S., *Wichale XVII*, Addis Ababa, 1964.

—— *Tewodros of Ethiopia*, Addis Ababa-Nairobi, 1966.

Rüppell, E., *Reise in Abessinien*, 2 vols., Frankfort, 1838-40.

Ryckmans, G., *Les noms propres sud-sémitiques*, Louvain, 1935.

—— *Les Religions Arabes préislamiques*, 3rd ed., Louvain, 1960.

Ryckmans, J., *L'Institution monarchique en Arabie Méridionale*, Louvain, 1951.

Sabelli, Luca dei, *Storia di Abissinia*, Rome, 1936-8.

Sahle Sellassie, *Shinega's village*, Univ. of California Press, 1964.

Salt, H., *A voyage to Abyssinia*, London, 1814.

Sanderson, G. N., *England, Europe and the Upper Nile, 1882–99*, Edinburgh University Press, 1965.

Sandford, C., *The Lion of Judah hath prevailed*, London, 1955.

Sauter, R., and Michaud, R., *Etiopia*, Zurich, 1968.

Schoff, W. H., *see Periplus*.

Sergew Hable Selassie, *Bibliography of ancient and medieval Ethiopian history*, Addis Ababa, 1969.

Shack, W. A., *The Gurage*, London, 1966.

Shihāb ad-Dīn, *see* Basset, R.

Simon, Jean, 'Notes bibliographiques sur les textes de la *Chrestomathia Aethiopica*', *Orientalia*, 1941.

—— 'Bibliographie éthiopienne (1946–51)', *Orientalia*, 1952.

Simoons, F. J., *Northwest Ethiopia*, Madison, 1960.

Steer, G. L., *Caesar in Abyssinia*, London, 1936.

Stern, H. A., *Wanderings among the Falashas in Abyssinia* (1862); 2nd ed. with intro. by R. L. Hess, London, 1968.

Strelcyn, S., *Catalogue des manuscrits éthiopiens (Collection Griaule)*, Tome IV, Paris, 1954.

—— *Prières magiques éthiopiennes pour délier les charmes* (*Rocznik Orientalistyczny* XVIII), Warsaw, 1955.

—— *Médecine et plantes d'Éthiopie*, Warsaw, 1968.

—— 'Catalogue of Ethiopian MSS of the Wellcome Institute of the History of Medicine in London', *BSOAS*, 1972/1.

Taddasa Tamrat, 'Some notes on the fifteenth century Stephanite "heresy" in the Ethiopian Church' in *RSE* XXII, 1966–8.

—— *Church and State in Ethiopia, 1270–1527*, Oxford, 1972.

Talbot Rice, D., *Byzantine Art*, Pelican, 1954.

Thomas, H. (translator), *The Discovery of Abyssinia by the Portuguese in 1520*, London, 1938.

Tisserant, E., *Ascension d'Isaie* (Traduction de la version éthiopienne), Paris, 1909.

Trasselli, C., 'Un Italiano in Etiopia nel XV secolo: Pietro Rombulo da Messina', *RSE*, I, 1941.

Trevaskis, G. K. N., *Eritrea. A colony in transition 1941–52*, Oxford, 1960.

Trimingham, J. S., *Islam in Ethiopia*, London, 1952.

Tubiana, J., 'Un culte des génies agrestes en Éthiopie', *RSE*, 1954.

—— 'Éléments de toponymie éthiopienne (tigre)' in *JA*, 1956.

Tucker, A. N., and Bryan, M. A., *Non-Bantu languages of North-Eastern Africa* (Handbook of African Languages, Part III), London, 1956.

Turaiev, Boris, 'Testi etiopici in manoscritti di Leningrado', *RSE*, VII/1, 1948.

Ullendorff, E., *Exploration and study of Abyssinia*, Asmara, 1945.

—— 'Tigrinya Language Council', *Africa*, 1949.

—— *Catalogue of Ethiopic MSS in the Bodleian Library*, Oxford, 1951.

—— 'The Obelisk of Matara', *JRAS*, 1951.

—— 'Studies in the Ethiopic Syllabary', *Africa*, 1951.

—— 'James Bruce of Kinnaird', *Scottish Historical Review*, October, 1953.

—— 'The Ethiopic manuscripts in the Royal Library, Windsor Castle', *RSE*, XII, 1953.

—— *The Semitic languages of Ethiopia*, London, 1955.

—— 'Hebraic-Jewish elements in Abyssinian (Monophysite) Christianity', *Journal of Semitic Studies*, July 1956.

—— 'An Aramaic *Vorlage* of the Ethiopic text of Enoch?' in *Atti del Convegno Internazionale di Studi Etiopici*, Rome, 1960.

—— 'The "Death of Moses" in the literature of the Falashas' in *BSOAS*, October 1961.

—— 'The Queen of Sheba' in *Bulletin of the John Rylands Library*, March 1963.

—— *An Amharic Chrestomathy*, London, 1965.

—— *The challenge of Amharic*, London, 1965.

—— 'BILKĪS' in *Encyclopaedia of Islam*, 2nd ed.

—— 'ERITREA', in *Encyclopaedia of Islam*, 2nd ed.

—— 'HABASH' in *Encyclopaedia of Islam*, 2nd ed.

—— *Ethiopia and the Bible*, British Academy and O.U.P., 1968.

—— 'An Amharic Language Academy?' in *Addis Reporter*, 27 June 1969.

—— 'Comparative Semitics', *Current Trends in Linguistics*, vol. 6, The Hague, 1971.

—— 'Some early Amharic letters', *BSOAS*, 1972/2.

Ullendorff, E., and Wright, S., *Catalogue of Ethiopian manuscripts in the Cambridge University Library*, Cambridge, 1961.

Ullendorff, E., and Beckingham, C. F., 'The first Anglo-Ethiopian Treaty' in *JSS*, Spring 1964.

Ullendorff, E., and Abraham Demoz, 'Two letters from the Emperor Yohannes of Ethiopia to Queen Victoria and Lord Granville' in *BSOAS*, XXXII, 1, 1969.

Ursin, M., *Aethiopien. Impressionen aus einem altchristlichen Land*, Mannheim, 1958.

U.S. Army, *Area handbook for Ethiopia*, Washington, 1960.

Varenbergh, J., 'Studien zur abessinischen Reichsordnung (Šer'ata Mangešt)' in *ZA*, vol. 30, 1915.

Walker, C. H., *The Abyssinian at home*, London, 1933.

Waterfield, G. (ed.), *First footsteps in East Africa* by Sir Richard Burton, London, 1966.

Wellesz, E., 'Studien zur aethiopischen Kirchenmusik' in *Oriens Christianus*, 1920.

—— *History of Byzantine music and hymnography*, Oxford, 1949.

—— (ed.), *Ancient and Oriental music*, London, 1957.

Wendt, K., 'Die theologischen Auseinandersetzungen in der äthiopischen Kirche zur Zeit der Reformen des XV. Jahrhunderts' in *Atti del Conv. Internaz. di Studi Etiopici*, 1960.

—— *Das Mashafa Milad (Liber Nativitatis) und Mashafa Sellase (Liber Trinitatis) des Kaisers Zar'a Ya'qob; CSCO* (4 vols.); (1) Eth. text 221/41—trans. 222/42, 1962; (2) Eth. text 235/43—trans. 236/44, 1963.

Wessel, K. (ed.), *Christentum am Nil*, Recklinghausen, 1964.

Whiteway, R. S. (trans. and ed.), *The Portuguese expedition to Abyssinia 1541–1543* (as narrated by Castanhoso, with extracts from Bermudez and Correa); Hakluyt Society, London, 1902.

Wissmann, H. von, *Zur Geschichte und Landeskunde von Alt-Südarabien*, Vienna, 1964.

Wissmann, H. von, and Höfner, M., *Zur historischen Geographie des vorislamischen Südarabien*, Wiesbaden, 1953.

Wolff, J. von, *Mammals of Ethiopia*, Min. of Agriculture, Ethiopia, 1955.

Wolska-Conus, W., *Cosmas Indicopleustès, topographie chrétienne*, Paris, 1968.

Worrell, W. H., 'Studien zum abessinischen Zauberwesen' in *ZA*, 1910.

Wright, W., *Catalogue of Ethiopic MSS in the British Museum*, London, 1877.

Wurmbrand, M., *The death of Aaron* (Ethiopian text edited, trans. into Hebrew, annotated and intro.); publ. by the Circle of Friends of the Faitlovitch Library, Tel Aviv, 1961.

—— *The Falasha Arde'et* (trans., annotated, and intro., in Hebrew); Tel Aviv, 1964.

Yohannes Gebre-Egzi'abher, Abba, *Ethiopian dictionary* (Tigrinya-Amharic), Asmara, 1956.

Zanutto, S., *Bibliografia etiopica: manoscritti etiopici*, Rome, 1932.

Zewde Gabra-Sellasie, 'The Process of Re-unification of the Ethiopian Empire 1868–89', unpub. Oxford D.Phil. thesis, 1971.

Zotenberg, H., *Catalogue des MSS éthiopiens de la Bibliothèque Nationale*, Paris, 1877.

GLOSSARY
of the most commonly used Ethiopian terms
(For transcription, see Preface)

———∿∿∿∿ｸﾞ◎ﾉﾉ∿∿∿———

ABBA	Title of ecclesiastics
ABBAY	Blue Nile
ABIET	Exclamatory formula; petition for justice; 'at your command'
ABUNA	(Abun—if not followed by the name). Title of the head of the Ethiopian Church. Sometimes also used as a courtesy prefix for the most senior clerics
ADDARASH	Palace, hall, seat of persons of rank
AG(W)DO	Round hut (tukul)
ALEKA	Chief—esp. of ecclesiastical institution; prior of monastery
AMBA	Flat-topped mountain
ATO	Title of respect—now generally prefixed to names as Mr.
AZMATCH	Military commander; often title of district chiefs
BAHR NEGASH	Ruler of the maritime province, i.e. Eritrea
BARNOS	Cloak
BERBERE	Pepper; chief condiment used in preparation of Ethiopian food
BERILLE	Bottle of decanter shape used especially for tedj
BERUNDO	Raw meat
BITWODDED	One of the most senior titles of the realm
BLATTA or BLATTENGETA	Counsellor. Title of senior official
BUDA	Evil spirit, esp. connected with the evil eye
CHIKKA	Village Chief
DANYA	Judge, arbitrator

DEBTERA	Cantor, precentor
DEGA	Highland regions—7,000 feet and above
DEJATCH	Abbreviated form of the next entry
DEJAZMATCH	'Commander of the Door'; originally: senior court official, general. Title of senior dignitaries, district chiefs, etc.
DIGLAL	Paramount Chief of the Beni Amer
DJABART(I)	Muslim nuclei in the Christian provinces of Ethiopia— physically indistinguishable from their Christian compatriots
ENDA	Kinship group
ETCHEGE	Premier monk of the realm; Prior of Debra Libanos Monastery
FALASHA	Indigenous Judaized tribe; cf. Chapter V
FESMI	Customary oath; solemn declaration made before a judge (Tigrinya form)
FETM	See previous entry (*fetm* is the Amharic form)
FITAWRARI	'Commander of the Spearhead'; title of intermediate seniority
GABBAR	Land-owning head of family; tributary subject
GE'EZ	The classical language of Ethiopia; Ethiopic
GEZZI	Formal injunction carrying legal force
GRAZMATCH	'Commander of the Left'; title of intermediate seniority
GULT(I)	Territorial fief; land held free of tribute
HABESHA	Indigenous name for Tigrinya
HEDMO	House of rectangular shape and usually of considerable size
INJERA	Round and flat bread; highly absorbent
ITEGE	Title of the Queen of Ethiopia
JANHOY	Title of Emperor of Ethiopia; originally probably a judicial invocation
JIHAD	(Arabic) Holy war of Muslims against unbelievers
KAHEN	Priest
KAMIS	Tunic
KANTIBA	Mayor, governor
KANYAZMATCH	'Commander of the Right'; title of intermediate seniority
KEDDASE	Holy Mass
KEREMT	Rainy season (June to September)
KES	Priest

KESHI	Tigrinya form of previous entry
KWERBAN	Eucharist
LIK	Superior, learned, doctor of the church
MAKWAMIYA	Prayer-stick
MAMHER	'Master', title of abbots
MAREB MELLASH	'Beyond the Mareb river', i.e. Eritrea
MASAFENT	'Judges' (see p. 78), princes
MASKAL	Feast of the Cross; 27 September
MATEB	Neck-cord (cross, amulet)
MESLENIE	District Chief
MIES	See under TEDJ
NA'IB	(Arabic) 'Deputy'; indigenous chieftain of Arkiko and Massawa, originally appointed by Ottoman Government
NEBURA ED	Chief of Aksum
NEGUS	King
NEGUSA NAGAST	King of Kings = Emperor
QUOLLA	Hot and low-lying areas
RAS	The most senior title—just below that of *negus*—comparable to 'Duke'
REST(I)	Hereditary ownership of land
SAWASEW	Indigenous study of grammar and vocabulary
SHAMMA	Toga-like garment commonly worn by Ethiopians
SHANQELLA	Negroes
SHARI'A	(Arabic) Muslim law
SHIFTA	Bandit
SHUM	Tribal or District Chief
SHUMAGALLE	Elders; members of the hereditary nobility (Tigre)
SOM	Fast
TABOT	Altar slab; Ark of the Covenant
TALLA	Indigenous beer
TEBEKA	Advocate
TEDJ	Ethiopian honey-mead
TEMKAT	Baptism
TENSA'E	Resurrection—Easter
TEZKAR	Memorial celebration for the dead
TSAHAFE TE'EZAZ	'Scribe of Orders', secretary; Minister of the Pen
TUKUL	Indigenous hut
WAT	Strongly spiced Ethiopian sauce; a type of curried stew

WOYNA DEGA   Intermediate zone—between 5,000 and 7,000 feet elevation

WOYZARO   Lady

ZAR   Demon, spirit

ZEGENI   (Tigrinya) see WAT

ZEMA   Plain-song; chant

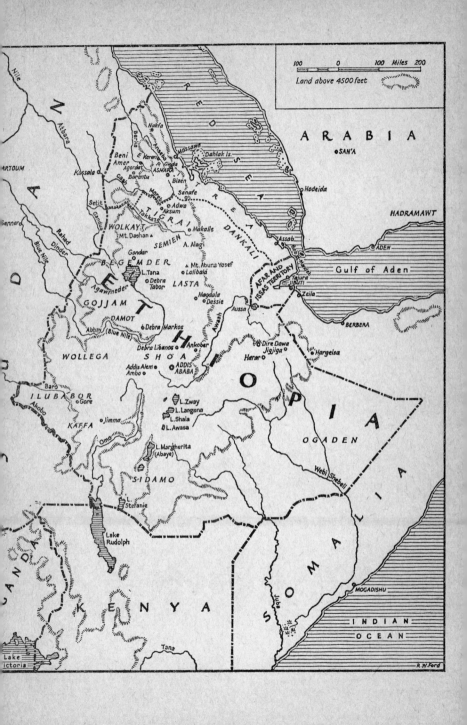

INDEX